Limiting Rights
The Dilemma of Judicial Review

In *Limiting Rights* Janet Hiebert addresses a dilemma of judicial review that threatens to undermine claims that what courts do can be distinguished from the discretionary decisions of policy makers and raises concerns about whether judicial review of the Charter of Rights and Freedoms is consistent with democratic principles. *Limiting Rights* is an in-depth exploration of who is, and who should be, responsible for determining whether legislation that conflicts with the entrenched rights of the Charter should nevertheless be upheld as a reasonable limit on protected rights.

Through an extended analysis of Supreme Court decisions involving limits on protected rights, Hiebert explores the issues surrounding judicial review. She looks at how difficult it is for judges to determine the reasonableness of legislative initiatives and examines the considerable influence exerted by Canadian politicians deciding which legislative activities will be considered justifiable limits on protected rights. Politicians have, in other words, helped define the very constraints that the Charter was intended to impose on them.

Limiting Rights sheds light on one of the most contentious issues in a political system with entrenched rights.

JANET L. HIEBERT is assistant professor of political studies, Queen's University.

Limiting Rights

The Dilemma of Judicial Review

JANET L. HIEBERT

McGill-Queen's University Press
Montreal & Kingston • London • Buffalo

© McGill-Queen's University Press 1996
ISBN 0-7735-1431-7 (cloth)
ISBN 0-7735-1437-6 (paper)

Legal deposit second quarter 1996
Bibliothèque nationale du Québec

Printed in Canada on acid-free paper

McGill-Queen's University Press is grateful to the Canada Council for
support of its publishing program.

Canadian Cataloguing in Publication Data

Hiebert, Janet, 1960–
    Limiting rights: the dilemma of judicial review
    Includes bibliographical references and index.
    ISBN 0-7735-1431-7 (bound)
    ISBN 0-7735-1437-6 (pbk.)
    1. Judicial review – Canada.   2. Legislative power – Canada.
    3. Civil rights – Canada.   4. Federal government – Canada.   5. Canada.
    Canadian Charter of Rights and Freedoms.   6. Canada – Constitutional
    law – Amendments.   7. Canada. Supreme Court.   I. Title.
    KE4248.H53 1996   347.71′012   C96-900197-5

This book was typeset by Typo Litho Composition Inc.
in 10/12 Baskerville.

Contents

Acknowledgments

This project began as a dissertation for the Department of Political Science at the University of Toronto. I had a wonderful committee, with Peter Russell as my supervisor, and two advisers, Jennifer Nedelsky and Stefan Dupré, who were inspiring and whose professionalism and courtesy I will strive to emulate in my professional life.

I owe a special thanks to Peter Russell. At a general level, Peter's pioneering and rich work on the judiciary, as a branch of government, provided encouragement and nourishment to students of Canadian politics such as myself who were interested in courts and judicial developments. More specifically, Peter's intellectual contribution to studying the political purposes and effects of entrenched rights, and his insightful observation that the principal effect of the Charter of Rights and Freedoms is not that it guarantees rights but changes the way decisions are made to establish limits on the extent to which the rights and freedoms can be enjoyed, inspired my dissertation. This book was born out of continued musings about political and judicial responsibilities for evaluating limits on rights.

I have benefited enormously from the ability to engage in exchanges with many colleagues whose conversations, stimulating comments, and critical observations about earlier drafts or articles have compelled me to refine and at times reassess my conceptions of rights and limits, individual and community, judicial review and democracy. I especially thank Kathy Brock, Matthew Mendelsohn, George Perlin, David Schneiderman, Keith Banting, Bev Baines, and David Mac Donald. I am particularly grateful to John Tait for his timely and constructive suggestions about the strengths and weaknesses of the manuscript. I feel extremely privileged to have benefited from his insights and wisdom. I also wish to acknowledge and thank my students in POLS 815 – Raj Chari, Nancy Loane, John McLean, and Nina Woods – whose penetrating questions helped in the development and clarification of my arguments.

Earlier versions of chapter 2 and chapter 6 were published in *Osgoode Hall Law Journal* and *Canada: The State of the Federation 1994*. I am grateful for the use of material published elsewhere and wish to thank the anonymous reviewers of those articles.

My greatest debt is to my husband Wayne, whose uncompromising support and unconditional love gave me, as a high school dropout, the courage to pursue my education. His willingness to quit his own job so that we could relocate for my graduate training and his cheerful endurance during our lean years permitted me to pursue, without distraction, my graduate education, without which this book would not have been possible.

Limiting Rights

1 Introduction

The Charter of Rights and Freedoms has been described as the single most important innovation of the constitutional changes of 1982[1] and the most radical break ever made with the Canadian constitutional and legal order "hitherto characterized by continuity and incremental development."[2] The Charter, by establishing formal rights as the standard for evaluating the justification of legislative and executive decisions and designating courts to assume an authoritative role in resolving citizen-state conflicts, represents a significant institutional change to the Canadian political system.

Much of the constitutional debate in Canada prior to the inclusion of the Charter in the constitution centred on conflicts between levels of government. What the Charter contributes to the constitutional setting is an alternative criterion and forum to resolve conflicts between governments and citizens. It is these changes in the responsibilities of courts and representative institutions that Charter enthusiasts hail when arguing that the Charter is the best means of protecting rights. The benefits of entrenchment, in their view, stem from its regulating impact on the state. Because the Charter imposes standards against which legislation can be evaluated and provides the mandate for courts to declare unconstitutional any legislative decision or executive act that departs from these standards, Charter enthusiasts believe that it will result in better protection for individual rights. As they see it, majoritarian preferences, discriminating customs, and parochial values will be replaced as policy considerations by principled and reasoned decision-making, detached and insulated from political influences.

The hopes of Charter enthusiasts are the fears of its critics, who are sceptical of a polity that encourages the structuring of its policy debates on the basis of formal rights. These sceptics have little faith in courts' abilities to evaluate legislation. In their opinion, courts and judicial review are neither the appropriate institution nor process for making important decisions affecting social policy. Furthermore, rather than encourage governments to be more responsible in taking Canadians' interests seriously in the formulation of policy, Charter sceptics anticipate the exact opposite and believe that the Charter will encourage elected representatives to avoid difficult and contentious policy decisions by taking refuge in the language of rights.

The unique structure of the Charter will have a decisive influence in determining whether the hopes of the enthusiasts or the fears of the sceptics are realized. The Charter establishes the rights and freedoms that must be respected yet provides explicit constraints on their exercise. This dual purpose of both recognizing fundamental rights and yet allowing limits upon them is served by the general limitation clause of section 1[3] which provides:

1. The Canadian Charter of Rights and Freedoms guarantees the rights and freedoms set out in it subject only to such reasonable limits prescribed by law as can be demonstrably justified in a free and democratic society.

The idea of including an explicit limitation clause has generated controversy about how it will affect judicial interpretations of protected rights. Debates about whether and how to formally limit rights were inherent in the struggle over the Charter from the very outset. Some considered the clause redundant, because in its absence Canadian courts would likely follow the lead of American judges who have "implied" limits by varying the level of protection for individual rights. Others worried that an explicit limitation clause would be harmful. Some feared that, because the clause would require that courts systematically entertain legislative arguments about why impugned policies impose reasonable limits, courts would become too deferential in accepting these arguments. Others worried that a general limitation clause would result in courts being drawn into the wholesale scrutiny of legislation on the basis of an imprecise standard or criterion that judges are ill-equipped to apply.

At all times the issue of explicit limits on rights remained an important part of the debate. In fact, it was so central that the provinces would probably not have agreed to entrenchment had the Charter not addressed some of their concerns about whether and how limits can be imposed on enumerated rights. Throughout the debate the provincial premiers argued for a Charter designed specifically to enable Parliament and the provincial legislatures to promote values that conflict with, and necessarily limit, protected rights.[4] Although the limitation clause that now appears in the Charter has changed considerably from the preferred wording of many of the provinces, the standard for limiting rights – a free and democratic society – is sufficiently broad that it imports into the Charter the context and opportunity for judicial and political debates about the justification of non-enumerated values that impose limits on protected rights.

Judicial review of the limitation clause will ultimately determine whether and to what extent Parliament and the provincial legislatures can promote non-enumerated values that conflict with protected rights. The idea that judicial review can encompass two analytically distinct functions – of determining whether an activity is protected under the constitution and evaluating whether it is reasonable and legitimate to impose limits on protected rights – may seem strange to those influenced by the American constitutional tradition where the Bill of Rights expresses rights as if they were absolute values. While American judges have adopted interpretive techniques of varying the level of protection for individual rights,[5] this manner of "balancing" conflicting rights is implicit, rather than explicit, and conveys different messages about the scope and primacy of protected rights. When the United States Supreme Court finds that a protected right has been infringed, no opportunity exists for further legislative activity in contravention of the Court's pronouncement. In Canada, once the Supreme Court has found that a right has been infringed it may still deem the legislatively imposed limit to be "reasonable." Alternatively, where the limit is not reasonable, Parliament or the provincial legislatures can invoke the notwithstanding clause of section 33 to explicitly override the Court's decision.[6]

The significance of the limitation clause in the Charter goes well beyond the symbolic recognition that rights are not absolute and will have to be limited when in conflict with other rights. Section 1 relates directly to one of the principal and most contentious issues in a political system with entrenched rights: how much discretion should representative institutions retain to promote policies that conflict, prima facie, with protected rights? Section 1, in establishing the principal and most visible way of establishing the boundaries and limits to which the protected rights will be enjoyed, has led early commentators to suggest that it "gives carte blanche to the Court to make of the Charter what it wills"[7] and that "the ultimate strength and vitality of Charter rights may well depend more upon the significance that Canadian courts assign to s. 1 than upon the resolution of any other single Charter issue."[8]

The premise of this book is that the tension between entrenched rights and limits is essential to understanding the political significance of the Charter. Peter Russell has observed that the main effect of the Charter is not to guarantee rights but to change the way decisions are made to establish limits on the extent to which the rights and freedoms can be enjoyed.[9] Building on that view, I will argue that the nexus between rights and limits, while important to any political system with entrenched rights, has a particular significance given the structure of the Charter.

The book has a decidedly institutional perspective. A core assumption is that the very nature of judicial decision-making has been influenced by the design of the Charter. In particular, the inclusion of an explicit limitation clause sets the stage for a debate between representative institutions and the courts: should the state promote policy objectives in the name of collective values or general welfare considerations if, in so doing, these conflict with individual rights?

The inclusion of an explicit limitation clause has encouraged the nation's highest judicial authority, the Supreme Court, to adopt a bifurcated approach to judicial review which distinguishes questions about whether a right has been infringed from inquiries into whether the limit is reasonable. The explicit recognition that rights are subject to limitations has influenced the Court's decision to avoid the American practice of implying internal limits on rights. In contrast, the Supreme Court has encouraged an extremely broad interpretation of rights in the initial stage of review, subject to case-by-case assessments of the reasonableness of governments' reasons for imposing limits.

This broad and generous interpretation of rights in the initial stage of judicial review has the consequence of subjecting a far greater range of legislative activities to Charter review than if the Court had developed internal limitations. Not only does this bifurcated approach increase the frequency with which the Court must review the reasonableness of impugned policies, but the criterion the Charter establishes for evaluating reasonableness – a free and democratic society – is sufficiently contested that it substantially enlarges the range of policy objectives that Parliament and the provincial legislatures may claim to be reasonable limits on protected rights.

This responsibility poses serious difficulties for courts. Because the standard the Charter establishes for limiting rights does not elicit obvious or uncontested answers, judges are required to pronounce on the claims of Parliament or the provincial legislatures that the policies they promote are both important and consistent with a free and democratic society. It has quickly become apparent that the Supreme Court is extremely reluctant to reject explicitly these claims.

However, even when the Court agrees that the impugned policy objective is consistent with a free and democratic society, reasonableness inquiries also require an evaluation of the merits of the legislation in terms of how the policy was conceptualized and drafted. This task, I will argue, is inherently difficult for the judiciary to perform. The complexity of policy development ensures that judges are poorly situated to assess whether better and more reasonable legislative means are available. Consequently, the Supreme Court has been confronted with a dilemma that both threatens to undermine its claim that judicial review can be distinguished conceptually from the discretionary judgments of public and political officials and also raises concerns about whether judicial review conflicts with democratic principles. The dilemma can be stated simply. Given the discretionary nature of reasonableness assessments, once the Supreme Court has accepted that the legislative objective is sufficiently important to warrant imposing limits on protected rights, should judges scrutinize the internal dynamics of a policy at the risk of second-guessing complex legislative decisions and potentially invalidating compelling objectives? Or should judges instead defer to governmental claims about the reasonableness of the impugned policy, at the risk of discouraging Parliament and the provincial legislatures from taking the responsibility of respecting protected rights as seriously as they should?

Contrary to conventional wisdom, which assumes that courts have exclusive responsibility for interpreting section 1, I will argue that because of the Supreme Court's reluctance to disagree with governments' claims that the policies they promote are consistent with a free and democratic society, when combined with the Court's difficulty in assessing the reasonableness of impugned policies, Parliament and the provincial legislatures have been able to exert considerable influence in determining which legislative activities will be considered justifiable limits on protected rights. In other words, they have helped define the very constraints that the Charter was intended to impose on them. This raises serious concerns as to whether the Charter will be effective in requiring that Parliament and the provincial legislatures respect fundamental rights when making policy choices.

The political history of the limitation clause will be examined in chapter two. The evolution of the clause reveals an ongoing and at times rigorous discussion on how much latitude Parliament and the provincial legislatures should have to pursue collective values which conflict with entrenched rights. Both federal and provincial drafters of the Charter saw section 1 as an opportunity to enable governments, in certain circumstances, to ensure the primacy of non-enumerated values over specified Charter rights.

Chapter three will examine different perspectives on how section 1 should be interpreted. The issue of how much discretion Parliament and the provincial legislatures should retain to pursue policies that impose limits on protected rights is controversial because this issue lies at the heart of debates about the relationships between citizens and the state and between individuals and community. The sheer breadth of the limitation clause, with its vague reference to democratic values, provides the setting for judicial and political deliberations about the meaning of democracy, the priorities that should be attached to conflicting values, and the standards that should be adhered to in the promotion of policies that pursue the public interest or the general welfare, however defined, and conflict with protected rights.

Chapter four will examine how and why the judicial task of interpreting the limitation clause has given rise to the dilemma that confronts the Supreme Court. The Court initially was reluctant to acknowledge openly the discretionary nature of the requirement that it review the reasonableness of impugned legislation. After sidestepping the issue for almost two years, the Court developed a general framework to evaluate the reasonableness of challenged policies. But it soon became apparent that these interpretive principles, despite their objective appearance, would not provide the basis for a coherent and consistent body of jurisprudence that did not also depend on subjective and discretionary judicial opinions about the importance of the impugned legislative objective. The Court's recognition of its own difficulties in assessing the reasonableness of complex social policy has influenced how section 1 is being interpreted and, consequently, what constraints are being imposed on Parliament and the provincial legislatures.

In chapter five the central tenets in the American and Canadian debates on the relationship between democracy and judicial review will be examined. American political and legal scholars have had more time to consider whether judicial review is consistent with democratic principles and over the years have experienced numerous judicial interpretations of the Bill of Rights that either challenge or facilitate political commitment to contentious values. Discussion of the democratic implications of judicial review under the Charter cannot help but be influenced by the longstanding American debate, particularly given that the American experience is already familiar to many students of Canadian law and politics. Much of the discussion of the democratic character of judicial review in the United States and Canada share similar premises: that the vague constitutional provisions require unelected courts to make substantive decisions that may give priority to some values and impose financial and policy obligations on governments; that in a democracy, elected legislators, accountable through periodic elections, should make these kinds of policy decisions; and that when an unaccountable political institution such as the judiciary invalidates the choices of a legislature, this is inconsistent with the democratic principle of representative government. The chapter concludes by recasting the way judicial review is assessed and argues that the limitation clause, which systematically engages courts in discretionary assessments of the merits of legislation, is central to the issue of whether and how judicial review of the Charter conflicts with democratic principles. The principal concern, from a democratic perspective, is not whether unelected judges are setting aside the decisions of those who are democratically elected. Rather, concerns arise when courts, despite judicial uncertainty as to whether the limit is reasonable, nevertheless uphold legislation that undermines fundamental rights or set aside legislation that prevents the pursuit of compelling and justifiable policy objectives.

The relationship between the Charter and federalism will be examined in chapter six. When entrenched rights were first included in the constitution many predicted that the Charter would undermine the territorial-based pluralism contemplated by Canadian federalism and would encourage the homogenization of public policies. This chapter will revisit this thesis by examining American and Canadian federalism and rights jurisprudence and will consider whether the structure of the Charter will allow for provincial diversity in its interpretation and application.

2 The Evolution of Reasonable Limits on Rights

One of the distinctive features of the Charter of Rights and Freedoms is the general limitation clause that precedes the enumerated individual and collective values. While Charter advocates of the late 1960s through the early 1980s expressed an unqualified enthusiasm and optimism for what could be achieved by entrenching rights, Charter drafters were more modest in their ability to capture all of the fundamental values in Canadian society. The significance of this clause is that it provides a means of reconciling the protected rights in the Charter with other fundamental values not specifically enumerated.

The debate about entrenched rights, which has been an important part of the national political agenda since the late 1960s, was carried out on two fronts. The larger issue centred on how best to protect fundamental values. Which branch of government, legislatures or courts, should make decisions about the appropriate bounds of state action in the pursuit of collective values and, in the event of conflicting values, who should determine limits on entrenched rights? The second front was extremely important in terms of reconciling those who would have preferred not to entrench rights to the Charter. This underlying debate reflected divergent views both as to the guidelines that ought to inform decisions about acceptable limitations on protected rights, and also how much latitude representative institutions should have to pursue policies that impose limits on protected rights. Participants in the debate looked to the European Convention on Human Rights, which includes specific limitations in the actual description of the enumerated rights and freedoms, as well as to the American example that is generally silent on limits and leaves most decisions about qualifying rights to the determination of the courts. In the end, the Charter reflected neither the European nor the American models. The limitation clause can be considered the Canadian contribution to systems of entrenched rights. While the idea of limiting rights was certainly not innovative, the method of doing so was.

The evolution of the limitation clause reveals a rigorous and changing political discourse about the nature of rights and limitations. The wording of the clause, the range of the collective values it seeks to protect, and its exact location in the Charter have fluctuated considerably since it was first proposed. In analysing the evolution of the clause this chapter will examine more than a decade of deliberations between federal and provincial officials on how best to limit protected rights; testimony before the Joint Parliamentary Committee on the Constitution by individuals and organizations concerned with the limitation clause; and interviews with government officials instrumental in drafting the clause.

EARLY DISCUSSIONS
OF ENTRENCHED RIGHTS

The subject of entrenched rights was placed on the national political agenda early in 1968 when the federal government announced its intention of proposing a federal-provincial conference to discuss a constitutional charter of rights. A policy paper written by then Justice Minister Pierre Trudeau, *A Canadian Charter of Human Rights*, identified the following categories of rights under consideration: political, legal, egalitarian, linguistic, and economic.[1] The government issued another policy paper the following year that involved a more detailed discussion of the rights the government wished to see entrenched.[2] Trudeau, in making his case for entrenched rights, argued that a constitutional Charter of Rights was not only a good thing in itself, in that it would provide recognition and protection of citizens' fundamental rights, but also that it would provide "the path for an orderly reform of our constitution."[3]

From these earliest Liberal government proposals to constitutionally entrench fundamental rights and freedoms has come the recognition that the rights contained are not to be enjoyed in any absolute sense. The first policy paper, which did not propose a specific limiting clause, suggested that the enumerated rights and freedoms, particularly freedom of expression and freedom of conscience and religion, may have to be limited for reasons of preserving public safety and order:

Freedom with respect to the individual's internal belief or conscience might well be considered absolute and not qualified in any way. It is the external

manifestation of the exercise or furtherance of beliefs which may give rise
to problems and the need for limitations in the interest of public safety and
order.[4]

The 1968 policy paper did not contemplate a specific limitation
clause. Instead Trudeau proposed two other means of qualifying the
entrenched provisions. The first, which he referred to as the "simple
form," was to list the right without any specific qualifications and leave
the determination of limitations up to the courts. Trudeau indicated
confidence in the judiciary's ability to develop the appropriate limits
on rights when the exercise of the right conflicts with an important social value:

Opponents of an unconditional declaration [of freedom of expression] fear
that such wording might restrict the application of Criminal Code prohibitions
against obscene or seditious publications, or provincial laws pertaining to defamation or film censorship. This is unlikely, however, for free speech as it developed in England was never equated with complete licence. It has long been
recognized, even before the Americans expressly guaranteed this right in their
constitution, that free speech was subject to limitations for the protection of
public order and morals. The United States courts have given the guarantees
of the First Amendment very wide scope, but have upheld laws which prohibit
speech inciting to unlawful acts, and laws which punish the publication of matter which is purely obscene with no significantly redeeming social value.[5]

The alternative approach considered by Trudeau was to specify circumstances, within the actual description of the right, in which limits
would be imposed. The model for this way of limiting rights was the
European Convention on Human Rights. Trudeau indicated that the
advantage of a highly specified set of limitations was that it removed
possible uncertainties of whether the enumerated right would conflict
with other social values. The disadvantage, he thought, was that this
method lacks flexibility and would be difficult to adapt to changing circumstances. His preferred method was to describe the rights without
any specific limitations.

The policy paper of 1969 was faithful to Trudeau's preference to
avoid explicit limitations, with one noticeable exception. It included a
clause to ensure that the federal Parliament, in times of emergency,
would not be paralysed by having to confine its activities to those that
did not conflict with enumerated rights. The proposed clause was accompanied by an explanatory note in which the public was advised
that it is sometimes necessary to limit certain human rights during
wars and similar emergencies. In the proposed Canadian Charter of

Human Rights of 1969, the limited nature of rights in emergency situations would be explicitly provided for in section 7:

It should be provided that where Parliament has declared a state of war, invasion or insurrection, real or apprehended, to exist, legislation enacted by Parliament which expressly provided therein that it shall operate notwithstanding this Charter, and any acts authorized by that legislation, shall not be invalid by reason only of conflict with the guarantees of rights and freedoms expressed Charter [sic].[6]

PROVINCIAL RESPONSES

The idea of entrenching rights was considered a highly innovative proposal in the late 1960s, despite the fact that the Canadian Bill of Rights had been enacted less than a decade earlier.[7] Notwithstanding the potential implications of the Bill of Rights in terms of the legislative authority of Parliament, a system of constitutionally entrenched rights, which would apply to the provinces as well as to the federal Parliament, was considered a significant modification to our parliamentary system of government and, in particular, a direct assault on the principle of "parliamentary supremacy."

The federal proposal to constitutionally entrench rights was not greeted with enthusiasm by many of the provincial premiers who, in contrast to Trudeau's view that a charter of rights would provide the path for an orderly reform of the constitution, did not see the need for constitutional reform to embrace entrenched rights. Many of the provinces had a different idea of what the priorities should be in terms of constitutional reform. They felt the more urgent constitutional matters were the distribution of powers, particularly the spending and taxing power; an amending formula; reform of federal institutions such as the Senate and appointments to the Supreme Court of Canada; and the inclusion of a constitutional clause dealing with regional disparities. Of all of these topics, the question of distribution of powers commanded the most attention among the provinces. In contrast, the federal government argued that it was more logical to discuss the distribution of powers after agreement in principle had been reached on those rights that would be placed beyond legislative competence.[8]

Trudeau could not persuade the provincial premiers to adopt a draft charter of fundamental rights at the 1968 constitutional conference. The issue, however, became the focal point of study for the next three years by the Continuing Committee of Officials and its Sub-Committee on Fundamental Rights.[9] The debate about entrenched rights during this period was carried on at a high level of abstraction. That the federal government did not have an articulated policy on entrenched rights was evident in the fact that anyone who wished could submit a proposal on the subject.[10]

The open nature and high level of generality of these early discussions had unfortunate consequences. The process of issuing general policy papers and reviewing submitted proposals without actually developing any specific drafts collapsed under its own weight. By the fall of 1970 the provinces had become impatient with the process of constitutional renewal and pressured the federal government for a settlement on patriation. The premiers had provided little input into these earliest proposals and many were largely unconvinced about the "benefits" of entrenched rights. Moreover, as the federal government expressed its ideas on the substance and scope of rights, not only was it apparent that some of the provinces had serious reservations about entrenched rights, but even those inclined to support a constitutional charter disapproved of the lack of explicit limitations on rights.

The provincial response to the Trudeau proposals for entrenched rights ranged from conditional support to categorical rejection. A major obstacle in negotiating an agreement was the desire of many of the provinces to retain the principle of "parliamentary supremacy." This desire informed the debate not only about whether to entrench rights but also the scope of limitations on protected rights should the provinces agree to the principle of entrenchment.[11]

The four western provinces were the most vocal in their opposition to entrenchment.[12] The chief critic of entrenchment in the early stages of constitutional review was then Manitoba Attorney General Sterling Lyon who blamed much of what is wrong with the United States on its Bill of Rights. The June 1969 defeat of the Conservative government in Manitoba, however, altered the complexion of western opposition. The new Manitoba premier, Edward Schreyer, did not share the previous administrations's opposition to entrenched rights. The three remaining western provinces that opposed entrenchment argued that the most serious implication of entrenched rights is that courts are given the final word on basic policy issues.

… Judicial review is a most undemocratic procedure, since it gives the court power to substitute their opinions for those of the electorate. Canada has always operated under the principles of responsible government, and the sovereignty of the people as expressed through their legislators who are accountable to the people. Judicial review would subject the opinion of the legislation and the operation of self-government to the opinion of the courts.[13]

The three westernmost provinces argued that Canadians are better protected under the principles of responsible government and parliamentary supremacy than their American neighbours who have a constitutional Bill of Rights. They claimed that the entrenchment of rights would result in Canadians rejecting a system "which works reasonably well in Canada" in favour of a system "that is working badly in the United States."[14] The western provinces also complained that restrictions on governments' policy-making abilities would occur to a greater extent at provincial than federal jurisdiction, since entrenched rights would undermine the provinces' control over property and civil rights.[15] The provinces' concern about the possible jurisdictional effects of entrenched rights informed the suggestion that the distribution of powers should be settled before the matter of entrenchment was resolved.[16]

Even those provinces which offered conditional support for entrenchment had reservations about Trudeau's approach to limitations on rights.[17] The subject of limiting rights had become an important issue in the negotiations for a constitutional charter of rights. Ontario, the most flexible of the provinces on the issue of entrenched rights, had serious reservations about Trudeau's preferred method for leaving almost all decisions about limitations to the courts. A brief submitted at the 1968 constitutional conference, which indicated conditional support for entrenched rights, expressed the Ontario view that any restatement of fundamental rights must not be done in a manner that would deny or conflict with other important values: "These rights should be expressed in a form which will reflect their development in our laws over the years; any new expression of them must be applied so as not to diminish any existing right recognized by law or usage."[18]

At a subsequent meeting called to discuss constitutional reform, Ontario addressed the need to explicitly qualify rights. The Ontario submission referred to the European Convention on Human Rights as an example of a charter "which defines the difference between one man's liberty and his interference with the liberties of others." Ontario took the view that if political rights were entrenched, the drafters should either adopt the kind of limiting mechanism of the European Convention, in which constraints are placed on the exercise of rights in the actual section in which the rights are specified, or include a general limiting clause in the preamble of the constitution.[19]

As federal and provincial officials met throughout the winter of 1970–71, it had become apparent that Trudeau's preferred method for stating rights without explicit limitations would have to be abandoned if the federal government was to gain provincial support for entrenched rights. The provinces categorically rejected the principle of entrenched rights in which there are no explicit qualifications but rather a reliance on the courts to fashion the appropriate limits. The provinces also disapproved of the 1969 proposal in which the only explicit limitation was for emergency situations, arguing that they might also have emergencies in which limitations on rights would be warranted. The provinces opposed the idea that limitations on rights be tied to emergency situations and felt that rights should be subject to qualifications at all times. The 1969 proposal was also criticized by rights activists, who claimed the clause would give carte blanche to Parliament in times of war.[20]

By the summer of 1971 all provinces were reconciled to the entrenchment of fundamental rights in what became known as the Victoria Charter. This accord, which soon collapsed, was the first and last time there was provincial agreement for entrenched rights until the 1981 accord. The Victoria Charter included the following basic political rights: universal suffrage and free democratic elections at least every five years; freedom of thought, conscience, and religion; freedom of opinion and expression; and freedom of peaceful assembly and association.[21]

A key factor in reconciling the provinces to entrenched rights was the agreement to include a general limiting clause. This would be contained in article 3, following the preamble in article 1 and a statement that no law of the federal Parliament or provincial legislatures shall abrogate or abridge the specified fundamental freedoms in article 2. This general limitation clause, which would serve as the prototype for subsequent Charter drafts, provided:

Nothing in this Part shall be construed as preventing such limitations on the exercise of the fundamental freedoms as are reasonably justifiable in a democratic society in the interests of public safety, order, health or morals, of national security, or of the rights and freedoms of others, whether imposed by the Parliament of Canada or the Legislature of a Province, within the limits of their respective legislative powers, or by the construction or application of any law.[22]

The inclusion of a general limitation clause in the Victoria Charter revealed the kinds of philosophical trade-offs in regards to rights and limitations that were then, and would increasingly become, necessary to secure provincial agreement. A clear relationship had emerged between the provinces' willingness to support the principle of entrenched rights and the scope of limitations on those rights. The provinces, especially those most concerned about the intrusion of entrenched rights on parliamentary supremacy, wanted limitations on rights to extend far beyond either the qualifications Trudeau expected the courts to make in the absence of an explicit directive or emergency situations that had been provided for in the 1969 policy paper.

The Victoria Charter reflected the provinces' view on the appropriate relationship between rights and limits. Article 3, which included the kinds of qualifications on rights permissible in the European Convention, would allow either level of government to impose limits on rights. The situations in which limits on entrenched rights were justified were described in extremely general terms that would give both provincial and federal governments significant latitude in enacting legislation that conflicted with the enumerated rights. Furthermore, the provision in the clause that the Charter should not prevent such limitations that arise from the "the construction or application of any law" was intended to amplify the impact of the limitation clause. This phrase was to serve as a directive to the courts that when faced with construing limits on a law, they should not reduce the effects of limitations.[23]

Despite the demise of the Victoria Charter, its provisions were studied the following year by the Special Joint Committee of the Senate and of the House of Commons on the Constitution of Canada. The committee supported the idea of a general qualifying clause and suggested that explicit limitations were preferable to "roughly formulated propositions in judicial minds." One of the benefits of the limiting clause, the committee suggested, was that it ought to eliminate the "simplistic argument that rights are absolute." While the committee supported the concept of a general limitation clause, it did not like the wording of article 3 of the Victoria Charter. The preferable way of limiting rights, the committee indicated, was to include a clause that states qualifications more generally:

In order to focus the principle of judicial interpretation more clearly ... we would prefer to state any such qualification more rather than less generally. We would therefore recommend that any limitations on the exercise of the fundamental freedoms should be only such "as are reasonably justified in a democratic society" without any further specification.[24]

For the next four years federal-provincial conferences were dominated by economic concerns and the subject of entrenched rights was not debated. The 1976 election of a separatist government in Quebec provided new impetus for constitutional renewal. Early responses to the election of the Parti Québécois did not occur on the intergovernmental stage; rather, individual provinces conducted their own studies on constitutional reform.[25] The federal government responded by establishing a Task Force on Canadian Unity. While the task force's report favoured the entrenchment of individual and collective rights, its recommendations in terms of language rights differed significantly from the goals of the federal government. As a result, the report was given little attention in subsequent constitutional debates.[26]

The next serious attempt at constitutional reform was the introduction of Bill C-60 in 1978. The bill, which included the section "Rights and Freedoms within the Canadian Federation," contained a number of enumerated rights that would apply only to the federal Parliament. While the Charter in Bill C-60 was a federal initiative, the federal government was hopeful that the provinces would voluntarily adhere to its provisions. As an incentive, the federal government promised to do away with disallowance and remedial legislation.

The Charter included a limitation clause that did not adhere to the recommendation made by the Joint Parliamentary Constitutional Committee six years earlier. Federal officials felt that the committee's recommendation was too vague and would adversely affect the enumerated rights and freedoms. In deciding on an alternative to the joint committee's limiting clause, federal officials considered three approaches: a general limiting clause similar to the one in the Victoria Charter; internal limitations tailored to the specific rights and included in the actual section in which the right was specified; and no explicit limitations but an exclusive reliance on the courts to determine the boundaries of rights.[27]

There were serious problems with the second and third approaches. The difficulty with including specific limitations within the actual definition of the right was that the provinces had previously expressed concern that if limits were placed on some of the rights and not others, courts might interpret those rights that were silent on limits, as limitless. The provinces were worried that the courts might not allow limitations on rights beyond the specific qualifications already included. Yet if more detailed limitations were attached in anticipation of the provinces' concerns, the Charter would be politically embarrassing: it would read like a negative bill of rights in which every time a right was granted, it was taken back.[28] As for the third approach, the provinces did not share Trudeau's faith in the ability of courts to impose the appropriate limits on rights in the absence of an explicit directive. The provinces had already indicated that the American approach, which is silent on limits, was unacceptable. Moreover, some federal officials had expressed reluctance to rely exclusively on courts to determine limits on rights, particularly in emergency situations. Given the provinces' concerns with internal qualifications and their categorical rejection of a charter which was silent on limits, it is not surprising that the federal government chose to include a limitation clause similar to what had already been agreed to six years earlier at Victoria. The limitation clause in Bill C-60 provided:

25. Nothing in this Charter shall be held to prevent such limitations on the exercise or enjoyment of any of the individual rights and freedoms declared by this Charter as are justifiable in a free and democratic society in the interests of public safety or health, the interests of the peace and security of the public, or the interests of the rights and freedoms of others, whether such limitations are imposed by law or by virtue of the construction or application of any law.[29]

The Charter in Bill C-60 was considerably broader than the Victoria Charter and included property, legal, and equality rights. Without provincial agreement this Charter would not constrain provincial legislatures. The federal government, however, was not in a strong bargaining position to compel provincial support. A number of the provinces were reluctant to be drawn into the discussion about entrenched rights, especially on the proposed legal and equality rights. They had been sceptical about supporting even the limited charter of rights in Victoria and were even more determined in their efforts to thwart this greater assault on parliamentary supremacy.[30] The unpopularity of the Trudeau government did not help the federal cause. Bill C-60 eventually died on the order paper when Parliament was dissolved in May 1979.[31]

Despite the demise of Bill C-60, its provisions were scrutinized by members of the Special Joint Parliamentary Committee on the Constitution.[32] The committee's recommendations were greatly influenced by the testimony of a number of witnesses who either opposed the wording of the limitation clause because they thought the scope of it was overly broad or wanted the clause removed entirely.[33] The joint committee reported that the instruction to the courts on how to interpret the Charter was not necessary. It recommended that the limitation clause be removed and replaced by a more explicit provision that would base the justification for limiting rights upon the invocation of the War Measures Act or similar legislation.[34] Like the clause in the 1969 policy paper, the specified grounds for limitations would be emergency situations such as war, invasion, or insurrection. Further, rights could only be qualified by the federal Parliament which alone is empowered to enact the War Measures Act. But the committee's proposed clause also included a recommendation that had not earlier arisen in discussions on how to limit rights. In contrast to earlier proposals, including the government's own explanatory note on section 25,[35] the determination of whether limits are justifiable would not be made by the courts, but by Parliament: "Clause 25 should be replaced by a clause which exactly specifies permissible limitations on protected rights and freedoms by the War Measures Act or similar legislation, and the Government should be required to justify to Parliament the invocation of such legislation."[36]

The joint committee's proposed limitation clause was not endorsed by the federal government. The committee sought to replace section 25 because it felt this clause was too excessive. But ironically, the recommendation was rejected by federal officials who knew from past experience that the provinces would not support a charter that tied limitations to emergency situations. The provinces' attitudes towards limitations on entrenched rights had changed little in the past six years. They continued to express concern that if the general limitation clause were to be replaced with an emergency clause, this might mean that rights were limitless in times of peace. Yet if provincial concerns were satisfied by extending the scope of the clause to situations other than war, the federal government would in effect be introducing a legislative override into the Charter. Further, the idea that limitations on rights be justified to Parliament was unacceptable to Trudeau. Another problem with the committee's proposed clause was that the continuing debate about the use of the War Measures Act in 1970 would subject the clause to criticism for encouraging the enactment of the War Measures powers.

NEW FEDERAL INITIATIVE

The federal government, unable to secure an agreement for entrenched rights in 1978, was in a stronger bargaining position two years later. The majority victory for the Liberal government in 1980, and the subsequent "success" in the May 1980 Quebec referendum, meant that the federal government had more influence over the constitutional agenda than it had enjoyed for some time.[37] In successfully campaigning for a No vote on the referendum question, Trudeau argued that there was a new political resolve and goodwill to reform the constitution and satisfy the government's promise of renewed federalism.[38]

However, when it became clear that an agreement with the provinces might not be possible,[39] the federal government committed itself to a public relations contest; it was determined to "sell" the Charter.[40] Its strategy was to design a charter which would appease some of the provinces' concerns with entrenched rights. But if an agreement with the provinces could not be reached, the federal government was prepared to act unilaterally, in which event it wanted to ensure that the Charter would attract public support. With this delicate balance in mind, the federal government introduced a significant change to the wording of the limitation clause. In response to provincial concerns, the federal government amended the clause to read: "The *Canadian Charter of Rights and Freedoms* recognizes the following rights and freedoms subject only to such reasonable limits as are generally accepted in a free and democratic society with a parliamentary system of government."[41]

At the time the amendment to the limitation clause was made, Ontario and New Brunswick were the only provinces that supported the federal government's constitutional package. It was thought that Nova Scotia might be convinced to support entrenched rights. Alberta, British Columbia, and Prince Edward Island were extremely reluctant to support a charter, while Manitoba and Saskatchewan opposed it outright. Newfoundland had not declared itself either way. Quebec was in a difficult position: the public declaration that the majority of Quebec citizens wanted to stay in Canada meant that the Quebec delegates had to appear to participate in the process of constitutional renewal but, for political reasons, it would have been difficult for the Lévesque government to support the federal initiative.[42]

The inclusion of the phrase "parliamentary system of government," which was intended to expand the scope of permissible limitations, was a federal attempt to reconcile more of the provinces to the Charter. The federal government had considered two strategies for increasing provincial support. It could either appease provincial concerns about the implications of entrenched rights by including a legislative override, or it could make the Charter more attractive to the opposing provinces by including the reference to a parliamentary system of government in the limitation clause. Federal officials chose the latter approach because they were hopeful that this broader clause would militate against some of the provinces' demands for a legislative override in the Charter.[43] While there were concerns that the new wording might encourage judicial deference to governments and pave the way for the courts to turn the Charter into the 1960 Bill of Rights, the broader limitation clause was felt to be the "lesser of two evils." With a limitation clause, even one broadly constructed, there was a chance that the courts would still curb parliamentary supremacy. With an override, however, federal officials were concerned that the provinces would be willing to use it which, they thought, would have serious and possibly irrevocable implications for entrenched rights.[44]

The intent of the federal government in including the reference to a parliamentary system of government was revealed during the hearings before the Joint Parliamentary Committee on the Constitution. A senior Justice official testified that the reference to a parliamentary system of government was a deliberate choice to reflect the concept of parliamentary sovereignty and to differentiate the Canadian political system from the American:

The reference to a parliamentary system of government, I think, was deliberate, to refer to the concept of parliamentary sovereignty and the things that go with that. I might say that some of the provinces attach a good deal of importance to this in the discussions on the Charter, the reference to the parliamentary system of government, to indicate to the Court some distinction between our system and the American system.[45]

Not only did federal officials change the wording of the limitation clause but, in an important symbolic gesture, they placed it in the lead position of the Charter.[46] This was intended to appease those opposing provinces who wanted to emphasize that rights are subject to limitations. The other purpose for stating that rights are subject to limits in section 1 was to meet the criticism that had plagued the federal government in earlier drafts, that these charters were more concerned with limiting and qualifying rights than in protecting them. The drafters thought it was preferable to be "up front" about limitations so they would not be accused of hiding their intent.[47] Despite the changes to the clause, provincial support for the Charter did not increase.

The Charter, including the limitation clause containing the reference to a parliamentary system of government, was scrutinized in 1980–81 by the Joint Parliamentary Committee on the Constitution. The hearings were significant because the debate about the presence and wording of section 1 reflected the witnesses' conception of the nature of rights and limitations. Moreover, the hearings provided firsthand explanations of federal drafters' views of the function and purpose of section 1.

Testimony revealed that the federal government considered the principal purpose of the limitation clause to be twofold: to ensure that rights are not interpreted by legislatures or courts as being absolute; and to underscore that traditional limits on rights should be honoured by the courts. In giving evidence before the joint committee, Deputy Justice Minister Roger Tassé described the purpose of section 1 as:

In effect, Mr. Chairman, that Section 1 is meant to bring forward the concept that these rights that are spelled out in the Charter ... are not absolute rights.

If you just take, for example, the freedom of expression, there are limits to the freedom of expression that already are spelled out in the Criminal Code and that will continue and should continue when a Charter of Rights like this is entrenched.

What the Section is meant to do is to bring that concept not only to the legislatures but also to the judges because in effect the judges when they are faced with cases where government action or parliamentary action, legislative action is being tested and being challenged, in effect they have to decide whether limits, restrictions, that may have been imposed, because again these rights are not absolute, are reasonable ones.[48]

The overwhelming majority of the witnesses who appeared before the committee were strongly opposed to the wording of the clause. Testimony came from a diverse group of individuals and organizations, including civil liberties groups, university professors, women's groups, ethnic associations, legal groups, police officials, and crown counsel. Many were willing to see a general limitation clause in the Charter as long as it was more narrowly constructed, while some opposed the clause in its entirety. As in 1978, the witnesses' principal concern with the limitation clause was that the wording created too broad a standard for permissible limitations. Critics called section 1 the "bathtub section" because the clause would make it so easy for lawmakers "to pull the plug on human rights and freedoms."[49] They argued that the clause as worded would permit so many encroachments upon protected rights that it would seriously impair the ability of the Charter to protect citizens' rights. Some critics went so far as to suggest that section 1 must be deleted otherwise its presence would open the door to "the very abuse to the supremacy of Parliament which the Charter is intended to check."[50]

One of the most influential critics, in terms of prompting changes to the wording of the limitation clause, was Walter Tarnopolsky, then president of the Canadian Civil Liberties Association. Tarnopolsky was critical of the phrase that had been a significant concession to the provinces – the reference to a parliamentary system of government. He argued that judges, who are not anxious to change the traditional Canadian relationship between legislatures and the courts, might interpret the reference to mean the retention of parliamentary supremacy and be unwilling to overturn legislation that encroached upon Charter rights. Of even more concern to Tarnopolsky, however, was the phrase "generally accepted." Tarnopolsky argued that this phrase was problematic because it would not be an adequate safeguard of fundamental human values given that many of the actions in our history, which are now considered to have involved the infringement of human rights, were generally accepted at the time. Tarnopolsky's concern was that the argument might be made that whatever Parliament enacts is "generally acceptable."[51]

Tarnopolsky also argued that the limitation clause did not clearly determine where the onus should lie for demonstrating the reasonableness or unreasonableness of a limitation. In his view, the onus should lie with the party who favours the restriction. Not only should the government bear the onus for demonstrating the reasonableness of a limitation, but the clause should require that limitations be prescribed by law:

… The onus has to be upon the one who argues that there are restrictions, and that has to be put in terms of being either necessary or demonstrably justifiable or demonstrably necessary; … the most important aspect of the Canadian Bill of Rights is not so much in the invalidation of parliamentary legislation as it is in the control of administrative acts, police acts, and with respect to that [*sic*] the limitations that are provided in international instruments require that they be provided specifically by law.[52]

FINAL WORDING

There is little doubt that the overwhelming criticism that the clause made it too easy for governments to limit protected rights pressured the federal government to rewrite the limitation clause. Then Justice Minister Jean Chrétien indicated that while the government was agreeable to narrowing the application of the clause, it was not willing to eliminate section 1 entirely because it felt the clause was necessary to maintain an equilibrium between the rights of citizens to be protected by the courts and the ability of elected representatives to legislate. In explaining changes in the clause, Chrétien stated that the purpose of the amendments was to narrow the scope of limits that could be applied to the rights and freedoms. Chrétien indicated that the federal government itself preferred a narrower limitation clause but had gone along with the broader wording as a concession to the provinces.[53] The amended clause, which is the phrasing that now appears in the Charter, provides:

1. The Canadian Charter of Rights and Freedoms guarantees the rights and freedoms set out in it subject only to such reasonable limits prescribed by law as can be demonstrably justified in a free and democratic society.

One of the most important changes in the wording was the replacement of the idea that rights are subject to such limits as are "generally accepted" by the more difficult requirement that rights be subject "only to such reasonable limits prescribed by law." Moreover, the reference to a parliamentary system of government, which many critics thought would result in judicial deference to Parliament and the provincial legislatures, was removed and the phrase "demonstrably justified in a free and democratic society" was included to place the onus for limiting a right squarely on the party seeking to limit it.

The change in the wording of the clause was significant not only because it made it more difficult for governments to limit protected rights but also because this was the first time the provinces' view was not represented in the drafting of the clause. The majority of the provinces' preference for parliamentary supremacy and their concomitant demand that limitations on rights be generous and explicit had largely informed the debate of the preceding decade. The provinces' preferred clause, such as the one in Victoria, included permissible limitations that were so generally stated that, when accompanied by the directive that the Charter should not prevent limitations arising from the "construction or application of any law," effectively allowed governments, not courts, to determine the scope of limitations.[54] The assumption was that limitations would almost always be justified by virtue of having being enacted. The intended judicial deference to governments' policies, which had been at the heart of provincial demands and had been reflected in the Victoria Charter, Bill C-60, and the September 1980 Charter, was replaced by the more difficult requirement that limitations be prescribed by law, demonstrably justified, and consistent with a free and democratic society.

It might seem strange that in 1981 the federal government was willing to deny the provinces' concern for a broadly constructed clause. Given that in the past, the federal government had felt it necessary to accommodate the provinces' demand for such a clause, why was it now willing to act without provincial consent? The answer lies in the dynamics of the constitutional process of 1980–81. The federal government had already committed itself to a public relations contest of selling the Charter. It had promised renewed federalism and was determined to have a revised constitution. The parliamentary committee's review of the proposed Charter served the federal cause. Once the federal-provincial negotiations had broken down in the fall of 1980 the federal government's strategy became one of focusing attention on the joint committee. As the hearings progressed it soon became apparent that the vast number of submissions were in favour of strengthening the Charter and making it more difficult for governments to limit protected rights. The committee hearings served both to build up public momentum for the Charter and to give the federal government an effective bargaining chip by which to deny provincial demands for a weaker Charter through a broader limitation clause. By the end of the committee process the federal government was able to go to the provinces and defend the new limitation clause with claims that the "public" supported a stronger Charter and that the joint parliamentary committee, with representation from all three parties, had fully debated and deliberated the issue of rights and their limits, and had strongly endorsed a more narrow limitation clause.

The opposing provinces had several objections to the amended clause: they wanted either to remove entire chunks of the Charter, particularly legal rights, to reinstate the reference to a parliamentary system of government in the limitation clause, or to go back to the kinds of limitations that were provided for in the Victoria Charter. However, at this point the federal government considered its bargaining strength sufficient to enable it to adopt a take it or leave it position. The revised wording of the clause did not change despite the provinces' attempts.

A contributing factor in the provinces' failure at this stage was the long-awaited decision by the Supreme Court on the constitutionality of federal unilateral action.[55] The Supreme Court's decision, handed down on 28 September, 1981, essentially upheld the legality of the federal proposal for unilateral action by a seven to two margin although this was qualified by a six to three ruling that unilateral action would be inconsistent with the political convention that provinces be consulted and in agreement with constitutional amendments. While the decision left the matter of what an agreement entailed somewhat uncertain, it clearly did not require unanimity. However, politically the decision clearly implied that the convention of provincial agreement ought to be obeyed. But this did not give the provinces an advantage because it was no longer safe to presume that interprovincial agreement could provide an absolute buffer against the federal position. Since convention was not deemed to require unanimity, the knowledge that no single province could block the reform process meant that each premier was in danger of being on the wrong side of the agreement. An indication that the pressures for compromise were significant is evident in the fact that an agreement was achieved a scant five weeks later. The critical issues to be resolved no longer included the nature of the limitation clause. By November 1981 the only issue left for debate on the scope of rights was whether there would be a legislative override and to which provisions it would apply.

OVERVIEW OF SECTION 1

The evolution of the limitation clause reveals an ongoing and at times rigorous discourse about what latitude legislators should have in pursuing policies that reflect non-enumerated values and conflict with entrenched rights. The debates about section 1 suggest differing views on what the relationship should be between rights and limits. One view is reflected in the testimony of the majority of witnesses who appeared before the 1978 and 1980–81 joint parliamentary hearings on the constitution. These critics, who either wanted significant changes in the wording of the 1980 clause or, in the absence of changes, its complete elimination from the Charter, shared a similar conception of what rights should look like if entrenched in the Charter. According to their view, protected rights should have primacy over legislation. While they acknowledged that rights can never be absolute and must be subject to limitations, they argued that governments should not be allowed to encroach upon protected rights unless they can demonstrate and justify that the policy at issue facilitates the functioning of the democratic system (the values of which the testimony seemed to presume are both obvious and uncontested), or is necessary because of an emergency situation. This view implies that the Charter is exhaustive of the fundamental values in Canada; the enumerated rights, therefore, should have primacy over all other policy goals. For those who view rights in these terms, the purpose of the limitation clause is really nothing more than to provide the self-evident statement that rights are not absolute. A similar effect could be achieved without an explicit limitation provision in which courts would fashion the appropriate limits on rights.

It was this conception of entrenched rights that informed the criticism during the 1980 hearings which implied that the drafters of the limitation clause were fickle for not being able to decide whether Canada should have entrenched rights or not. The drafters were told repeatedly to make up their minds about what kind of political system they wanted for Canada: were we to have parliamentary supremacy or a Charter regime? As Professor Cohen admonished the drafters:

To the extent that you want to have an equilibrium between a charter regime and parliamentary supremacy, you must accept the fact that, once you introduce a charter regime, parliamentary supremacy is modified for ever to that extent. That is a plain legal and political fact, and you cannot have the best of both worlds, except in an emergency.[56]

A second view is that of the provinces and, to a lesser extent, the federal government. The suggestion that Charter drafters were fickle would have been less objectionable to the provincial premiers than the federal drafters given that the majority of provincial premiers remained sceptical about the virtues of entrenched rights throughout the debate. Far from being inconsistent, most of the premiers did not waver in their belief that if rights are entrenched they must be accompanied by explicit limitations to ensure their ability to legislate in areas that conflicted with Charter rights.

To understand fully the position of the majority of the provinces on the issue of limits on rights, it is helpful to reconsider the nature of the debate underlying the discussions about entrenched rights. At the time of the 1980–81 joint hearings, the larger issue about whether or not to entrench rights was still far from being resolved. An important issue in the debate continued to be which institution, legislatures or courts, is best suited to make political decisions about the appropriate limits on protected rights when they conflict with general welfare concerns or collective values. At times this conflict appeared irreconcilable. The premiers continued to argue that a limitation clause must be sufficiently broad to permit governments significant latitude in determining their policy agendas. Saskatchewan Premier Allan Blakeney was a leading critic of the suggestion that the limitation clause should be more narrowly constructed. His support of the 1980 limitation clause and, in particular, the reference to a parliamentary system of government, was consistent with his belief that governments, rather than courts, are better equipped to determine the appropriate limits on rights. In arguing for the retention of the clause, Blakeney made no secret of the fact that he viewed this section as a good way of moderating the impact of entrenched rights.

I could certainly go along with entrenching and with a non obstante clause, because basically the courts are good places to decide individual cases of human rights issues, but bad places to decide broad social policies in the guise of deciding issues of human rights.

Therefore what we need is some basis whereby the legislatures can over-ride if, in the course of deciding an issue about a single citizen, they have made a decision which affects broad public policy.

I had thought that the resolution before this Committee was not too bad in that regard, because it has Section 1 which is a kind of non obstante clause in advance.

You may think that is too comprehensive, but the suggestion of deleting Section 1 raise [*sic*] all my apprehensions, because we are then left with a very large number of judgments to be made by judges.[57]

One might be tempted to suggest that the dynamics of the constitutional process of 1980–81 enabled the federal government to choose a Charter Regime. By winning the battle over the limitation clause, the federal government was able to deny provincial demands for a broadly constructed clause and ensure that the Charter reflects its own view on the appropriate relationship between entrenched rights and limits. But there are reasons to question whether the adoption of a more narrowly constructed limitation clause ensured that the Charter reflected the critics' view concerning limits on entrenched rights and whether the federal government shared the critics' conception of the relationship between rights and limits.

Despite Cohen's suggestion that Charter drafters must choose between two mutually exclusive political systems, it is difficult to conclude that the inclusion of a more narrowly constructed limitation clause has meant that representative institutions no longer have discretion to promote values that conflict with protected rights. While the provinces were unable to secure their preferred limitation clause, they were successful in negotiating a legislative override which allows legislatures to override certain Charter rights for a period of five years, after which the declaration must be re-enacted.[58]

Federal officials and Charter commentators are quick to argue that by the fall of 1981 the discussions about the override were not related to the limitation clause: the wording of the limitation clause had crystallized and the issue for debate was whether there would be an override and to which provisions it would apply.[59] Nonetheless, it is important to remember the federal government's strategy of the preceding year. [In its attempt to secure provincial support and avoid the political difficulty of acting unilaterally, the federal government had considered introducing a legislative override. Instead it decided to broaden the scope of the limitation clause and include the reference to a parliamentary system of government because officials hoped it would militate against provincial demands for an override. The federal government assumed that the provinces would not demand a legislative override if entrenched rights were subject to a broad limitation clause that encouraged judicial deference to governments' policy goals. It seems reasonable to suggest, however, that once the broad limitation clause was withdrawn and it was made clear that governments would bear the burden of demonstrating the justification for limits on entrenched rights, the override became more important to the provincial premiers.

It should also be questioned whether the federal government shared the critics' conception of the relationship between rights and limits. It is not clear that the Trudeau government's view on the nature of limitations, in the period following the two policy papers of the late 1960s, reflected a coherent or singular intent. Until the 1980–81 joint parliamentary hearings the federal government did not seriously dwell upon the issue of where the onus should lie for demonstrating the reasonableness or unreasonableness of a limitation. A senior Justice Department official confirmed that the drafters had not addressed the issue of onus until early 1981 when Tarnopolsky criticized the limitation clause for being unclear in this regard. This forced the federal drafters to re-examine the impact of the limitation clause. Up until that time they had assumed that when the courts determined limits, they would address the issue of onus.[60] The fact that the drafters had not addressed this issue before the hearings is also evident in testimony before the joint committee by Barry Strayer, then assistant deputy justice minister (public law):

It was the belief of the drafters that by going to these words demonstrably justified or can be demonstrably justified, it was making it clear that the onus would be on the government, or whoever is trying to justify the action that limited the rights set out in the charter, the onus would be on them to show that the limit which was being imposed not only was reasonable, which was in the first draft, but also that it was justifiable or justified, and in doing that they would have to show that in relation to the situation being dealt with, the limit was justifiable.

... Before, there was no indication as to who had the onus of proving that the limit was reasonable or unreasonable, or whether it was generally accepted or not generally accepted. This seems to put the onus, appears to put the onus on the government that has to try to uphold some kind of limit to the rights set out in the charter.[61]

Given the broad applicability of the limitation provisions that had preceded the revised 1981 clause, it seems remarkable that the federal government did not address the issue of onus earlier. The most plausible explanation is that the federal position regarding limitations on rights was not as far from the provinces' view as one might expect from scrutinizing the rhetoric of the Charter debate. The proposed limitation provisions in the Victoria Charter, Bill C-60, and the 1980 clause, which referred to a parliamentary system of government, were so broadly constructed that they would almost certainly have encouraged judicial deference to legislatures. Without an explicit directive that legislatures demonstrably justify limits, courts would have leaned heavily in favour of upholding limits on rights; the individual litigant would have assumed the difficult burden of demonstrating that a limitation is unreasonable. Since an intended consequence of the early limitation clauses was to encourage judicial deference to legislatures, it is unlikely that the federal government could have shared the critics' conception of rights – that decisions about limits on rights should be removed from the political arena – and yet not be concerned with the issue of onus.

The federal government hardened its view on limitations in the final stages of the Charter debate. When faced with the overwhelming criticism that the limitation clause as worded undermined the purpose of the Charter, federal officials were forced to re-examine their view. It would have been a great embarrassment if the federal government, as the leading proponent of entrenched rights, endorsed a limitation clause that was widely criticized for rending Charter rights a "verbal illusion."[62] This charge was even more damning in light of the unbridled optimism of Liberal government members' promises of being able to forever guarantee Canadians' rights.[63]

CONCLUSIONS

Section 1 now reflects a requirement that governments demonstrably justify limitations on rights that is far more difficult to meet than that envisaged earlier by either the provinces or the federal government. While the different conceptions of the nature of rights and limitations make it difficult to ascribe a singular intent to the clause, it is clear that its inclusion was intended by both federal and provincial drafters to ensure that governments, in certain circumstances, be able to ensure the primacy of non-enumerated values over specified Charter rights. Both federal and provincial officials were in agreement that the purposes of the clause were twofold: to ensure that governments are able to exercise discretion to pursue policies that reflect values that are not specifically enumerated in the Charter; and to permit governments some measure of influence on judicial decisions about when these policies are justified. Judicial review will ultimately determine whether section 1 is interpreted in a manner consistent with what the political drafters had in mind for the clause.

3 Approaches to Limits

Despite the substantive changes made to the limitation clause, which make it significantly more difficult to impose limits on protected rights, the contested nature of democracy and the lack of specific guidelines as to what constitutes a democratic objective could give Parliament and the provincial legislatures the opportunity to promote a wide range of non-enumerated values that conflict with protected rights. The question of how much discretion legislatures should retain to impose limits on protected rights lies at the heart of debates about the relationship between citizens and the state and individuals and community. The limitation clause of section 1 provides the context and opportunity to engage in a broader debate within and around liberal theory: should the state promote policy objectives in the name of collective values or general welfare considerations if, in so doing, these conflict with individual rights? It also inspires diverse opinions on how courts should interpret the Charter. This chapter will examine these perspectives on the nexus between protected rights and limits and their likely implications for the political process.

Evaluations of the Charter have been influenced by scholarly pursuits of a rights-based liberal ethic. The concept of rights is important for liberalism because it provides an ordering principle for conflicts between individuals and the state. While those espousing the liberal rights ethic disagree on which rights are fundamental (some are sympathetic with the welfare state[1] while others counter that redistributive policies violate property rights[2]) liberals agree that political decisions should promote outcomes that are general in their application and do not interfere with individual choice. Liberalism characterizes the normative role of the state in terms of neutrality. The state should be guided by "principles which are 'neutral' among various conceptions of what is worth pursuing in life,"[3] which allows individuals the freedom to pursue their own life choices.

[Liberalism] supposes that political decisions must be, so far as is possible, independent of any particular conception of the good life, or of what gives value to life. Since the citizens of a society differ in their conceptions, the government does not treat them as equals if it prefers one conception to another, either because the officials believe that one is intrinsically superior, or because one is held by the more numerous or more powerful group.[4]

Conceptual problems underlie liberalism's portrayal of neutrality and freedom. To assess liberalism's prescriptive portrayal of freedom, as being dependent on a politics of "neutral concern,"[5] it is necessary to explore commonly shared liberal assumptions of freedom. Liberal assumptions of neutrality are intricately linked with claims about how the law and the market facilitate freedom. The essential assumption behind these claims is that a formal system of rights can intelligibly define a boundary, to be enforced by the state, which delineates the individual's private sphere from either arbitrary public or private encroachment.

F.M. Hayek's theory of the law/market relationship speaks to many of the assumptions of liberalism, although liberal scholars often fail to elaborate explicitly on this relationship. According to Hayek, the ability to choose without being subject to another's will is necessarily linked with the market. The market provides a means of effectively coordinating human activities, without deliberate or coercive orders from an authoritarian source, provided that there is a known demarcation of general rules that restrict individual action. The Hayekian conception of freedom can be considered a process that facilitates predictability – a crucial requirement if order is to predominate in a society in which individuals pursue their own particular ends.[6] This process ensures that individual action can be guided by foresight; individuals not only make use of their knowledge and abilities but can anticipate, with a high degree of confidence, what they can expect from others.

What links the market and the law is the role of the state to enforce contract rights; this is seen as a "decisive condition for mutually advantageous collaboration between people, based on voluntary consent rather than coercion." The rule of law ensures that neither the common law nor the market systematically favour a particular outcome and make some individuals' goals easier to obtain than others. The enforcement of contracts by the state is therefore an essential condition of freedom, viewed by Hayek as ensuring that the "whole network of rights created by contracts is as important a part of our own protected sphere, as much the basis of our plans, as any property of our own."[7] Because freedom is defined as the ability to choose, without being thwarted by another's will, the use of the state apparatus for any objective other than to improve the rules of the common law or the market will threaten freedom because it will distort the mutual adjustment of spontaneous activities in the market:

[The] conflict between the ideal of freedom and the desire to "correct" the distribution of incomes so as to make it more "just" is usually not clearly recognized. But those who pursue distributive justice will in practice find themselves obstructed at every move by the rule of law. They must, from the very nature of their aim, favor discriminatory and discretionary action. But, as they are usually not aware that their aim and the rule of law are in principle incompatible, they begin by circumventing or disregarding in individual cases a principle which they often would wish to see preserved in general. But the ultimate result of their efforts will necessarily be, not a modification of the existing order, but its complete abandonment and its replacement by an altogether different system – the command economy.[8]

The most sweeping challenge to liberal claims about the freedom/market relationship have come from the Critical Legal Studies movement. Many associated with this movement dispute liberal claims that a formal system of rights can intelligibly bound the private/public spheres; that the common law itself is neutral in that it is equally facilitative of all goals and purposes; that the market belongs to the private sphere; and that it is a product of a natural order that does not implicate the state. They argue that the market is simply one choice among many and that entitlements of private property exist only to the extent the state is prepared to recognize and support these in the face of competing claims.[9]

Critics contend that liberalism's claims of its ability to facilitate freedom in a neutral manner does not stand up to empirical challenge. Liberal principles are inherently difficult, if not impossible, to adhere to when put into practice. There simply is no deductive process by which judges can derive the "right" legal answers from abstractions such as freedom or property.[10] Empirical studies of the evolution of the common law suggest that when a set of legal rules is no longer useful in resolving conflicts between competing legal concepts or cannot be justified by appealing to tradition, jurists have either changed the rules or developed a new theory to justify them. For example, a study of the common law on torts and contracts reveals that with the recognition by the end of the nineteenth century of the impossibility of simultaneously protecting both competitive and property interests, formal judicial reasoning gave way to legal attempts to balance the conflicting interests. Thus with the development of tort and contract law, judicial decisions could not be "deduced from abstract doctrines such as property and competition."[11] Similarly, analyses of nineteenth- and early twentieth-century attempts to unify the law, to articulate a coherent rule of law, question the "objective" or "immutable" qualities of the law. As Grant Gilmore argues, the development of contract law was guided by the objective of developing an abstract and absolute doctrine to replace a series of loose rules and practices which were not yet a "systematically organized, sharply differentiated body of law."[12]

These critical evaluations of developments in the law raise doubts about the liberal vision of freedom. The sheer scope of the transformation of the common law makes it problematic to assume that these changes were neutral or equally facilitative of everyone's freedom. Rather than considering legal rules as being neutral in promoting freedom, they should be viewed as a manifestation of particular choices that facilitate or constrain particular kinds of actions. But if the essential liberal claim is in doubt – that a formal set of rights provides an intelligible means of regulating state coercion – then so is the subsequent claim that alternatives to this liberal model are inimical to freedom. The threshold for freedom can no longer be measured in terms of the absence of state intervention, other than to protect contract rights and common law rules. Rather, the questions become: what values and outcomes are desirable and justified, and what legislative and judicial actions are required to promote these?

While the origins of liberal claims of neutrality can be traced to the common law and are directed at the intervention of the state into the economic realm, the essential liberal premise – that freedom is dependent on a politics of neutral concern which presumes that the state must not interfere with individual choice – has also been persuasive in the realm of constitutional rights. Despite these conceptual difficulties, those who are most hopeful about the Charter's salutary effects emphasize the Charter's regulatory impact on legislatures to prevent them from promoting public objectives or community values that interfere with individual freedom. Freedom is defined largely in negative terms – as the absence of state intervention – which presumes that the purpose of the Charter is to erect a boundary to separate the private realm of individual freedom from the public realm of state activity. According to this view, the state interferes with individual freedom and choice when legislatures promote policies that conflict with individual rights.

RIGHTS SHOULD BE PARAMOUNT

Those most influenced by the liberal rights ethic believe that rights should be interpreted broadly and subject to limits only when in conflict with other protected rights. This perspective on the appropriate interpretation of the Charter is that the limitation clause of section 1 serves as little more than a symbolic statement that rights are not absolute and may have to be limited when in conflict with other rights. Therefore, it does not provide the means or opportunity for legislatures to promote other values that conflict with protected rights. The only time it is acceptable for legislation to restrict rights is to reconcile actual conflicts between existing Charter rights. This perspective will be referred to as the "rights should be paramount" approach.

Those who believe that rights should be paramount to all other policy or societal objectives have found considerable intellectual support in the works of American liberal scholars such as John Rawls and, to a greater extent, Ronald Dworkin. While Rawls argues of individual "inviolability" founded on justice that cannot be overridden even by the welfare of society as a whole and cannot be subject to political bargaining or "to the calculus of social interests,"[13] Dworkin is even more explicit in his advocacy of the supremacy of rights. Rights, Dworkin argues, are best understood as trumps over political decisions that promote other societal or community objectives. Dworkin's concept stems from his assumption that the American constitutional system rests on a particular liberal moral theory – one that assumes that individuals have moral rights against the state.

If someone has a right to something, then it is wrong for the government to deny it to him [sic] even though it would be in the general interest to do so. This sense of a right (which might be called the anti-utilitarian concept of a right) ... marks the distinctive concept of an individual right against the State which is the heart ... of constitutional theory in the United States.[14]

One of the clearest expressions of the Dworkian view in the context of section 1, that protected Charter rights should have primacy over all other values, is found in the work of Lorraine Weinrib. She argues that the Supreme Court does not first recognize and uphold Charter rights only to make policy decisions about limiting them at a later stage. Rather, what the Court is doing in section 1 is advancing the very values that underlie the protected rights in the Charter: "the same values undergird limits on rights as inform the rights themselves."[15] The task of the Court, as Weinrib sees it, is to uphold the values in the Charter which, she assumes, are identical to and exhaustive of the requirements of a free and democratic society. Weinrib argues that the frame of reference for defining rights and interpreting limits is the same because "rights have emerged as crystallizations of the concept of a 'free and democratic society'"[16] and provide the *exclusive* standard against which limits on rights should be justified:

The courts are to forward an ideal of political ordering, one that reflects the very purpose for which rights were entrenched, even as they entertain arguments to justify limits upon those rights. The judicial task is to monitor adherence by Canadian governments to their constitutional commitment to freedom and democracy in the second stage of Charter argument [the section 1 consideration], just as in the first, [the interpretation of a right] because the exclusive standard set for limits on enumerated rights and freedoms forwards the same values as does their entrenchment.[17]

Weinrib does not anticipate that interpretations of the scope of protected rights or review of section 1 arguments will turn on competing interpretations of democracy or contested claims about which rights are essential to a democratic system. Her argument that only those values that are already contained within the Charter justify limiting a protected right assumes that reasons for advancing alternative policy values are either unwarranted, because they are motivated primarily by the desire to minimize costs or maximize administrative convenience, or are of secondary importance, and therefore subordinate, to protected rights. In either case, the promotion of non-enumerated values is repugnant to, rather than consistent with, a free and democratic society. In the face of legislatures' utilitarian calculus what is required of courts will be readily apparent.

The Court's various comments on section 1 justification, when read together, epitomize the view that convenience, commonly held preferences and usage are repugnant not only to the rights-guaranteeing aspects of the Charter, but moreover to section 1 justification ... Interests specified as rights and freedoms are by definition granted at the expense of the collectivity, to the extent that a majoritarian measure of cost, convenience and custom prevails ... If, despite constitutional entrenchment, these values remained defeasible to the tides of the political marketplace, then the effect of the entrenchment of the Charter, like the enactment of the Canadian Bill of Rights, would indeed be without legal meaning or institutional coherence. That conclusion would deny the supremacy of the Constitution.[18]

The usefulness of a "rights should be paramount" perspective as a prescriptive approach to judicial review can be questioned for reasons both methodological and ideological in nature. As a prescriptive approach to judicial review, the assumption that protected rights should have primacy over all other values does not confront the vagueness in which constitutional rights are understandably articulated. The Charter is no exception to the tendency to express constitutional values in general, broad strokes. The Charter provides little direction as to the specific circumstances that are protected by its vague and general provisions. As a result, courts are required to make substantive policy decisions about the content of rights. The vagueness and ambiguity of the Charter's provisions, referred to as "limp balloons" into which judges must decide how much air to blow,[19] confers considerable discretion on the judiciary to determine the full scope of the Charter's protection. For example, it is not clear from the Charter's wording why freedom of expression should be interpreted as protecting the right to solicit for prostitution purposes or why the right to vote is not interpreted as embracing qualitative considerations such as the relative weight of each individuals' vote.[20] These decisions are not the product of universal principles but are the product of judicial reasoning or policy determinations.

The limitation clause of section 1 is even less determinate of specific outcomes. The difficulty for courts is that the values integral to a free and democratic society are contested. Furthermore, inquiries into the reasonableness of impugned legislation presume scrutiny of the merits of legislation. The subjective nature of these inquiries affords considerable judicial discretion notwithstanding judicial attempts to formalize "objective" guidelines. Reasonableness inquiries, which are highly discretionary, will be examined in more depth in chapter four.

A fundamental objection to a "rights should be paramount" perspective is its indifference to the inevitable judicial discretion in defining rights or determining reasonable limits and the concomitant possibility of judicial fallibility. Notwithstanding the rhetorical appeal of speaking to principles, the enumerated rights and the limitation clause are sufficiently vague to ensure that the Charter is determinate of few rights-based disputes. While conflicts between competing rights are acknowledged, entrenchment is assumed to have resolved disputes about the relative importance of competing values clearly in favour of those explicitly provided for in the Charter. Given the uncertainty as to which values are actually protected, it is troubling to assume that only those claims of entitlement that can be neatly collapsed into rights-based language are worthy of protection and that legislatures should not play a role in defining the interests, values, and rights considerations that justify imposing limits on protected rights.

As a method for judicial review, a "rights should be paramount" perspective has a conservative force that may undermine the Charter's ability to adapt to other values fundamental to Canadians. The Charter was not the product of prodigious intellectual or philosophical collaborations on how to encapsulate the most important rights and values of liberal democracy. Rather, it was largely a political and bureaucratic exercise reflecting the various political compromises between eleven governments and the pressures exerted by academics, civil libertarians, aboriginal, and women's and other interest groups. Nevertheless, one should be sceptical about the assumption that the political drafters of the Charter have captured all of the fundamental values that we, our children, and their descendants will value in the future. For the assumption that only those rights specifically enumerated should be protected and that non-enumerated values cannot be justified could have a chilling effect on political debate about whether other fundamental but non-enumerated values should be upheld under the Charter. In rejecting the legitimacy of other values because they do not have the same status as rights, and therefore do not warrant constitutional protection, the language or terms of the debate are altered to the extent that other values are difficult to promote. How can society, after all, compromise fundamental constitutional principles?

From an ideological perspective, a "rights should be paramount" approach can be criticized for the limited vision of liberalism it promotes. By assuming that the enumerated rights must have primacy over all other societal values, this view promotes a single theory of rights – liberal individualism – which does not address the pluralistic values and diverse cultures of Canada. Those who believe that the Charter gives primacy at all times to individual rights, except where collective rights are specifically entrenched, find support in the work of Dworkin. Dworkin argues that while governments may have to assess competing rights and make choices about which right should be given priority, only individual rights count. Collective rights should never triumph over individual rights.

The existence of rights against the Government would be jeopardized if the Government were able to defeat such a right by appealing to the right of a democratic majority to work its will. A right against the Government must be a right to do something even when the majority thinks it would be wrong to do it, and even when the majority would be worse off for having it done. If we now say that society has a right to do whatever is in the general benefit, or the right to preserve whatever sort of environment the majority wishes to live in, and we mean that these are the sort of rights that provide justification for overruling any rights against the Government that may conflict, then we have annihilated the latter rights.

In order to save them, we must recognize as competing rights only the rights of other members of the society as individuals.[21]

Dworkin's twin assumptions – that rights should be conceptualized as trumps against other societal objectives, and that it is constitutionally improper for governments to advance collective or general welfare values that conflict with individual rights – have gained currency in Canada. They have found expression in constitutional debates about the legitimacy of recognizing Quebec as a distinct society;[22] they are often characteristic of the arguments presented to courts in legal factums, particularly in the context of section 1 arguments;[23] and they are reflected in the work of Weinrib when she argues that collective values should not be able to limit protected individual rights:

The Court provides a list of some of the elements essential to a free and democratic society: respect for the inherent dignity of the human person, commitment to social justice and equality, accommodation of a wide variety of beliefs, respect for cultural and group identity, and faith in social and political institutions that enhance the participation of individuals and groups in society. Given this list of examples of the values essential to a free and democratic society, the reference to "collective goals of fundamental importance" should not be taken to suggest that section 1 limits rights for the good of the collectivity – or, the majority – at the expense of those who claim the protection of the rights ... The phrase "collective goals of fundamental importance" must be understood to refer to the maximization of these interests on the principle of equality of enjoyment, rather than to benefits for a fortunate number at the expense of the rest.[24]

Despite the growing ascendency of this perspective, Canada's political culture diverges in important ways from the unencumbered primacy of individualism. There has been in Canada little counterpart to the theorizing by early American thinkers of how best to limit government to protect individual rights, principally property. Canada's failure to embrace a strictly individualistic political culture can perhaps be attributed to the inheritance of tory and socialist influences,[25] the influence of federalism and its objective of promoting community values, or the need for the state to assume a role in developing a foundling economic and industrial base.[26] Certainly, Canada's political culture has never represented a liberal monolith.

Another ideological concern arising from a "rights should be paramount" approach is the likelihood that it would foster a negative interpretation of rights. At its core is the assumption that rights serve as vetoes over state actions that impose limits on individuals to promote broader societal values. Thus rights are defined as freedom from interference. This approach to judicial review would make it difficult for legislatures to implement progressive or affirmative policies that seek to promote qualitative considerations such as equity or fairness, intended to improve conditions for under-represented or underprivileged groups, which require limiting individual rights.

An example of how a negative interpretation of rights might undermine broader societal considerations is aptly demonstrated by a lower court decision about the legitimacy of election spending limits. A 1983 Alberta decision found that legislation to regulate the amount of expenses made by those other than registered candidates and parties in elections was an unconstitutional violation of speech. The legislation was part of a larger regulatory scheme that was intended to limit the amount of money spent in federal elections. Limits on independent expenditures were to ensure the integrity of candidate/party limits which would be undermined by parallel campaigns by individuals or interest groups to promote or oppose candidates and parties. Regulations on the amount of election spending, in place since 1974, are premised on the assumption that fairness and equity should prevail as central principles in the election process. The rationale is that money should not have an undue influence by allowing those with superior financial resources to monopolize the commercial media, alter the agenda, and create cynicism about the integrity of the election. Spending limits also promote fairness by establishing a low economic threshold for election participation which, along with partial reimbursement, ensures that the requirements for seeking office do not discriminate against those of modest means.[27]

The Alberta decision interpreted freedom of expression wholly from a negative perspective – freedom from interference. The result of the decision was to cast doubt on whether the principles of Canadian elections, fairness and equity, can be preserved in the face of unregulated election advertising by individuals and interest groups.[28] The issue has yet to be resolved and revised legislation, which has again been overturned in Alberta,[29] is in the process of being appealed.

INTERNAL LIMITATIONS

The method for determining when and how to limit rights is not dictated by the structure of the Charter. Many of the participants in the

Charter debate, particularly critics of earlier drafts of the limitation clause, believed that the presence of an explicit qualifying provision was unnecessary. Critics argued that a formal system of rights necessarily entails that courts devise strategies for building implicit limitations on rights.[30] The inclusion of an explicit limitation clause has not silenced suggestions that when interpreting the Charter, courts should follow the American course of fashioning internal qualifications on rights.

A second approach to interpreting the Charter would be to collapse the interpretation of rights and consideration of limits into a single process. Judicial review of the Charter would not proceed in two analytically distinct stages, as is the case in the "rights should be paramount" approach, in which the interpretation of whether a right has been infringed is separate from the inquiry into the reasonableness of limits. Rather, arguments about the justification for limits would be incorporated into the process of defining a protected right to determine if it has been infringed.

Two concerns underlie this approach. One is to ensure that fundamental rights are adequately protected, the other that courts are not involved in the wholesale assessment of legislative decisions, including activities not intended by the Charter's drafters to be subject to judicial review.

Paul Bender is a leading advocate of internal limitations. He believes that this approach will ensure that fundamental rights and freedoms are better protected than if courts too readily assume that all governmental action conflicts with protected Charter interests. His worry is that if rights are interpreted too broadly, the necessary and frequent recourse to section 1 will encourage judicial deference to legislative decisions:

Constitutional standards of permissible justification that will be developed for dealing with such inquiries may very well turn into extremely weak and deferential standards. Such deference may be essential in order to allow government the wide degree of latitude that is necessary when it seeks to deal – often tentatively and experimentally – with the full range of new and complex economic and social problems that seem constantly to confront modern society. That large degree of deference, however, may be quite inappropriate where fundamental rights and freedoms are at stake; such rights might, indeed, all but disappear as a practical matter if weak and deferential standards of governmental justification come to be employed in Charter cases across the board. If, on the other hand, the scope of Charter scrutiny of governmental justifications is restricted to legislation and government behaviour that invades the limited category of fundamental interests that the Charter does, indeed, protect, courts will likely take Charter rights more seriously and apply relatively strong constitutional standards of justification – standards that will make these rights truly meaningful as a constitutional matter.[31]

Bender's second reason for favouring internal limits is that it provides the most prudent way for courts to evaluate the justification of legislative objectives that may conflict, prima facie, with protected rights. Bender argues that treating section 1 as a separate phase of judicial review is inappropriate both as a matter of "proper technical analysis" of the Charter and as good human rights policy. Underlying his advocacy of internal limits is the assumption that the Charter should not implicate every conceivable legislative objective. If rights are interpreted abstractly and only then subject to limits, courts will become involved in the wholesale assessment of legislative decisions, including activities not intended by the Charter's drafters to be subject to judicial review:

It is a serious mistake to assume that the Charter has constitutionalized all concerns about legislation and governmental practices that may affect individual or commercial interests, thus requiring courts, in every case in which such legislation or practices are attacked, to ask whether there is a constitutionally adequate justification for the challenged rules or activities.[32]

Bender does not believe courts are well placed to evaluate the reasonableness of legislative decisions because this inquiry is inherently subjective and value laden. Thus, courts can minimize the requirement of having to balance legislative justifications and protected rights by defining rights and excluding, at the outset, those circumstances not intended to be protected by the Charter. By so doing, the frequency and range of issues that require judicial decisions about the reasonableness of legislation will be reduced substantially.

Bender's argument suggests there is a categorical distinction between the policy role of courts when applying reasonable limits as opposed to interpreting rights. Yet the vague manner in which protected rights are stated gives courts considerable discretion to define what circumstances are actually protected. Judicial decisions about whether freedom of association protects collective bargaining or whether freedom of expression includes commercial advertising require substantive judicial policy decisions that are difficult to distinguish, as categorically as Bender does, from subjective considerations of the reasonableness of policy. Nevertheless, Bender believes that the interpretation of whether a right exists is consistent with judicial experience and expertise in interpreting statutes, common law precedents or division of powers, whereas decisions about the merits and reasonableness of legislation are not.

> It would be unfortunate ... if courts were to forego the opportunity to further the development of the Charter in the area in which, by training, competence and tradition, they are most well-equipped to contribute, and instead concentrated their energies exclusively in the most subjective and value laden of Charter inquiries – that of balancing governmental justifications against protected Charter interests.[33]

This approach to the Charter can be criticized for placing too great a burden on the individual to show that a right has been violated. While litigants bear the onus for demonstrating that a right has been infringed, the directive in section 1 requires that the government, or the party seeking to limit a right, demonstrably justify the reasonableness of limits. Yet if courts adopt a single approach to interpreting the Charter, one that combines the interpretation of a right with reasonableness assessments, the litigant would have to demonstrate that a right has been infringed amidst governmental arguments that, first, the impugned policy serves an important societal purpose that is more important than the prima facie rights violation, and second, given the lesser importance of the rights-based claim, it should not be accorded constitutional protection. In other words, an internal limitations approach would effectively shift the burden of persuasion to litigants who would have to disprove governmental claims about the reasonableness and importance of legislative objectives.

For example, if this approach were adopted for reviewing legislation which restricts election spending by individuals or interest groups, those defending the policy would try to convince the court that freedom of expression does not include the right of non-candidates to spend money on election advertising. Their arguments might be two fold: that since the purpose of elections is to elect candidates and choose a government, the right to spend money in elections should be confined to registered candidates and parties; and that this interpretation is justified given the importance of promoting a fair and equitable election where money does have an undue influence on outcomes. Consequently, no right was infringed. Litigants would have the burden of persuasion that, although they are not the principal participants in election campaigns, freedom of expression should nevertheless embrace a right by individuals and groups to advertise.

The prospect that individual litigants might have to argue that a protected right has been infringed against assumptions of reasonableness generated considerable controversy during the 1980–81 parliamentary committee hearings on the Charter. Given the tradition of parliamentary supremacy, many argued that unless the Charter made it absolutely clear that legislation would not be presumed to be constitutional, and that governments bore the burden for demonstrating the reasonableness of limits, courts might be overly deferential in assessing the reasonableness of legislation. This criticism was a compelling one, particularly in light of earlier political attempts to design the limitation clause to ensure that individual litigants would have to prove the unreasonableness of a limitation; the assumption in these clauses was that limits on rights would almost always be deemed reasonable, by virtue of having been enacted.

Concerns that an internal limitations approach would make it difficult for individual litigants to challenge legislation successfully are amplified by the structure of the limitation clause. In light of the vague and contested nature of the standard for justifying limits on rights – a free and democratic society – representative institutions could argue that a broad range of policies, reflecting non-enumerated values, are reasonable under section 1. The superior resources of governments to compile evidence and expert opinions testifying to the importance of the impugned legislation would increase the difficulty for litigants who would have to counter this evidence. This practice could undermine the extent to which the Charter is effective in providing individuals protection from unnecessary or overly intrusive state action.

A different problem with an internal limits approach is that it increases the likelihood of freezing the definitions of rights. If courts apply internal or definitional limits to restrict the scope of rights, it would be considerably more difficult subsequently to alter the definition to embrace changing attitudes about the substantive content of rights. Equality rights provide a good example of the need to allow definitions to evolve. Judicial interpretation in the 1970s did not recognize the need for equality to reflect and accommodate women's biological function of child-bearing. As a result, the Supreme Court concluded that unemployment insurance policy, which imposed greater burdens on pregnant women than on other applicants, did not violate women's equality. The Court's reasons were based on the observations that UIC did not differentiate on the basis of sex because it did not "treat unemployed women differently from other unemployed persons, be they male or female," and thus the differentiation on the basis of pregnancy did not constitute sexual discrimination.[34] Fifteen years later the Supreme Court overruled its earlier interpretation of equality by recognizing that equality does not exist when women are expected to assume the entire costs of child-bearing. In contrast to its earlier interpretation, the Court upheld the claim that discrimination based on pregnancy amounts to discrimination against women and therefore violates equality. In the Court's revised opinion, pregnancy cannot be separated from sex.[35]

The fact that the Charter was seen as establishing a different standard for rights protection from the Bill of Rights, which was the basis for the earlier decision, provided the Court ample opportunity to reverse its interpretation to reflect a change in societal understandings of the substantive content of equality.[36] However, this was a unique set of circumstances. An internal limitations approach would make it difficult for the Court to change or expand the definition of a right if an earlier court had imposed definitional limits that specifically denied constitutional protection for the claim in question. Given the principle of stare decisis which underlies the common law, an internal limitations approach would require that a court explicitly reverse a prior decision if, at a later date, it had determined that a Charter right embraces a situation formerly excluded. Thus an internal limitations approach would constrain the Charter's capacity to evolve and embrace changing circumstances and values. The risk of freezing rights is reduced with a two-stage approach to judicial review where rights are initially interpreted broadly and in which the reasonableness of limits are assessed on a case-by-case basis.

A further criticism of an internal limitations approach is that it would create a complicated jurisprudence that would make it difficult to distil the principles that govern judicial decisions about when limits on protected rights are justified. In the absence of an explicit limitation clause, American courts have developed a range of procedural means to evaluate limitations on rights. A search of the literature on the procedural and substantive concerns that underlie American judicial evaluation of legislation reveals little discussion or agreement by American scholars on what the standards for limiting rights are or how they should guide legislative proposals that conflict, prima facie, with protected rights. Instead, what is revealed in the literature and jurisprudence is a "morass of complex and inconsistent exclusive standards."[37] The emergence of clear and coherent judicial standards for determining the reasonableness of legislation is particularly important for Canada. Given the relative newness of the Charter, policy-makers are still learning how to adapt their objectives to the standards in the Charter. In light of the prevalence of collective and cultural aspirations in the Canadian polity, the need for policy-makers to understand the standards they must adhere to when promoting those objectives that conflict with protected rights is particularly pressing.

EXPANSIVE APPROACH TO
DEMOCRATIC VALUES

A third approach to interpreting the Charter and, as chapter four will reveal, the one closest to what the Supreme Court itself has adhered to, is a two-stage approach that would interpret rights broadly while recognizing that values other than those already protected may justify limiting them. This approach will be referred to as an expansive approach to democratic values. Rather than confine democratic values to those rights specifically enumerated in the Charter, it recognizes that legislatures may promote democratic values that cannot be easily captured by the specific rights' language of the Charter but are nevertheless sufficiently important to warrant imposing limits on protected rights.

The principal advantage of this approach is that it responds to the ideological constraints imposed by a rights should be paramount approach. If the only justification for limiting protected rights is to give effect to other protected rights, the Charter itself will be considered exhaustive of all fundamental values. The assumption that only those rights specified in the Charter, or derivative of them, can justifiably limit protected rights represents an ideological and institutional constraint on the values that can be promoted legitimately by the legislatures. It excludes those values which cannot be captured by the specific, and highly individualistic, language of the Charter.

Accepting a role for legislatures to promote values other than those specifically enumerated helps to overcome the narrowness of the Charter in recognizing fundamental rights and freedoms. While the Charter gives limited recognition to collective rights, the extent to which they are protected by the Charter should not be overstated. The collective rights that are entrenched – most notably minority education rights – can be thought of as both collective and individual rights; they are entitlements conferred on individuals but can be called upon only in a collectivity (where numbers warrant). Minority education language rights can be distinguished, conceptually, from other collective rights such as aboriginal or association rights (collective bargaining and striking) that reflect a collective orientation that is not dependent on or derivative of an individual right. The extent to which the Charter embraces collective values that cannot be reduced to an individual right is minimal. Multicultural rights, for example, do not constitute substantive entitlements of their own but represent an interpretive guide for how other protected rights are interpreted. Aboriginal rights also do not represent new substantive entitlements but provide an interpretive principle for judges in light of earlier aboriginal treaty or pre-Charter rights. The extent to which other protected rights in the Charter will embrace collective values depends largely on judicial assumptions about the philosophical content of these.

The ideology of liberalism, with its emphasis on individual freedom, will inevitably influence judicial determinations. A telling example of the Supreme Court's approach to collective values is that a majority would not recognize a collective right to strike as a protected form of freedom of association in part because striking does not have any individual analogy.[38] The majority decision on striking underscores the distinction between different kinds of collective values. Whereas minority education language rights are individual entitlements that depend on quantitative considerations to become constitutionally relevant (where numbers warrant), collective values such as aboriginal rights or collective bargaining represent community or association values that may not be derivative of individual rights or have an individual analogy. Constitutional recognition for the latter relies on subjective and philosophical assumptions about the relevance or justification of these values.

Despite the Charter's emphasis on individual rights, collective values continue to find ample expression in the Canadian polity. While the Charter requires legislatures to exercise greater sensitivity towards individual rights when developing policy, legislative examples abound with attempts to reconcile individual rights with policies intended to promote general welfare values such as fairness and equity, protect vulnerable individuals, or facilitate public safety.[39] One example is federal rape shield legislation (to prevent a women's sexual past from being raised in court as a defence to sexual assault charges), which seeks to promote the collective security of women despite possible implication for individual legal rights.[40] More telling examples of collective elements in the Canadian polity are the cultural differences that distinguish aboriginal and Québécois from other Canadians and from each other. Aboriginal and Québécois cultural objectives are defined in terms of community and cultural values that reflect collective assumptions and aspirations difficult to conceptualize purely in individual terms.

An expansive approach to democratic values would enable legislatures to promote values that are not specifically enumerated as justifiable limits on protected rights. The Charter would be seen not as an exhaustive statement of protected rights but as the framework for fundamental values in Canada that could be amplified where legislatures can convince courts that the non-enumerated values they wish to promote, which may reflect cultural or community objectives, are both pressing and substantial and consistent with a free and democratic society.

Having argued that the limitation clause is a way of conferring constitutional recognition on community or collective values that are not specifically enumerated, it is important to emphasize that not all community values may justify limiting protected rights. While this approach to section 1 would enable legislatures to promote a broader range of values than under a rights should be paramount approach, they would still be expected to defend and justify the reasonableness of their choices. In this sense, the criterion that should be satisfied is similar: policies that pursue objectives inimical to democratic values would be excluded. But, unlike a rights should be paramount approach, democratic values would not be confined to those values specifically enumerated in or derivative of the protected individual rights in the Charter. The issue of how the justification of collective or non-enumerated values should be assessed will be explored in chapter five.

A second advantage of this third approach to interpreting the Charter is that it offers more robust protection for rights than under an internal limitations approach. Only after the court decides that a right has been infringed would it consider arguments about whether and why the limit is reasonable. Unlike a definitional limits approach, governments would bear the onus for demonstrating the reasonableness of their impugned policies rather than individual litigants having to argue the unreasonableness of legislation. To again use the example of election spending limits, under this third approach the legislation would be considered a limit on freedom of expression, because it regulates the amount of money individuals can spend to purchase advertising to express opinions on candidates. The most important and difficult question would be whether the limits were reasonable. Individual litigants would not have to disprove the reasonableness of the legislation. Rather, the government would have to convince the court that the objective of promoting fair and equitable elections by regulating election expenses is consistent with a free and democratic society and that the legislative means were reasonable. The onus would be on the federal government to demonstrate that alternative and less restrictive measures were neither practical nor effective. The advantage of this approach is that it does not paralyse representative institutions by having to eschew compelling democratic objectives that cannot be neatly encapsulated in the language of individual rights, yet it requires that these policies be justified in democratic and reasonableness terms.

One criticism of this approach is that a bifurcated method of judicial review unnecessarily engages courts in assessments of the merits and reasonableness of policy, a task that is considerably different from what has traditionally been associated with the judicial function. It is this

task, implicit in judicial review but enhanced by inquiries into the reasonableness of legislation, which lies at the heart of proposals to impose internal limits on protected rights. While those who favour
internal limitations might be guilty of exaggerating the different policy
ramifications of interpreting rights as opposed to assessing the reasonableness of legislation, the complexity of policy development gives rise
to compelling concerns about courts' capacity to scrutinize the merits
of policy choices. These concerns have a particular resonance for
the third approach to section 1. Because courts, under this approach,
would both interpret rights broadly and recognize that non-enumerated values may justify imposing limits on protected rights, conflicts
would arise more frequently between rights claims and governmental
objectives.

But the increased chance of conflict is not, by itself, justification for
rejecting this approach in favour of either of the first two methods
of review. While this third approach to judicial review of the Charter
makes visible the tension between rights and limits, the Charter should
be seen as a welcome obligation and requirement on representative institutions to justify policy choices in terms of their effects on protected
rights. This obligation is not fulfilled by altering the level of protection
for rights and making it more difficult for litigants to demonstrate that
a right has been infringed.

Furthermore, it confuses the issue to treat internal and external limitations as representing mutually exclusive approaches. It is highly unlikely that courts will interpret rights without making some decisions
about the proper scope of rights. It seems inconceivable in a liberal democracy that freedom of expression, for example, would be interpreted so broadly as to give constitutional protection for violent forms
of expression, such as physical assault or murder, subject only to reasonable limits. For a court to conclude that any expressive activity is entitled to constitutional protection, no matter how violent or morally
repugnant, would strain the credibility of judicial review. Courts must
provide some scope and content to the Charter's vague provisions
independent of and prior to considerations of the reasonableness of
legislative objectives. To do otherwise would be to trivialize the significance of fundamental rights and values.

But there is a difference between defining rights and values, as a way
of making sense of them and making them relevant to the Canadian
constitutional setting, and the kind of balancing of values contemplated by an internal limitations approach. An expansive interpretation of democratic values would not prevent courts from exercising
discretion to exclude from the Charter's protection those circumstances that do not warrant constitutional recognition. But the context

for doing so would be the importance of the value at stake, rather than an attempt to accommodate and reconcile conflicting rights and policy values.

CONCLUSIONS

It is difficult to appreciate the political significance of the Charter without understanding the tension between entrenched rights and limits. The limitation clause of section 1 relates directly to one of the principal and most contentious issues in a political system with entrenched rights: how much discretion should Parliament and the provincial legislatures retain to pursue policies reflecting values in conflict with protected rights. Although it is certainly true that the Charter has modified the constitutional principles upon which the Canadian state rests, considerable room for debate remains on the question of how the polity should reconcile concerns for individual rights with general welfare, collective, or community values.

An expansive approach to democratic values is the most compelling of the approaches to judicial review because it both protects litigants from having to assume the undue burden of "disproving" the reasonableness of legislation and yet enlivens the Charter to embrace important but non-enumerated values. Both individual and collective values are relevant to Canadian conceptions of democracy, yet the latter are not adequately captured by the highly individualist language of the Charter. While this particular approach to section 1 may increase the frequency in which courts must review the reasonableness of legislation, the Charter ensures that the policy contribution assumed by judicial review in the legislative process cannot be eliminated. The challenge posed by the Charter is not how to engage in creative interpretive techniques that would minimize this policy role but rather how to assess the justification of the potentially broad range of policies that claim to forward democratic values. Courts must decide not only whether the objectives promoted are consistent with democratic values and sufficiently important to limit a protected right, but also whether the means of advancing these objectives are justified. How the Supreme Court responds to its responsibility of reviewing the reasonableness of impugned policies will be the subject of the next chapter.

4 The Supreme Court on Section 1

The inclusion of a formal system of rights in the constitution has significantly increased the policy contribution judicial review assumes in the
legislative process. Courts must now give content to the general and
vague provisions of the Charter and assess the reasonableness of legislative decisions that conflict with protected rights. The Charter of Rights
and Freedoms has changed the way decisions are made about the scope
of citizens' rights by giving to courts much of the responsibility, formerly
held by legislatures, for determining the appropriate limits on rights.[1]

With the power to review legislative decisions about limiting rights,
courts have the potential to give priority to a different range of values
than those espoused by legislatures. What is not clear, however, is how
the judiciary will qualify rights. The presence of section 1 is not simply
a symbolic recognition that rights are not absolute. The evolution of
the clause reveals that section 1 was intended to enable legislatures,
under some circumstances, to limit rights when they consider a more
pressing value to be at stake. But if drafters of the Charter envisaged
section 1 as a way of occasionally preserving the abilities of legislatures
to determine the primacy of particular policies or values, they were taking a considerable risk in entrusting the amended clause to the courts
for interpretation. The abandonment of the concept that limitations
on rights are those which are "generally accepted" in a democratic society, and its replacement by the more difficult requirement that rights
be subject only to such limitations which are "demonstrably justified,"
weakens the impetus for judicial deference towards legislative decisions which limit rights. Moreover, the deletion of the reference to a
"parliamentary system of government," which was intended as a spe-

cific reminder to the courts of the significance parliamentary supremacy has played in the constitutional order, is a further undermining of judicial signals to defer to legislative choices that limit rights.

The wording of the existing clause provides no indication that it should be read as a way of enabling legislatures to make discretionary decisions about whether a specific right should be limited. It gives no direction as to when or how rights should be limited or what standards should be invoked for determining the reasonableness of legislation that encroaches upon a protected right. The limitation clause does not address the level of judicial scrutiny that should be afforded legislation in conflict with protected rights. The clause indicates that governments must demonstrate the justification of their reasons for limiting enumerated rights but it does not instruct courts on how to recognize when an objective is valid or determine whether the means are warranted. As a result of the Charter, judges are now engaged directly in one of the most difficult tasks facing liberal democracies: how does a democratic society distinguish between allowable state action and the protected sphere of human activity? In the specific context of section 1, the questions become what kinds of legislative objectives are worthy of limiting protected rights and how much latitude should be given to legislatures to design and administer their policies?

This chapter will analyse Supreme Court decisions involving section 1. It will evaluate how the reasonableness of legislation, in conflict with protected rights, is being assessed. The hierarchical nature of the Canadian judicial system and the impact of Supreme Court decisions on other courts, particularly those cases of a constitutional character, render it of particular significance for a student of constitutional politics. The importance of Supreme Court decisions is not only that they are binding on all other courts and are the final word in all areas of law, but also in the "prospective light they throw on relationships in our society affected by the principles and rules they enunciate."[2] In the constitutional sphere these written decisions address the appropriate bounds of government action in the pursuit of collective values and general welfare objectives. In assessing the Court's approach to section 1, particular attention will be paid to how the Court copes with the judicial discretion inherent in the task of measuring legislation against the vague and contested concept of a free and democratic society. How the Court responds to this challenge is vitally linked to the question underlying this chapter: is the interpretation of limits on protected rights resulting in priority being given to a different range of values than those espoused by legislatures?

Judicial review of the limitation clause of section 1 represents the most significant change in judicial responsibilities introduced by the Charter. Section 1 systematically engages courts in policy making of a kind different from what is incurred in the normal course of judicial responsibilities. It must be recognized that the very exercise of judicial power has legislative consequence. It would be a mistake to presume that the law-making powers of courts are restricted to the constitutional realm. Canadian judges have long exercised influence on public policy in their capacity of developing the common law, interpreting statutes, and umpiring division of powers disputes, as well as in their non-adjudicative capacity of sentencing in criminal courts and serving on royal commissions.[3] When interpreting the common law, judges are required to make substantive choices between conflicting precedents and between competing philosophical assumptions (the decision, for example, of whether striking as an incident to collective bargaining is a political or economic activity).

The law-making consequences of judicial power are particularly pronounced in the constitutional realm. The Charter is replete with unqualified provisions requiring content and scope to determine what values are actually protected by vague phrases such as "the right to life, liberty and security of the person." Open-ended phrases such as freedom of expression can engage the courts in an inquiry into the merits of legislative enactments to regulate such things as advertising in magazines, the content of television or cinema films, what election participants may spend on election advertising, or attempts to shield the names of juveniles or sexual assault victims from media attention. Further, courts will have to engage in normative and philosophical inquiries as to whether legislative objectives, which impose limits on protected rights, are justified in the context of a free and democratic society. Yet little agreement exists as to whether the values that are essential to a free and democratic society are confined to those rights specifically enumerated or derivative of them, or also embrace collective or other non-enumerated values. An even greater challenge facing the courts in evaluating the reasonableness of impugned legislation is that these judicial inquiries require implicit, if not explicit, scrutiny of the merits of legislation. This responsibility takes courts even further away from their traditional judicial function. They must now also evaluate arguments about whether alternative or more reasonable measures should be sought.

Three stages can be identified in the Court's development of an approach to interpreting the reasonableness of legislative decisions that conflict with protected rights.

STAGE 1: ORIGINS OF AN APPROACH

In early Charter jurisprudence the Court established that the Charter has altered significantly the role and function of courts in Canadian political life. Some early commentators speculated that the Charter would not have a substantial impact on how courts evaluate legislation because conservative Canadian judicial culture has been reluctant to question the role of legislatures in resolving important social and political questions.[4] But the Court took little time to dispel such suggestions. The Court seemed almost anxious to distance itself from earlier decisions, which were characterized by a reluctance to scrutinize legislative objectives in conflict with the provisions in the Canadian Bill of Rights.[5] The Court recognized the Charter as the supreme law of Canada and suggested that it represents a "new yardstick of reconciliation between the individual and the community and their respective rights."[6] Characterizing itself as "the guardian of the Constitution," the Court stated that it must bear in mind that it no longer has reason to be uncertain or ambivalent about the requirements of judicial review. Rather, the Charter "has sent a clear message to the courts that the restrictive attitude which at times characterized its approach to the *Canadian Bill of Rights* ought to be re-examined."[7]

Another indication that the Court would treat the Charter of Rights in a qualitatively different manner was the approach it adopted for interpreting the enumerated rights. The Court suggested that the interpretation of rights should be generous rather than legalistic if the Charter was going to serve future generations and secure for Canadians the full benefit of its protection. The Court established early on that the proper approach is a purposive one, which will enable it to delineate the nature of the interests Charter Rights are meant to protect.[8] Justice Dickson, as he was then, expanded on what is meant by a purposive approach when he explained that the purpose of the particular right or freedom in question is to be sought by reference to the character and the larger objectives of the Charter itself, to the language chosen to articulate the right, to the historical origins of the concept, and, where applicable, to the meaning and purpose of the other rights and freedoms with which it is associated within the text of the Charter.[9] The virtue of a purposive approach, the Court argued, is that it will enable courts to scrutinize more rigorously legislation challenged under the Charter by providing a "more vigorous protection of constitutional rights by obviating the individual litigant's need to prove effects violative of Charter rights."[10]

The Court's determination to interpret rights broadly increases the range of legislative activities that will be found to conflict, prima facie, with the Charter. But in its early cases, despite the frequency in which legislation was found to infringe upon protected rights, the Court avoided the task of systematically scrutinizing the reasonableness of impugned policies. The Court's first two years were characterized by a tension between its new course of constitutional jurisprudence and its reluctance to develop a consistent approach to determine whether legislatively imposed limits on individuals rights are reasonable or demonstrably justified under section 1. During the first two-year period the Court set aside legislation for conflicting with protected rights in five of its fifteen cases yet showed little concern for weighing the impact of its decisions on government policies in the public interest.[11] Instead, members seemed preoccupied with the need to deny the policy contribution judicial review assumes in the legislative process. The Court repeatedly asserted that it was merely applying the standards in the Charter, not inquiring into the merits of legislation. The assumption was that by refraining from making pronouncements on the merits of legislation, the Court was not participating in the policy process.

An example of how the Court has attempted to distinguish the legal nature of its task from the kinds of policy considerations necessary to determine the priority that should be attached to conflicting values is the judgment of Justice Bertha Wilson in *Operation Dismantle* v. *the Queen*. In this case Operation Dismantle, a coalition of peace, labour, and other interest groups challenged the government's decision to allow testing of the cruise missile in Canadian airspace. The basis of the challenge was that the government's policy increased the chances of nuclear war and therefore violated the section 7 right to life, liberty and security of the person and the right not to be deprived thereof except in accordance with the principles of fundamental justice. In this decision Wilson stated that the question before the Court was not whether the government's defence policy was sound but whether it violated the appellants' rights under section 7.

… it is important to realize that judicial review is not the same thing as substitution of the court's opinion on the merits for the opinion of the person or body to whom a discretionary decision-making power has been committed … The question before us is not whether the government's defence policy is sound but whether or not it violates the appellants' rights under s. 7 of the Canadian Charter of Rights and Freedoms. This is a totally different question.[12]

Although Wilson suggested that the Court could distinguish its (proper) legal task from an (improper) inquiry into the merits of the legislation, she did not elaborate on how the Court could decide the validity of the claim, which was based on the assumption that the government had wrongly decided to allow testing of the cruise missile in Canadian airspace and therefore had increased the risk of nuclear war, without inquiring into the soundness or merits of that policy.[13]

Judicial assertions that review of legislative decisions does not engage the Court in a normative inquiry into the merits of policy stand in stark contrast to the Court's perception, as recently as 1976, of the subjective task of resolving disputes between conflicting values. For example, in *Harrison* v. *Carswell* Justice Dickson declined to discuss the merits of the competing arguments involved in a dispute as to whether peaceful picketing in a shopping centre was an illegal trespass on private property. In his view, the resolution of competing social values is inherently arbitrary and therefore best left to elected representatives:

The submission that this court should weigh and determine the respective values of society of the right to property and the right to picket raises important and difficult political and socio-economic issues, the resolution of which must, by their very nature, be arbitrary and embody personal economic and social beliefs.[14]

Even though it did not discuss what standards should be invoked to review legislation in conflict with a protected right in its early cases, the Court found that the legislation had shortcomings that could not possibly meet a section 1 test. One technique the Court used to avoid assessing directly the merits of legislation that conflicts with a protected right was to find that where the legislative intent runs directly contrary to the purpose of the Charter right, the legislation cannot be considered to represent a reasonable limit within the meaning of section 1. This technique was used in *A.G. Quebec* v. *Quebec Association of Protestant School Boards*. Quebec's Bill 101 restricted access to English schools to those children with at least one parent who had received all of his or her elementary education in Quebec in English, children of newcomers whose parents were living in Quebec when the law was passed but who had been educated in English outside the province, and children with older brothers or sisters already enroled in an English-language school. The issue at stake was whether this legislation violated section 23 of the Charter. This law was more restrictive than the Charter's minority education language rights that guarantee public education in English or French to the children of citizens whose first language, or whose primary school instruction in Canada, was in the language of the English or French linguistic minority population of the province in which they reside.[15]

The Court avoided assessing the Quebec government's arguments that sections 72 and 73 of Bill 101 were justified in light of demographic, migration, and assimilation patterns. The Court speculated that "the framers of the Constitution would not have drafted s. 23 of the Charter as they did" if they had not intended that it should override Quebec's school language instruction policy and argued that section 23 had been entrenched to establish new national constitutional norms for the issue of school instruction policy.[16] Given the specificity of the intent of section 23, the Court argued that it could not accept the claim that Bill 101 imposes a reasonable limit on section 23. The effect of the legislation, in the Court's view, was not to limit but to amend minority education language rights guaranteed in the Charter. Thus, despite the absence of a framework or general approach to evaluate section 1 arguments, the Court concluded:

The provisions of s. 73 of Bill 101 collide directly with those of s. 23 of the Charter, and are not limits which can be legitimized by s. 1 of the Charter. Such limits cannot be exceptions to the rights and freedoms guaranteed by the Charter nor amount to amendments of the Charter.[17]

The idea that legislation that conflicts directly with the intent of a protected right will not be eligible for section 1 consideration was also relied on in *R.* v. *Big M Drug Mart,* a case involving a challenge to the federal Lord's Day Act on the basis that it violates freedom of conscience and religion.

A second technique used by the Court to avoid engaging in a section 1 inquiry was to declare that the contentious legislation would not conform with the necessary, although undeclared, standards for limiting a Charter right. In *Singh et al.* v. *Minister of Employment and Immigration* Justice Wilson, writing for the three members of the Court who relied on the Charter to decide the case, indicated that whatever standard eventually emerges under section 1, the government could not possibly have satisfied it in this case.[18] The *Singh* case involved a challenge to the process of administering claims for Convention refugee status based on section 7 of the Charter. Wilson J. held that the procedure for determining refugee status claims was inconsistent with the requirements of fundamental justice because, in the absence of an oral hearing, it did not provide the refugee claimant with an adequate opportunity to state a case and to know the case that has to be met. She was not persuaded by the principal claim of the minister of employment and immigration that the Immigration Appeal Board was already subjected to a considerable strain in terms of the volume of cases it was required to hear and that the requirement of an oral hearing in every case where an application for redetermination of a refugee claim had been made would constitute an unreasonable burden on the board's resources. The inquiry to determine whether legislation that infringes upon a Charter right can be justified under section 1, she stated, must be conducted in light of a commitment "to uphold the rights and freedoms set out in the other sections of the Charter."[19] In her view, the minister mistakenly had assumed that the reference to "reasonable" in section 1 refers to the administrative procedures of the legislation in question:

The issue in the present case is not simply whether the procedures set out in the Immigration Act, 1976 for the adjudication of refugee claims are reasonable; it is whether it is reasonable to deprive the appellants of the right to life, liberty and security of the person by adopting a system for the adjudication of refugee status claims which does not accord with the principles of fundamental justice.[20]

Given that the determination of whether legislation imposes a reasonable limit depends not upon the reasonableness of the administrative procedures but whether it is reasonable to limit an individual's Charter right, Wilson found that the government's argument amounted to little more than utilitarian considerations of costs and administrative convenience.

In light of the Court's inclination to deny that judicial review assumes a policy contribution in the legislative process, it is not surprising that the Court tried to avoid the section 1 issue. By finding that legislation imposed limits that were in direct conflict with a protected right, or that the legislation did not conform with the necessary, although undeclared, standards to be saved by section 1, the Court avoided having to assess the justification of the legislative objective. In the absence of a general approach to section 1 the Court has projected the image not of engaging in ad hoc assessments of the worth of conflicting values but of merely upholding Charter rights against unjustified state encroachments. The Court's early judgments reflect the assumption that the essential purpose of the Court in Charter review is to protect individuals' rights from encroaching state activities – a task courts can fulfil by confining their inquiry to legal, as opposed to policy, considerations. Judgments contain considerable discussion of the need to interpret Charter rights in the broadest possible manner but little acknowledgment that one consequence of a broad, purposive interpretation of rights will be that legislation will frequently be found to conflict with the Charter, in which the courts will have to assess conflicting values and claims.

Some may wonder where concern lies with the Court's handling of its early cases. Although provincial and federal governments were unsuccessful in their first five cases involving section 1, the Court's decisions regarding legislation found to impose an unreasonable limit do not seem horrendous. Indeed, with the exception of Bill 101 which is controversial because it generates divergent views about the appropriate relationship between collective or cultural objectives and individual rights, these early decisions are more likely to be applauded than lamented by those familiar with the Charter. Consider, for example, the following decisions. The idea that Convention refugees can be denied status and have their application rejected without even knowing the case they have to meet offends basic conceptions of procedural fairness. The Lord's Day Act, which relies on criminal sanctions to enforce compliance with the religious day of observance chosen by the Christian majority, no longer seems appropriate for a society which has such a large multicultural population and has signified its commitment to multiculturalism in the Charter. In other cases the Court found that warrantless searches by combines officials violate the right against unreasonable search and seizure[21] and that a minimum period of imprisonment for driving without a valid driver's licence or under suspension violates the principles of fundamental justice in section 7.[22] The idea that combines officials could enter a specific corporate office as well as others "elsewhere in Canada" without a warrant or without the approval of an objective third party does not seem a reasonable limit on privacy and the right to be secure against unreasonable search or seizure. The fact that someone who drove while suspended would be liable to an automatic jail sentence even though he or she did not know of the suspension violates a basic foundation in criminal law – the principle of mens rea.

It is not the actual decisions themselves that are troublesome. The concern lies with the Court's reliance wholly on negative liberty and its concomitant reluctance to address the requirement that it evaluate the importance of the impugned legislation. As a result, little consideration has been given to the values underlying the contentious policy or to the consequences of invalidating the legislation. The cases the Court hears will not always be so easy to resolve in a way that seems intuitively correct. The policies promoted by governments as a reasonable limit on a protected right may be more pressing, involve conflicting philosophical principles about which values should take precedence, and evoke different opinions of how best to achieve a desired goal.

STAGE 2: DEVELOPMENT OF
A GENERAL APPROACH

After almost two years of avoiding the section 1 issue, the Court developed in *R. v. Oakes* an interpretive framework to evaluate the reasonableness of legislation found to conflict with protected rights. This in itself was a significant departure from earlier suggestions that when interpreting the Charter, the Court is not required to consider the soundness of an impugned policy but is engaged in the "totally different question" of determining whether that policy violates an individual's protected right. In *Oakes* the Court recognized that it would have to evaluate the merits of contentious policies to determine whether protected rights should be qualified for general or collective goals of fundamental importance.

The *Oakes* test, which continues to be cited routinely, consists of two criteria. The first is that the impugned legislative objective must be "of sufficient importance to warrant overriding a constitutionally protected right or freedom." At a minimum, the objective must relate to concerns that are "pressing and substantial" in a free and democratic society before it can be characterized as sufficiently important. Once a sufficiently significant objective has been recognized, the government must show that the means chosen are reasonable and demonstrably justified. This criterion of proportionality has three components:

i) the measures adopted must be rationally connected to the objective and cannot be arbitrary, unfair or based on irrational considerations;
ii) the means should impair "as little as possible" the right or freedom in question; and
iii) there must be a proportionality between the effects of the measure and the objective.[23]

On the surface the *Oakes* test appears to make it difficult to justify limits on protected rights. Not only do governments bear the burden of demonstrating the justification for the legislation, but the Court has suggested that as a general rule it will be operating under the assumption that the limit is not justified. But despite appearances, the Court set the groundwork in *Oakes* for recognition of constitutionally valid objectives separate from and independent of the specific protected rights in the Charter. The Court indicated a sensitivity, lacking in its earlier judgments, to claims that government action which appears to conflict with a specified right in actual fact might facilitate another value equally entitled to constitutional protection. In other words, by recognizing that a protected right might have to give way for "collective goals of fundamental importance" the Court not only gave explicit recognition that it will have to evaluate competing values but tacit acceptance that Charter values extend beyond the specific enumerated provisions.[24]

The indication that the Court might have to look beyond the Charter suggests that judicial review will engage the justices in normative inquiries concerning the values essential to a free and democratic society. But there is little in the *Oakes* test to inform this kind of inquiry. Then Chief Justice Dickson indicated that the reasonableness of legislation should be measured against the values and principles essential to a free and democratic society which are the "genesis of the rights and freedoms guaranteed by the Charter" and provide "the ultimate standard against which a limit on a right or freedom must be shown, despite its effect, to be reasonable and demonstrably justified". The difficulty for the Court is that the requirements of a free and democratic society are neither obvious nor uncontested. The first hurdle of the test – establishing that the objective is pressing and substantial – may involve philosophical disputes about the kinds of values worthy of constitutional protection. Convincing the Court that the policy responsible for limiting a right is worth pursuing, that it represents a "pressing or substantial interest," may depend more on individual justices' policy preferences, ideology, or views about the appropriate division of institutional labour than on anything in the *Oakes* judgment or in the Charter itself.

Judicial Decisions after Oakes

Despite the unified front suggested by the almost habitual way the *Oakes* criteria are referred to by all members of the Court in cases involving section 1, the judgments after *Oakes* reveal significant variance in how justices apply the test.[25] These decisions reflect different normative conceptions of which values are essential in a free and democratic society and varying assumptions of the appropriate bounds of judicial authority in a parliamentary democracy. Almost immediately after outlining the criteria for conducting a section 1 inquiry a majority of the Court began relaxing the requirements governments must meet to demonstrate the justification of a limit.

In *R. v. Jones*, one of the first cases involving section 1 following *Oakes*, the three judges who found that a protected right had been limited cited *Oakes* yet went on to uphold the reasonableness of the impugned policy in the absence of evidence or argument about its justification.[26] The *Jones* case involved the question of whether sections 2(a) and 7 of the Charter were infringed by the requirement under the Alberta School Act that a person who gives instruction at home or elsewhere have that instruction certified. At the heart of the dispute was an impasse between the Calgary Board of Education and Jones, a fundamentalist pastor. Both demanded the other make the first move in the inquiry to determine whether a group of children were receiving adequate instruction outside the public school system.

The deference shown to the provincial government in *Jones* was not only indicated by upholding the legislative objective but was also directed at the way the policy was administered. The Calgary School

Board offered no evidence to demonstrate why it should not take the initiative of inspecting academies wishing to avail themselves of exempting students from public schools or approved private schools. Despite a lack of evidence, the majority decision, written by Justice La Forest, accepted as self-evident the justification of the Calgary School Board's policy that it should not take this initiative. His decision reads as if he did not feel bound by the *Oakes* test.[27] Although he described the objective as a compelling one he did not address the issue of whether the legislation passed the proportionality criterion outlined in *Oakes*.

The legitimate, indeed compelling, interest of the state in the education of the young is known and understood by all informed citizens. Nor is evidence necessary to establish the difficulty of administering a general provincial educational scheme if the onus lies on the educational authorities to enforce compliance. The obvious way to administer it is by requiring those who seek exemptions from the general scheme to make application for the purpose.[28]

This decision provided an indication that for some judges the interpretation of section 1 is influenced by the assumption that the Court should extend considerable deference both in recognizing the validity of the legislative objective and in determining whether the design and implementation of the objective is justified. In this case La Forest cautioned his colleagues that the Court must recognize that a certain amount of pragmatism is required in the legislative attempt to strike a balance between fairness and efficiency. It is not the duty of the Court to scrutinize the exact balance sought, he held, unless the administrative scheme is manifestly unfair.

Some pragmatism is involved in balancing between fairness and efficiency. The provinces must be given room to make choices regarding the type of administrative structure that will suit their needs unless the use of such structure is in itself so manifestly unfair, having regard to the decisions it is called upon to make, as to violate the principles of *fundamental* justice.[29]

The assumption in this statement is that where the Court has found that a legislative objective is valid, the legislature should be allowed considerable latitude to design and administer its policy. The Court, in other words, should not be too strict in its application of the proportionality test, lest this make the administration of the legislative goal unmanageable.

That members of the Court would confer significant discretion upon legislatures to pursue policy objectives was reaffirmed in *R. v.*

Edwards Books.[30] The reasons, in this case, were not confined to practical considerations due to the complexity of policy development. A second reason was to give legislatures sufficient opportunity to pursue policies intended to protect vulnerable groups. At issue was whether the requirements under the Retail Business Holidays Act that Ontario retail businesses close on Sunday for a secular common pause day violated freedom of religion. The objective of the legislation was to establish a common day of rest for retail workers. Chief Justice Dickson, writing for the majority, found that the act did violate freedom of religion of Saturday worshippers but was reasonable under section 1. In considering the reasonableness of the secular pause day, he held that courts should be flexible when administering the proportionality test in *Oakes* in cases where the legislative objective seeks to protect the interests of a vulnerable group. In his view, the retail employees targeted in this act were vulnerable because these workers, predominantly female, tended to be poorly paid and were generally not unionized. Their vulnerable economic position made it difficult for them to stand up to their employers or to find a job elsewhere if they wished to a day of rest in common with their family and friends.[31]

Although Dickson acknowledged the limited and dated evidentiary materials available to the Court for the section 1 evaluation, he nevertheless accepted the claim that the objective was sufficiently important to justify limiting protected rights. In reviewing the proportionality criteria, he reminded his colleagues that the Court has been careful to avoid "rigid and inflexible standards" when applying the proportionality elements of *Oakes*[32] and warned the Court against interpreting the Charter in a manner that would prevent governments from protecting the interests of those who are vulnerable – in this case, retail employees: "I believe that the courts must be cautious to ensure that [the Charter] does not simply become an instrument of better situated individuals to roll back legislation which has as its object the improvement of the condition of less advantaged persons."[33]

The *Jones* and *Edwards Books* cases provide two rationales for deferring to legislative choices that limit protected rights: first, given the complexity of policy-making, courts should not frustrate the pursuit of valid legislative objectives by requiring a difficult proportionality threshold; and second, where the objective is to ameliorate the position of disadvantaged groups, courts should not scrutinize too closely the legislative balance struck between conflicting interests, otherwise the Charter will become an instrument of powerful groups to overturn progressive policies.

These rationales, which have the effect of giving legislatures significant discretion in designing policy objectives under section 1 and in making choices about the benefits and burdens of policies, were reaffirmed in subsequent cases and by other members of the Court.[34]

Other Approaches to Assessing the Reasonableness of Limits

Three other perspectives have emerged on how to evaluate section 1 that reveal differing assumptions about the normative requirements of democracy or the institutional responsibilities of judges: to protect the autonomy of individuals from interference by the state; to develop and maintain an appropriate division of institutional labour; and to ensure that the Charter cannot be used to interfere with public safety.

Personal Autonomy.   Justice Wilson's approach to the Charter has been influenced by her liberal assumptions about the need to protect individual personal autonomy from the state. An early indication of Justice Wilson's normative approach, which centred on her conception of liberty, appeared in her dissenting judgment in *Jones*[35] and was developed further in *R. v. Morgentaler.* At issue in *Morgentaler* was whether federal legislation, which prohibited abortions unless a woman's life or health was endangered, violated the principles of fundamental justice in section 7. Section 251 of the Criminal Code required that a woman carry a fetus to term unless she could meet the particular criteria established as a defence to criminal prosecution. The Court, by a five to two majority, held that the legislation violated section 7. The decision is complex because three separate judgments were written on the majority side which differed considerably on such fundamental issues as defining the purpose of the legislation and whether there is a substantive constitutional right to an abortion.[36]

Only Justice Wilson was willing to state explicitly that there is such a right. Her discussion of the ambit of the right to liberty in section 7 revealed how she conceptualizes the relationship between rights and limits in the Charter. While her assumptions are founded in liberalism, it is not the market that demarcates the public from the private sphere; rather it is individual autonomy in the realm of personal decision-making. For Wilson the Charter is primarily an individual rights document and the role of the Court is to determine the parameters of the individual's private sphere.

The *Charter* is predicated on a particular conception of the place of the individual in society ... The rights guaranteed in the Charter erect around each individual, metaphorically speaking, an invisible fence over which the state will not be allowed to trespass. The role of the courts is to map out, piece by piece, the parameters of the fence.[37]

Having outlined the role of the Charter, which is to delineate the individual's private sphere in which the state cannot constitutionally enter, Wilson outlined her normative assumptions of the content of liberty:

An aspect of the respect for human dignity on which the *Charter* is founded is the right to make fundamental personal decisions without interference from the state. This right is a critical component of the right to liberty ... This right, properly construed, grants the individual a degree of autonomy in making decisions of fundamental personal importance.[38]

For Justice Wilson, a woman's decision to terminate her pregnancy is an intensely personal matter, and as such is the kind of issue that affects an individual's autonomy and should be protected by the liberty provision in section 7. Having found that liberty in section 7 embraces a right to decide for oneself whether to have an abortion, Wilson had little difficulty concluding that section 251 violated this right by regulating for a woman "something that she has the right to decide for herself."[39]

Wilson speculated about whether an abortion law could be justified. While Parliament would be justified under section 1 to authorize limits on a woman's right to have an abortion in order to protect the fetus, the question that would have to be addressed is "at what point does the state's interest in the protection of the fetus become 'compelling' and justify state intervention in what is otherwise a matter of purely personal and private concern?" While she felt that this decision ultimately belonged to the legislature "which is an position to receive guidance on the subject from all the relevant disciplines," the impugned legislation was not justified under section 1 because it takes this decision away from women at all stages of pregnancy. Thus it does not pass the proportionality test in *Oakes* because it does not impair a woman's right "as little as possible."[40]

Justice Wilson's view of the state, seen primarily in terms of hindering the autonomy the Charter is intended to protect, has resulted in her being less receptive to arguments that impugned policies are justified. Given the premium she places on freedom from interference, it is not surprising that she has been the one member most likely to adhere to a strict application of the *Oakes* criteria, particularly the proportionality elements. In the Court's first one hundred cases, from 1984 to 1989, Wilson rejected governments' section 1 argument that legislation was justified as a reasonable limit in twenty-three of twenty-nine cases.[41] The *Oakes* test has served her well because she has been reluctant to challenge directly the validity of legislative objectives. The attraction of the *Oakes* criteria is that Wilson can find that legislation interfering with liberty is invalid on the narrower grounds that it has not been designed to exact only a minimal impairment on a protected right.

Appropriate Division of Institutional Labour.   More than any other member of the Court, the decisions by Justice McIntyre, often in dissent, reflect the belief that the Court should minimize its role of scrutinizing the merits of legislation under section 1. His decisions imply that the test established in *Oakes* may not be appropriate because it increases the frequency in which legislation is implicated by the Charter. McIntyre believes the requirement that courts assess the reasonableness of legislation is a task that courts are ill-equipped to perform. Thus he believes the Court should confine definitions of rights to what is clearly provided for in, or derivative of, the express values entrenched in the Charter. In doing this the Court can reduce the instances in which it must scrutinize the reasonableness of impugned policies. McIntyre has been the judge least likely to find that a protected right has been infringed. A survey of justices' dissenting and concurring opinions, which are often written to establish a significant departure from the interpretation advanced in the main opinion on the majority or dissenting judgment, confirms that more than any other member, McIntyre supports a narrower interpretation of the Charter section in question. He has also been the judge most likely to find that a protected right has not been infringed.[42]

The first indication of Justice McIntyre's views on these issues appeared in his concurring reasons in three cases involving claims by unions of a right to collective bargaining and to strike. In all cases a majority of the Court rejected the claim that the right to strike, as an incident to collective bargaining, is protected under the Charter.[43] McIntyre, in a concurring opinion, asserted that organized labour and business are equally strong and that courts should not give labour an advantage over business by recognizing a right to strike. However, institutional concerns about the role of the Court were also important factors in his decision. He expressed concern that if the Court upheld a right to strike and engage in collective bargaining, it would be drawn into the dispute by having to evaluate whether government attempts to regulate strikes were justified under section 1. But in his view, decisions about the justification of back-to-work legislation or other prohibitions on strike actions and lockouts were not amenable to the kind of principles and precedents with which the judiciary is familiar.

There are no clearly correct answers to these questions. They are of a nature peculiarly apposite to the functions of the Legislature. However, if the right to strike is found in the Charter, it will be the courts which time and time again will have to resolve these questions, relying only on the evidence and arguments presented by the parties, despite the social implications of each decision. This is a legislative function into which the courts should not intrude.[44]

McIntyre believed that the Court could minimize its incursion on the legislative realm by confining the scope of protected rights to the specific values underlying the Charter. "Where no specific right is found in the *Charter* and the only support for its constitutional guarantee is an implication, the courts should refrain from intrusion into the field of legislation. That is the function of the freely-elected Legislatures and Parliament."[45]

Nowhere have Justice McIntyre's attempts to confine the scope of judicial review to the rights clearly protected in the Charter been more evident than in his dissenting opinion in *R. v. Morgentaler.* He viewed the Court's responsibility in that case not as having to "solve nor seek to solve what might be called the abortion issue, but simply to measure the content of s. 251 against the Charter." Since the Charter does not protect explicitly a right to abortion, the Court should not create this right.

Difficult choices must be made and the personal views of judges will unavoidably be engaged from time to time. The decisions made by judges, however, and the interpretations that they advance or accept must be plausibly inferable from something in the *Charter.* It is not for the courts to manufacture a constitutional right out of whole cloth.[46]

Justice McIntyre's approach, in essence, amounts to a tacit rejection of the two-stage analysis in *Oakes* in which rights receive a "large and liberal" interpretation initially and are subject to qualification only in the second stage of review if the government in question can demonstrate that its objective is sufficiently important to justify limiting a protected right. McIntyre's difficulty with this approach, which may explain his refusal to sign the *Oakes* judgment, is based on the initial generous interpretation of the right. His judgments reflect the view that the Court should establish definitional limits on rights in the initial stage of review to reduce the frequency of instances in which legislatures' policy choices must be evaluated. Although the Court must "clothe the general expression of rights and freedoms contained in the Charter with real substance and vitality" and give full effect to the Charter interpretations while avoiding the "idiosyncratic view of the judge who is writing," the Court can do so, he implied, without "abandoning its traditional adjudicatory function in order to formulate its own conclusions on questions of public policy."[47] The way to prevent overt incursions into the legislative sphere, he believes, is to confine the content of Charter guarantees to the purposes given specific expression in the Charter.

Justice McIntyre's concerns have not gone unnoticed by Charter analysts. Peter Russell, for example, while sympathetic to McIntyre's concerns, suggests his comments are unfair because the provisions in the Charter are stated in such general terms that they must be infused with meaning:

> ... McIntyre J. states that "it is not for the courts to manufacture a constitutional right out of whole cloth." If this is meant as a criticism of what his colleagues in the majority were doing, it is an unfair – although not an inaccurate – complaint. For cutting more precise constitutional rights out of the vague generalities of the *Charter* is precisely what judges have been doing and must do. Phrases like "freedom of conscience," "freedom of expression," "freedom of association," "the right to liberty," "principles of fundamental justice," and "the right to equal benefit of the law without discrimination" are very whole pieces of cloth indeed.[48]

The Charter and Public Safety.   Another indication that section 1 does not provide an authoritative standard to evaluate the reasonableness of impugned policies is the decision by the Court to virtually ignore the proportionality criterion in a pair of cases involving public safety on roads and highways. In these cases, *R. v. Thomsen* and *R. v. Hufsky,*[49] a unanimous Court was extremely reluctant to allow the procedural rights of drivers to interfere with discretionary attempts by police officials to ensure public safety on roads and highways. The section 1 standard was barely evident in these cases as the Court assumed, with little or no scrutiny of the reasonableness of the legislative means, that the impugned policies were justified. After finding that the purpose of the legislation was pressing, the Court ruled that the legislation passed the proportionality criterion in *Oakes* without actually addressing the three elements. The decisions reflect considerable deference to the legislation and imply that a strict application of the *Oakes* criteria would undermine road safety. That Justice Wilson signed these decisions is particularly surprising given that she, more than any other judge, has been more willing to apply a strict interpretation of the proportionality test.

The *Thomsen* case involved the question of whether it was reasonable to deny an individual, who had been stopped at a roadside screening device, the right to retain and instruct counsel without delay and to be informed of that right.[50] In determining whether the limit was justified,

Justice Le Dain was particularly sympathetic to the role played by roadside breath testing, which he saw as increasing the detection of impaired driving as well as increasing the perceived risk of its detection. His deference to the legislation was evident in his decision not to apply the proportionality test which he justified by restating the warning made by Dickson in *Edwards Books* that the Court should be careful to avoid rigid and inflexible standards when articulating the standard of proof and describing the criteria comprising the proportionality requirements.[51] Similarly, in *R. v. Hufsky*, which involved the question of whether a random spot check infringed a driver's right not to be arbitrarily detained under section 9 and the right to be secure against unreasonable search in section 8, Le Dain again virtually ignored the proportionality criteria. In ruling that random spot checks violate section 9, he held that in view of the importance of highway safety and the role played by a random check in increasing both the detection and the perceived risk of detection of motor vehicle offences, the limit was reasonable. He implied that maintaining the safety of highways is too important to subject it to a requirement of more precise legislative drafting that might undermine its effectiveness:

If the stopping of motor vehicles [to improve highway safety] is not to be seriously inhibited, it should not, in my respectful opinion, be subjected to the kinds of conditions or restrictions reflected in the American jurisprudence … which would appear seriously to undermine its effectiveness while not significantly reducing its intrusiveness.[52]

STAGE 3: HOW MUCH DEFERENCE SHOULD BE ACCORDED LEGISLATURES?

The *Oakes* decision is widely accepted as providing the Court's most authoritative statement of how to evaluate the reasonableness of legislation that conflicts, prima facie, with protected rights. But the most significant contribution of *Oakes* actually occurred after the decision was rendered. It lies in the realization that a large and liberal interpretation of protected rights in the initial stage of review, if accompanied by a strict application of the proportionality criteria, will result in the frequent invalidation of government objectives. It has quickly become apparent that a majority of the Court is not comfortable with this possibility.

While no government was successful in demonstrating the reasonableness of legislation before *Oakes*, since then the Court has been far more receptive to section 1 arguments.[53] The Court's initial flurry of judicial activism prompted questions of whether judicial review of impugned legislation is resulting in courts giving priority to a different range of values than those espoused by legislatures; the Court's decisions in the post-*Oakes* period give rise to a different query. This period compels one to ask whether, and to what extent, the Charter is effectively constraining the policy choices of governments.

What distinguishes the third stage of judicial review from the period preceding it is the tacit recognition of the Court that the *Oakes* test does not provide guidance on what has become a crucial question for the Court: how much discretion should legislatures be accorded to pursue worthwhile objectives? The section 1 exercise, more than any other aspect of judicial review of the Charter, engages the Court in an undertaking that is distinguished from what judges generally encounter by virtue of precedents, experiences, and expertise. The evaluation of reasonableness involves policy analysis: a task that requires subjective evaluations of the merits of legislation and discretionary assessments of whether better or alternative legislative means are available. This analysis of alternative means incorporates the uncertain task of assessing expert analysis of conflicting social science evidence, comparative experience and informed best estimates, all of which may reflect choices between numerous alternatives, make distinctions between who will benefit or be affected by the policy, anticipate circumstances that may undermine objectives and represent part of a complex system of incentives and objectives.

The complexity of policy development makes it difficult to undertake careful and prudent policy analysis by judges (or others) who are external to the policy process or who lack the resources, relevant information, and analytical skills to evaluate conflicting social science evidence. It is therefore not surprising that the Court found the *Oakes* criteria of limited guidance when assessing the reasonableness of impugned policies. The difficulty of analysing the merits of policy encouraged individual justices to read into the standard their particular normative perspectives of liberty or democracy or institutional assumptions about the appropriate role of courts in a representative democracy.

The glaring contradiction between the seemingly objective standard in the *Oakes* test and individual judges' ad hoc and discretionary section 1 interpretations has encouraged renewed attempts by the Court to formalize its collective approach to the proportionality criteria by establishing new guidelines as to when judicial deference to the objective of legislation, and more importantly to the design and implementation of that objective, are appropriate. These revised guidelines about judicial deference do not, and are not purported to, resemble objective standards. Rather, they clearly are discretionary in appearance and effect and reflect subjective assessments by members of the Court about the importance of policy objectives and the degree of latitude required by legislatures when making choices about the benefits and burdens of policy. In its attempt to impart some general guidelines into a standard so loose that it resembled the proposition "it all depends,"[54] the threshold for reasonableness has changed significantly.

Section 1 Revisited

Three guidelines can be identified in the Court's attempts to formalize its collective approach to evaluating the reasonableness of legislation. The first is that legislatures do not have to prove empirically that a problem exists that needs to be remedied by legislation. The second guideline is the Court's collective acceptance of former Chief Justice Dickson's normative position, that the Court should give legislators broad latitude when pursuing policies to protect the interests and needs of vulnerable groups in society. In accepting this principle, the Court has developed the corollary position that deference is more appropriate in the context of social policy than in criminal law. A third guideline is that the Court should evaluate the nature of the infringement in the context of a hierarchy of rights in which the difficulty of limiting a protected right will depend on whether the infringed right relates to a core or universal right as opposed to a more marginal or peripheral claim.

1. *Justification for Legislative Objectives.*   How is the Court to recognize when legislative objectives are sufficiently compelling to justify limiting protected rights? The values integral to a free and democratic society are controversial and there is little in the Charter to help judges. Just as academic commentators disagree on how to recognize objectives compelling enough to limit protected rights, the Court has encountered similar disagreements. Former Chief Justice Dickson has been the member most willing to confront the issue of whether the values in a free and democratic society that justifiably limit protected rights are confined exclusively to those in the Charter. In his view they are not; the values in a free and democratic society go beyond those rights specifically entrenched.

Obviously, a practical application of s. 1 requires more than an incantation of the words "free and democratic society." These words require some definition, an elucidation as to the values that they evoke ... Undoubtedly, these values and principles are numerous, covering the guarantees enumerated in the Charter and more.[55]

The Court has accepted the proposition that values other than those specifically enumerated can justify imposing limits on protected rights. While the issue of whether section 1 can justify non-enumerated values has not generated opposition on the Court, considerable debate has taken place around the issue of what threshold a legislature must satisfy to demonstrate that its policy represents a sufficiently compelling objective to justify limiting rights. Specifically, debate has centred around the issue of whether the legislature must demonstrate empirically that a social problem exists that warrants legislative redress.

Justice Wilson, a principal participant in the debate, has argued that impugned legislative objectives are only justified in limiting protected rights when indication exists that serious social problems would occur in the absence of legislative redress. Her concern that the Court was being overly deferential arose in her minority dissent in a case that considered whether the Charter applies to hospitals and, if so, whether mandatory retirement infringes equality. She disagreed with the majority decision that the Charter does not apply to hospitals and concluded that mandatory retirement violates equality in a manner that is not justified under section 1. She acknowledged that while the Court, in some situations, has not required evidence to prove a government's assertion that a pressing and substantial concern exists that must be addressed, where there is dispute on the importance of the impugned policy "it is incumbent on the party bearing the burden of proof under s. 1 to establish the pressing and substantial concern." As she argued, the purpose of section 1 is not to justify *any reasonable legislative action* but rather to *uphold only those policies that are intended to address real problems.* In her view, where no evidence exists to support the allegation of a significant problem, the first branch of the Oakes test has not been satisfied: demonstration that the objective is sufficiently important to limit a protected right.[56]

The purpose behind [the pressing and objective component] of the *Oakes* test is to ensure that constitutional rights and freedoms will only be sacrificed where it is reasonable and justifiable to do so. The concept of constitutional entrenchment requires that rights and freedoms be curtailed only in response to real and not illusory problems.[57]

Justice Wilson elaborated on what she meant by real problems in *R. v. Chaulk* by suggesting that it is inappropriate for Parliament to rely on s. 1 to justify a "prophylactic measure designed to fend off a hypothetical social problem that might arise."[58] The issue in this case was whether section 16(4) of the Criminal Code violates the presumption of innocence. This section establishes a presumption of sanity which can be rebutted only if "the contrary is proved." Wilson disagreed with the majority decision that while the provision violates the presumption of innocence it is a reasonable limit under section 1. Parliament, she argued, must have had some reason to assume that it was necessary to impose a persuasive burden on an accused to prove his or her insanity and, therefore, should be prepared to justify the problem that compels it to limit the presumption of innocence. She argued that in the absence of evidence of an existing problem, the Court's decision to uphold the reasonableness of the legislation is contrary to its own guidelines in *Oakes* and asked of her judicial colleagues: "Do we wish to go down this path and justify infringements of guaranteed Charter rights on a purely hypothetical basis?"[59]

In *R. v. Zundel* Justice McLachlin similarly argued that the Court should not be so quick to accept claims that legislation is necessary in the absence of some indication that harm might otherwise occur. The issue in this case was whether the Criminal Code prohibition against wilful publication of false statements or news infringes freedom of expression. The majority decision, written by McLachlin, found that the legislation restricted freedom of expression and is not justified under section 1. The charge arose following the publication of a booklet entitled *Did Six Million Really Die?* which argued that the Holocaust is a myth perpetrated by a worldwide Jewish conspiracy. The relevant legislation under which Zundel had been charged was enacted in 1892, which led McLachlin to argue that the Court must consider the intent of Parliament when the section was enacted or amended. It is inappropriate, she held, for legislatures to assign objectives or invent new ones according to the perceived current utility of the impugned provision. Thus the proscription of false news originally intended to protect the wealthy and the powerful from discord or slander cannot be simply transformed into a contemporary mechanism for protecting vulnerable social groups. While the application and interpretation of objectives may vary over time, it is not proper for new or different purposes to be invented when legislation conflicts with protected rights.[60]

In concluding that the legislative objective could not be considered worthy of limiting protected rights – the only decision to date since *Oakes* where a majority has found that the legislative objective itself is not reasonable, as opposed to the way the legislation was drafted – McLachlin discussed the need for the Court to have more to rely on than assertions that harm would otherwise occur.

If the simple identification of the ... goal of protecting the public from harm constitutes a "pressing and substantial" objective, virtually any law will meet the first part of the onus imposed upon the Crown under s. 1 ... Justification under s. 1 requires more than the general goal of protection from harm common to all criminal legislation; it requires a specific purpose so pressing and substantial as to be capable of overriding the Charter's guarantees.[61]

Despite the positions of Justices Wilson and McLachlin that the requirement for limiting a protected right should be sufficiently rigorous and must address established problems, harm, or likelihood of harm, a majority of the Court has required a less rigorous standard for proving the importance of the policy objective. Not only are governments not required to demonstrate that harm will occur in the absence of the legislation, they need not demonstrate a causal link between the effects of the impugned objectives and the harm or problem the legislation is intended to address. This became clear in two cases where Parliament has sought to limit freedom of expression to address concerns related to hate literature and obscenity.

A majority of the Court rejected explicitly the requirement that Parliament demonstrate harm would occur in the absence of prohibitions against hate literature. In *R. v. Keegstra* the Criminal Code provisions, which prohibited the wilful promotion of hatred against identifiable groups, were challenged for violating freedom of expression. While the Court recognized that expression was limited, the majority found the limits were justified under section 1 even in the absence of proof that hate literature causes harm. In dispelling claims that Parliament must demonstrate empirically that harm or a serious problem exists Dickson argued: "It is clearly difficult to prove a causative link between a specific statement and hatred of an identifiable group. In fact, to require direct proof of hatred in listeners would severely debilitate the effectiveness of s. 319(2) in achieving Parliament's aim."[62]

The principle that government need not demonstrate a causal link between the restricted activity and the harm or problem it addresses was reaffirmed in *R. v. Butler* by Justice Sopinka in a case that involved a challenge to Criminal Code prohibitions of obscene materials. Harm in this case was defined as antisocial attitudinal changes arising from exposure to obscene material.[63] Sopinka, who wrote the majority decision, acknowledged disagreements in academic opinion as to whether there is a causal relationship between obscenity and the risk of harm to society at large but nevertheless decided against imposing a requirement that harm be demonstrated. All that is required it that "Parliament had a *reasonable basis*" for fearing that harm would occur. In his view, a sufficient connection exists between criminal sanction, which "demonstrates our community's disapproval of the dissemination of materials which potentially victimize women," and the objective of restricting the negative influence that such materials have on changes in attitudes and behaviour.[64]

2. *Protection of Vulnerable Groups against Rights-based Challenges by Powerful Interests.*   The Court has collectively endorsed the principle, first advocated by Chief Justice Dickson in *Edward Books*, that legislatures be given broad discretion to determine how best to strike the appropriate balance between promoting social objectives intended to help vulnerable groups in society and respecting the rights of those adversely affected.[65] A majority of the Court held that because of the difficulty in policy development for legislatures to identify, with certainty, what would constitute the most prudent as well as least restrictive means of implementing compelling policy objectives, the Court should not scrutinize rigorously the exact compromise struck:

In matching means to ends and asking whether rights or freedoms are impaired as little as possible, a legislature mediating between the claims of competing groups will be forced to strike a balance without the benefit of absolute certainty concerning how that balance is best stuck ... Where the legislature mediates between the competing claims of different groups in the community, it will inevitably be called upon to draw a line marking where one set of claims legitimately begins and the other fades away without access to complete knowledge as to its precise location. If the legislature has made a reasonable assessment as to where the line is most properly drawn, especially if that assessment involves weighing conflicting scientific evidence and allocating scare resources on this basis, it is not for the court to second guess.[66]

The collective acceptance of this principle was again affirmed in *Chaulk* when Chief Justice Lamer held that the Court should be mindful of the difficulty in recognizing which legislative means would be the least intrusive way of accomplishing an objective: "Parliament may not have chosen the absolutely *least* intrusive means of meeting its objective, but it has chosen from a range of means which impair [protected rights] as little as is reasonably possible. Within this range of means it is virtually impossible to know, let alone to be sure, which means violate Charter rights the *least*."[67]

Similarly, Justice Sopinka dismissed arguments that the Court should impose a rigorous standard whereby legislatures must choose the least restrictive approach of promoting an objective. Rather than choose the "perfect scheme," all that is required of a legislature is that its policy be appropriately tailored *in the context of the infringed right*.[68] As Sopinka held in *Butler*: "This Court will not, in the name of minimal impairment, take a restrictive approach to social science evidence and require legislatures to choose the least ambitious means to protect vulnerable groups."[69]

Even Justice Wilson has been cautious about applying strictly the minimal impairment requirement where legislatures are attempting to reconcile the interests and values of competing groups:

It seems to me that this Court has agreed that a form of "reasonableness" test may be preferable to a strict application of the minimal impairment branch of *Oakes* in those circumstances where the Legislature must mediate between the claims of competing groups, and especially where, in doing so, it opts to protect the interests of the disadvantaged and disempowered. In those cases, the Court will defer to the choice of the legislature so long as alternative measures for meeting or promoting the government's goals are not clearly superior.[70]

In relaxing the minimal impairment criterion the Court has justified its decision not only in terms of the complexities of policy-making but also because of its own inabilities to effectively scrutinize legislatures' decisions. It has indicated an increased awareness that the difficulty judges face when evaluating the reasonableness of policy is particularly acute when identifying whether less restrictive means provide a practical or workable alternative. In recognition that judges are not as well situated to evaluate a particular legislative scheme as are those working within the legislative realm, particularly in the social policy context, the Court has become reluctant to question governmental claims that less restrictive means are not available. As Justice La Forest stated in *McKinney*:

In undertaking [review of whether legislation impairs a right as little as possible] it is important again to remember that the ramifications of mandatory retirement on the organization of the workplace and its impact on society generally are not matters capable of precise measurement, and the effect of its removal by judicial fiat is even less certain. Decisions on such matters must inevitably be the product of a mix of conjecture, fragmentary knowledge, general experience and knowledge of the needs, aspirations and resources of society, and other components. They are decisions of a kind where those engaged in political and legislative activities of Canadian democracy have evident advantage over members of the judicial branch ... This does not absolve the judiciary of its constitutional obligation to scrutinize legislative action to ensure reasonable compliance with constitutional standard, but it does import greater circumspection than in areas such as the criminal justice system where the courts' knowledge and understanding affords it a much higher degree of certainty.[71]

However, the Court is not as reticent about scrutinizing the balance struck in criminal legal matters. Where a legislature is not mediating between different groups but can be characterized "as the singular antagonist of the individual whose right has been infringed," particularly in cases involving legal rights, the Court has indicated that deference may not be appropriate. In these cases the Court itself can assess "with some certainty" whether the least drastic means for achieving the purpose have been chosen:

> When striking a balance between the claims of competing groups, the choice of means, like the choice of ends, frequently will require an assessment of conflicting scientific evidence and differing justified demands on scarce resources. Democratic institutions are meant to let us all share in the responsibility for these difficult choices. Thus, as courts review the results of the legislature's deliberations, particularly with respect to the protection of vulnerable groups, they must be mindful of the legislature's representative function ...
>
> In other cases, however, rather than mediating between different groups, the government is best characterized as the singular antagonist of the individual whose right has been infringed. For example, in justifying an infringement of legal rights enshrined in ss. 7 to 14 of the Charter, the state, on behalf of the whole community, typically will assert its responsibility for prosecuting crime whereas the individual will assert the paramountcy of principles of fundamental justice ... In such circumstances, and indeed whenever the government's purpose relates to maintaining the authority and impartiality of the judicial system, the courts can assess with some certainty whether the "least drastic means" for achieving the purpose have been chosen, especially given their accumulated experience in dealing with such questions ... The same degree of certainty may not be achievable in cases involving the reconciliation of claims of competing individuals or groups or the distribution of scarce government resources.[72]

3. *Hierarchy of Rights and Limits.*   One response the Court has had to the question of whether judicial deference is appropriate is to establish a hierarchy of rights and corresponding burdens which legislatures must satisfy. This hierarchy presumes that the difficulty for justifying limits on protected rights will depend on judicial assessments of whether the infringed right relates to a core, or universal right, as opposed to a more marginal or peripheral claim.

The very presence of section 1 has encouraged the Court initially to interpret rights initially, in a broad manner. It has generally avoided defining rights by means of imposing internal (or definitional) limits on them. For example, the Court's reluctance to impose internal limits on freedom of expression ensures that a wide range of rights claims – from communication for prostitution purposes to commercial advertising – will conflict with legislative actions and will require that courts scrutinize the reasonableness of these impugned legislative activities.[73]

Former Chief Justice Dickson has been a central proponent of a core-periphery approach and has used it in many cases, particularly those dealing with freedom of expression, as a means of addressing the nature of the burden legislatures must satisfy to demonstrate the reasonableness of impugned policies. For example, when reviewing the reasonableness of legislation that criminalized communications for the purpose of prostitution, Dickson implied that because this form of expression is not as important as other forms, it is easier to limit.[74] He also affirmed explicitly this principle in *R. v. Keegstra* when he indicated that the Court "must ask whether the expression prohibited ... is tenuously connected to the values underlying s. 2(b)" which would make restrictions "easier to justify than other infringements." In his view, expression intended to promote the hatred of identifiable groups "is of limited importance when measured against free expression values."[75]

The core-periphery distinction has been applied by a majority of the Court in other cases[76] but figured particularly prominently in *R. v. Butler.* In this case Sopinka distinguished obscenity from more fundamental forms of expression and reaffirmed the principle that expressive activities that did not directly relate to core values would be easier to limit.

In my view, the kind of expression which is sought to be advanced does not stand on an equal footing with other kinds of expression which directly engage the "core" of the freedom of expression values.

This conclusion is further buttressed by the fact that the targeted material is expression which is motivated, in the overwhelming majority of cases by economic profit. This Court [has determined] that an economic motive for expression means that restrictions on the expression might "be easier to justify than other infringements."[77]

Implications of the Evolving Section 1 Standard

After an early debate about whether a legislature must demonstrate that a compelling societal problem requires legislative action, the Court has become overwhelmingly deferential to governmental assertions about the importance and justification of the legislative objective, particulary in the context of social policy. On only three occasions, and only once since the Court developed general interpretive principles in *Oakes*, has a majority of the Court rejected claims that a legislative objective is sufficiently compelling to warrant limiting a protected right.[78]

The willingness of the Court to accept governmental claims about the importance of the legislative objective has meant that the section 1 exercise focuses almost exclusively on the proportionality criteria, the most important element of which is the minimal impairment rule.[79] It is this which represents the most significant shift in the Court's approach to reviewing the Charter.

The Court has acknowledged that the minimal impairment test requires that judges "do a comparative analysis of effectiveness, feasibility and cost of all possible measures."[80] But this presents the Court with a dilemma. Once the Supreme Court has accepted that the legislative objective is sufficiently important to warrant imposing limits on protected rights, should judges scrutinize the internal dynamics of a policy – its relationship between objectives and effects and its structure of incentives and burdens – at the risk of second-guessing complex legislative decisions and potentially invalidating compelling objectives? Or instead should judges defer to governmental claims about the reasonableness of the impugned policy, at the risk of discouraging legislatures from taking the responsibility of respecting protected rights as seriously as they should?

Judicial concerns about the complexities and uncertainties of policy development, and the possibility of invalidating legislative choices intended to improve conditions for the vulnerable, have influenced the Court to the point of effectively removing what was the most important and most difficult aspects of the proportionality criteria in *Oakes*. This was that the legislative means should impair "as little as possible" the right or freedom in question. The current standard in Supreme Court jurisprudence for "reasonable" in section 1 bears little resemblance to the Court's earlier declaration that the issue is not whether the impugned legislative act is reasonable but whether it is reasonable to deprive individuals of their Charter rights.[81] No longer are limits on rights considered "exceptions to their general guarantee" in which the presumption is that "the rights and freedoms are guaranteed unless the party invoking s. 1 can bring itself within the exceptional criteria which justify their being limited."[82] Limits on rights are now acceptable as long as legislatures have a "reasonable basis" for fearing harm.

Under its modified approach to section 1 proportionality considerations, legislatures are no longer required to choose the optimum, or least restrictive, means to accomplish their objective, but must establish only that the legislative choice is "reasonable" under the circumstances.[83] As Chief Justice Lamer stated in *Chaulk*, the Charter does not require that Parliament "roll the dice" in its effort to achieve "pressing and substantial" objectives in order to adopt the absolutely *least* intrusive provision."[84]

With the more relaxed criterion of "reasonableness" the Court has also indicated that when imposing limits on protected rights for compelling social purposes, legislative decisions can reflect previous attempts to promote the policy. If less restrictive means have not been effective, legislatures should not be frustrated in promoting valid policies by having to eschew more effective means because of the need to restrict rights as minimally as possible.[85]

Exceptions to the Deference Principle

While the Court's evolving section 1 standard has reduced the extent to which the Charter imposes constraints on legislatures, it would be misleading to conclude that the Charter has no effects on policy choices. Even though its latest stage is characterized by overwhelming deference to impugned legislation, in a handful of cases the Court has found that legislation that conflicts with protected rights is not reasonable under section 1. One of these decisions was *Sauvé v. Canada (Attorney General)* in which a unanimous Court held that provisions in the Canada Elections Act that disqualified prisoners from voting did not represent a reasonable limit. The Court, in a single sentence, held that the legislation "is drawn too broadly" and fails to meet the minimal impairment component of the test.[86] The Court also set aside federal legislation in *Osborne v. Canada (Treasury Board)* which prohibited public servants from engaging in work for a political party or candidate. The Court held that the legislation violates freedom of expression and applies unnecessarily to public servants who are carrying out clerical or other duties that are divorced from the exercise of discretion that could be affected by political considerations.[87]

A different exception to the Court's growing deference to the policy choices of legislatures can be found in two 1994 cases in which the Court seems to have revitalized the third component of the proportionality criterion of the *Oakes* test. This involves the balancing of the legislative objective against the infringement of the protected right and, in theory, is to determine whether the infringement is too substantial in light of the benefit of the law. However, this third component has in the past been virtually neglected and has been considered by some as redundant.[88]

The Court has revisited the third component of the proportionality test in *Oakes* in *Dagenais* v. *Canadian Broadcasting Corporation* and has given it more prominence. As a result, even when a legislative objective is pressing and substantial, the means chosen are rationally connected to that objective, and the Court has not insisted that legislatures choose less restrictive alternatives, the Court may still be willing to rule that the actual salutary effects of the legislation are not substantial enough to justify the legislation.

The third step of the second branch of the *Oakes* test requires both that the underlying *objective* of a measure and the *salutary effects* that result from its implementation be proportional to the deleterious effects the measure has on fundamental rights and freedoms. A legislative objective may be pressing and substantial, the means chosen may be rationally connected to that objective, and less rights-impairing alternatives may not be available. Nonetheless, even if the importance of the objective *itself* (when viewed in the abstract) outweighs the deleterious effects on protected rights, it is still possible that the actual *salutary effects* of the legislation will not be sufficient to justify these negative effects.[89]

The motivation for the revised thinking on the proportionality criterion was the concern, expressed by Chief Justice Lamer, that without this new formulation situations may arise where the Court upholds legislation that achieves its objective only partially yet implements measures that have deleterious effects on fundamental rights and freedoms. The Court has rephrased the third component of the *Oakes* test as follows: "There must be a proportionality between the deleterious effects of the measures which are responsible for limiting the rights or freedoms in question and the objective, *and there must be a proportionality between the deleterious and the salutary effects of the measures.*"[90]

This case dealt with the issue of a publication ban restraining the CBC from broadcasting a fictional program dealing with child abuse in a Catholic orphanage until the end of criminal trials in Ontario. The majority ruled that even though the legislative objective of ensuring a fair trial was pressing and substantial, in this situation "a [publication] ban which has a serious deleterious effect on freedom of expression and has few salutary effects on the fairness of a trial" cannot be authorized.[91]

The Court re-emphasized this new approach to proportionality in *R. v. Laba*, a case dealing with a Criminal Code provision making it a criminal offence to sell precious metals unless the individual can establish that he or she is the owner or agent of the metal. The purpose of the legislation was to deter criminal transactions dealing with the selling of stolen precious metals. The majority judgment, written by Justice Sopinka, confirmed the Court's reticence about requiring that Parliament always rely on the least restrictive legislative means to accomplish its objective. Nevertheless, in his opinion Parliament could have accomplished its objective by requiring an evidentiary, as opposed to a legal or persuasive, burden on the accused. By failing to do so, Parliament had chosen a legislative response in which the salutary purposes were not in proportion to the deleterious effects:

> The [impugned legislation] permits the conviction of a wide range of innocent people and thus constitutes a serious violation of s. 11(d). This flows [in part] from ... the burden of proof on the balance of probabilities is an onerous one which many innocent people may be unable to meet ... Even if I were persuaded that the imposition of a legal burden was clearly more effective in achieving Parliament's objective, I would find that it fails the proportionality test because of the excessive invasion of the presumption of innocence having regard to the degree of advancement of Parliament's purpose.
>
> On the other hand, I believe that the imposition of an evidentiary burden upon the accused is justified even though it still impairs the right to be presumed innocent. I find it unlikely that an innocent person will be unable to pint to or present some evidence which raises a reasonable doubt as to their guilt. Although the imposition of an evidentiary burden violates the presumption of innocence I find that this only minimally increases the likelihood of an innocent person being convicted and represents a justifiable limitation upon the right to be presumed innocent.[92]

What is interesting about Sopinka's approach in this case is that while he reaffirmed the Court's willingness to grant representative institutions broad latitude when choosing between alternative legislative means, he signalled that the Court may no longer be willing to uphold legislation where the burdens imposed outweigh the salutary effects the objective was intended to serve.

The Court's revised approach to the proportionality criterion may serve to mitigate the effects of the Court's tendencies both to give broad latitude to legislatures when choosing between a range of legislative means and also to defer to the legislatures' judgment that the policies they pursue warrant imposing limits on protected rights.

While it is too soon to know how often, and with what effects, the Court will utilize this revised approach to proportionality, one can speculate about why the Court felt compelled to revisit the issue. Peter Hogg's view, that the proportionality criterion is simply a reformulation of the first component of *Oakes* – whether the objective is sufficiently important to justify imposing limits on protected rights – is persuasive. As Hogg argues, if the legislative objective is sufficiently important to justify imposing limits on a protected right, and the objective was pursued by means that infringe the protected right "as little as is reasonably possible," it is difficult to appreciate how the law could fail the proportionality test.[93] However, one problem with Hogg's formulation is that it is not consistent with the Court's more recent tendencies to defer to Parliament's choice of legislative means. In light of the complexity of policy development, in which it is difficult to evaluate the effects and benefits of alternative legislative means, the Court has given legislatures broad latitude when choosing between a range of legislative measures and has not insisted on means that impair rights as little as necessary.

One concern that arises from this judicial deference is whether the specific legislative regime is sensitive enough to protected rights that may be unduly or unnecessarily impaired. One possible outcome of the reformulated proportionality test is that while the Court may not formally impose an obligation on legislatures to choose the least restrictive legislative means to accomplish their policy objective (minimal impairment), it may nevertheless be willing to set aside the legislation if it deems that the benefits that the policy is intended to achieve do not outweigh the measure's deleterious effects. Thus this revised proportionality rule seems to be an alternative way of requiring that legislatures exercise more care in ensuring that their policies respect rights as much as possible and impose measures which impair rights as little as practically possible.

Secondly, the revised approach to proportionality accomplishes something for the Court that it has otherwise been reluctant to do – to disagree with representative institutions about the worthiness of a legislative objective and thus disallow the objective. Concerns about the legitimacy of judicial review and its consistency with democratic norms of representative government are likely responsible for the Court's reluctance to rule some policy objectives as wholly inconsistent with the Charter. It is much easier for judges to find fault with the legislation on safer grounds: that the legislation is not carefully enough designed rather than that the objective itself is found wanting. The revised proportionality test enables the Court to give the appearance of assessing the reasonableness of legislation without disagreeing directly with legislatures' judgment about the merits of the policy objective. It allows for an alternative way to ask what is essentially the same question, albeit in a disguised form: is the objective important enough, or does it exact too high a price, to justify limiting a protected right?

While these two cases are exceptions to the Court's inclination to defer to social policy decisions, it is also important to note that the Court has been less willing to recognize the reasonableness of policies that limit the legal rights of sections 7–14. This is consistent with the Court's evolving approach to section 1 which developed a caveat for deferring to complex social policy decisions that mediate between the interests and claims of different groups. This caveat, it will be remembered, holds that deference is less appropriate in conflicts involving legal rights. This distinction suggests that the Court may take two different paths when reviewing the reasonableness of legislative means, one for social policy and one for criminal legal policy. In the context of social objectives, the Court will be more willing to give legislatures considerable leeway in developing policy and choosing between alternative means because representative institutions are responsible for mediating between different groups. Further, the uncertainties and complexities of policy development present judges with particular difficulties in distinguishing between options. However, in the context of criminal legal rights, greater precision in choosing between objectives and effects is required because the effects of policy choices can undermine individuals' legal rights, which the Court traditionally has been charged to protect, and because the Court is more confident of its own capacity to scrutinize whether legislation imposes too great an impairment on individuals.

Among the most significant decisions since *Morgentaler* in which legislation has been set aside for violating legal rights in a manner not consistent with section 1 is *R. v. Seaboyer.* In this case a majority of the Court set aside rape shield provisions in the Criminal Code for violating the principles of fundamental justice in section 7 and the presumption of innocence in section 11 (d). Justice McLachlin, who wrote the majority opinion, did not dispute the importance of the legislative objective to abolish an outmoded, sexist use of evidence. Nevertheless, she did hold that the effects of the legislation were too extreme. Her objection to the legislation was its potential to exclude evidence "of critical relevance to the defence." In her view, evidence of a woman's sexual history may be relevant in addressing the issues of whether consent had been given as well as whether the woman was a reliable witness.[94] Justice McLachlin concluded that judicial discretion was an appropriate means of distinguishing between evidence that is necessary and evidence that is both irrelevant and prejudicial. In the absence of revised legislation, the Court advanced guidelines for judges to determine when they should and should not include evidence of a woman's sexual past.[95] New legislation has since been enacted that explicitly defines consent. Other cases in which parts of the Criminal Code have been set aside for violating legal rights in a manner not consistent with section 1 include *R. v. Bain* and *R. v. Morales.*[96]

If the Court continues to make this distinction between social and legal policy, the Charter's constraints on legislatures will most likely be felt in the realm of criminal legal policy. However, the majority of violations involving legal rights do not arise from statutory provisions but rather result from discretionary conduct of police officials or others who exercise power on behalf of the state. In the context of the latter, section 1 applies only to limits that are prescribed by law. Violations of rights that arise from the conduct of police or other public officials, and which are not related to the operating requirements of a statute, result in judicial inquiries under section 24(2) as to whether the evidence should be included or excluded in legal proceedings. It is in this context that the Charter is having its greatest effects on policy. Not only do a substantially larger portion of Charter cases involve legal rights, but the Court has been extremely active in its protection of the procedural rights of those accused of breaking the law. While it has long been assumed that Canadian courts are less sympathetic to protecting the rights of the accused, a comparative survey of Canadian and American high court decisions reveals that the Supreme Court of Canada has, since the Charter, protected the interests of accused and suspected persons at least as much as the United States Supreme Court and in a number of instances has protected them more. This is especially true of the right to counsel, the privilege against self-incrimination, and the definition of offences.[97]

CONCLUSIONS

The Court's interpretation of protected rights and limits in the immediate post-*Oakes* period differs markedly from its pre-*Oakes* jurisprudence. The Court's reluctance to acknowledge the policy contribution that judicial review assumes in the legislative process resulted in an early tendency to think of judicial review primarily in negative terms – to protect individual freedom from the state. Despite this initial inclination, in the post-*Oakes* period the Court has acknowledged that legislation, which on its face limits a protected right, might actually enhance a valid constitutional purpose. This is evident in the Court's willingness to uphold a diverse range of legislative values as being sufficiently important to restrict protected rights even though many of these are not easy to conceptualize as enumerated rights. Among the non-enumerated policy objectives that a majority of the Court has upheld as a reasonable limit are the Sunday Retail Holiday Act which promoted a common pause day for retail workers but discriminated against large and small retailers' abilities to enjoy freedom of religion; an adjudicator's order limiting freedom of expression by requiring a reference letter be written by a disgruntled employer on behalf of a unjustifiably dismissed employee and dictating the terms of the letter; Quebec consumer legislation prohibiting advertising aimed at children; legislation authorizing roadside stops resulting in arbitrary detention and denial of the ability to contact a lawyer and denying the presumption of innocence for criminal prosecution; and prohibitions against obscene materials and hate literature.

This change in the Court's orientation coincides with its acknowledgment, after almost two years, that it can no longer avoid a section 1 inquiry. But in exercising greater sensitivity to the proposition that legislation may foster values essential to a free and democratic society rather than hinder them, the Court has had to assess the constitutional worth of impugned legislation by a standard which, despite its semblance of establishing an objective and determinate framework, is not determinate of particular outcomes.

The inherent difficulty for judges to identify whether better legislative means are available has meant that the Court has been confronted with a dilemma. Should it scrutinize impugned legislation closely, at the risk of second-guessing complex legislative decisions, or defer to governmental claims about reasonableness, at the risk of discouraging legislatures from taking the responsibility of respecting protected rights as seriously as they should?

In responding to this dilemma the Court has assumed a deferential posture in the realm of social policy. Only once since *Oakes* has a majority of the Court ruled that the legislative objective itself is unreasonable and does not justify imposing limits on protected rights. The Court's reluctance to challenge the constitutional validity of legislative objectives and its tendency to resolve section 1 claims on the narrower grounds of procedural defects means that governments have the opportunity to reintroduce the contentious legislation in an alternative form.

Furthermore, what appeared in *Oakes* to be the stringent requirement that legislatures place limits on protected rights only when these constitute minimal impairment to an affected right, has devolved to the substantially lesser requirement that governments have a "reasonable basis" for making policy choices that conflict with protected rights. This devolution in the reasonableness standard has substantially reduced the extent to which the Charter constrains the choices of legislatures, particularly in the realm of social policy.

The Court's dilemma raises important questions of whether judicial review is consistent with democratic principles. As it becomes increasingly obvious that *Oakes* does not provide self-evident answers to the questions of when deference to legislative objectives is appropriate, despite renewed attempts by the Court to formalize its collective approach to the issue of how to apply the proportionality criteria, the role of the Court in section 1 issues can be seen for what it really is: the struggle of judges to determine the reasonableness of policies despite the absence of determinate principles and few resources, expertise, and analytical skills suitable for complex policy assessments.

If judges cannot base their decisions on a common and authoritative standard, one is compelled to ask what justification exists for discretionary judicial opinions to veto discretionary political ones. Stated differently, if the judicial task of reviewing the reasonableness of policies cannot be distinguished, categorically, from the kinds of subjective philosophical and policy considerations that originally shaped the legislative decision, what is the justification in a democratic society for an unelected, unrepresentative, and unaccountable body to second-guess legislative decisions?

That the Court's jurisprudence, to date, does not represent a significant departure from the priorities espoused by legislatures in no way lessens the significance of democratic concerns. After barely a decade of experience with the Charter it is too soon to make predictions about the likely legacy of an entrenched Charter. Further, it may be short sighted to assume that the effects of judicial review are measurable exclusively by counting how much legislation has been upheld or set aside.

There is an alternative way of casting the democratic question. Given the Charter's intent of providing a framework of fundamental values that should be respected, why should courts defer to legislatures? The Court's response to its dilemma has resulted in a devolving section 1 standard on reasonableness. But by accepting governmental claims that policies represent sufficiently important objectives to warrant limiting rights and easing the standard required to demonstrate that the policy is reasonable, what assurances do courts have that legislatures have taken the Charter seriously in their policy calculations?

These different perspectives on the question of whether judicial review is consistent with democratic principles will be explored more fully in the next chapter.

5 Judicial Review and Democracy

The Charter of Rights and Freedoms raises important questions about the democratic character and legitimacy of judicial review. While judicial review in Canada has been practised for more than a hundred years in disputes over the division of powers, the Charter has added an important new dimension to this exercise – the assessment of whether legislative or executive decisions conflict with protected rights. This new authoritative role for courts invites divergent opinions about whether judicial review conflicts with democratic assumptions of representative government.

The question of how to distinguish between allowable government action and the protected sphere of human activity is one of the most difficult and contentious issues facing liberal democracies. Decisions to trench upon protected rights, which in Canada are primarily of an individual nature, for the sake of the public interest or the attainment of a particular collective value will always be subject to controversy and debate. Some will contest the decision about which value deserves primacy, while others will dispute the design and administration of the legislative objective.

The Canadian polity is only beginning to realize that the ideas of codifying and protecting rights are deceptively simple ones.[1] Canadians have not yet been exposed to many divisive judicial outcomes in which Charter-based entitlements are fundamentally at odds with deeply held values. While a handful of judicial decisions have been contentious, these cases have not generally been of the kind that challenge Canadians' intuitive, moral, and political senses of what is just or fair or engage the polity in protracted and contentious discussions of the merits of values in conflict with protected rights.[2]

Canadians have had little more than a decade to observe and assess the political significance of the Charter of Rights and Freedoms. This lack of experience contrasts with Americans who have had more time to ponder the relationship between democracy and judicial review and have experienced numerous judicial interpretations of the Bill of Rights that either challenge or facilitate political commitment to contentious values. It will be helpful to compare emerging Canadian thoughts on the relationship between judicial review and democracy with the longstanding legitimacy debate in the United States. Not only is there a greater emphasis on comparative experiences when trying to understand domestic political phenomenon, but the American experience is already familiar to many of those who are interested in the Charter. Many Canadian scholars have trained in the United States or have studied the works of American constitutional scholars, and members of the Supreme Court of Canada have been extremely willing to call upon American constitutional case law when interpreting the Charter and developing the scope of its provisions. Furthermore, the United States has combined federalism with a system of entrenched rights which makes it highly relevant for comparative study of the political significance of entrenched rights. This chapter will examine central tenets of the American and Canadian debates on the democratic character of judicial review. It will set out many of the principal concerns when unelected courts are able to set aside the decisions of representative institutions. Democratic concerns are just beginning to be addressed by those who study the Charter and, as rights-based jurisprudence accumulates, will likely be discussed with increasing frequency and maturity.

AMERICAN JUDICIAL REVIEW AND DEMOCRACY DEBATE

Debate about the legitimacy of judicial review has been an enduring theme of American legal and political thought. There is no consensus on how courts should interpret the constitution from a democratic perspective. This is clear from both the continued scholarly discussion and theorizing about courts' proper constitutional role, and also from the controversy surrounding judicial appointments to the nation's highest court. American politics and government texts are careful to point out that judicial review is not explicitly provided for in the constitution. Nevertheless, there is little questioning of the rationale of judicial review in a democratic political system. But in spite of the acceptance of judicial review, there continues to be a robust debate over the appropriate parameters of judicial power. Considerable attention has focused on what role courts should assume when scrutinizing impugned legislation, whether the constitution itself provides a sufficient framework for courts to resolve conflicts, and whether, and how, the open-ended and dated text should be embellished to reflect changing norms and values.

Early Thoughts on Judicial Review

One of the early authoritative discussions of the democratic character of judicial review came from James Bradley Thayer who, in 1893, examined the question of how the United States could come to adopt the remarkable practice of striking down actions of the legislature or the executive, in light of the absence of any express judicial power. Although Thayer thought there was no inherent need for judicial review, he nevertheless was willing to recognize a legitimate judicial capacity to strike down legislative or executive acts, provided that the inconsistency was so significant that there could be no doubt that the impugned act was unconstitutional.[3]

Thayer's consideration of the democratic implications of judicial review was broader than the obvious concern that unelected courts could invalidate the choices of democratically elected legislators. He was apprehensive that an over-reliance on courts to determine questions about constitutional obligations would undermine the necessary political resolve to make difficult decisions about competing choices or values, particularly when the constitution does not speak authoritatively as to the correct decision. The danger of judicial review, as Thayer saw it, was that the public and legislators might relinquish responsibility for making difficult moral and prudential decisions:

It has been often remarked that private rights are more respected by the legislatures of some countries which have no written constitution, than by ours. No doubt our doctrine of constitutional law has had a tendency to drive out questions of justice and right, and to fill the minds of legislators with thoughts of mere legality, of what the constitution allows. And moreover, even in the matter of legality, they have felt little responsibility; if we are wrong, they say, the courts will correct it. Meantime they and the people whom they represent, not being thrown back on themselves, on the responsible exercise of their own prudence, moral sense, and honor, lose much of what is best in the political experience of any nation; and they are belittled, as well as demoralized. If what I have been saying is true, the safe and permanent road towards reform is that of impressing upon our people a far stronger sense than they have of the great range of possible mischief that our system leaves open, and must leave open, to the legislatures, and of the clear limits of judicial power; so that responsibility may be brought sharply home where it belongs.[4]

Since Thayer, generations of American political and legal scholars have tried to reconcile judicial review with democracy. Participants in the debate generally assess judicial review from one of the following precepts: democracy, as defined and interpreted in light of explicit or implicit constitutional norms; democracy as primarily an institutional process and arrangement for accountable representative government; and democracy as embodying certain fundamental rights that require judicial elucidations given the vagueness and age of the constitutional text.

Democracy and the Requirement of Interpretivism

In the United States there exists a long tradition to attempt to confine judicial review to textual interpretations of the constitution or to the framers' intents. Enforcing the constitution, according to this perspective, means basing decisions on the premises that are explicitly contained or implied in the document itself. While this approach is not always justified specifically in terms of democratic theory, assumptions about what democracy entails are implicit in discussions of the legitimacy of judicial review.

Those who espouse an "interpretivist" or "originalist" theory of judicial review[5] assume that it is illegitimate for an unelected institution to stray beyond stated societal norms, as contained in the constitution. To attach to the constitution meanings other than those derived from the text or from historical record is to impose, under the guise of constitutional interpretation, specific value or policy choices that are not the privilege or responsibility of an unelected and non-accountable court. Democratic concerns of contemporary proponents of interpretivism are derived from the following assumptions: the democratic foundation of the United States is the constitution which sets out the terms for the exercise of government power and the separation of powers; these terms represent a social contract; a fundamental premise of this contract is that the political system is based on representative and accountable government; judicial review is inherently anti-democratic in that it is neither representative nor accountable; and the only legitimate exercise of judicial review is to uphold the constitutional values as stated in the text or implied from the intent of the framers. As Robert Bork, one of the best-known contemporary interpretivists, argues, the constitution preserves Americans' liberties by providing that all of those given the authority to make policy are directly accountable to the people through regular elections.[6]

Majority tyranny occurs if legislation invades the areas properly left to individual freedom. Minority tyranny occurs if the majority is prevented from ruling where its power is legitimate. Yet, quite obviously, neither the majority nor the minority can be trusted to define the freedom of the other. This dilemma is resolved in constitutional theory, and in popular understanding, by the Supreme Court's power to define both majority and minority freedom through the interpretation of the Constitution. Society consents to be ruled undemocratically within defined areas by certain enduring principles believed to be stated in, and placed beyond the reach of majorities by, the Constitution.

But this resolution of the dilemma imposes severe requirements upon the Court. For it follows that the Court's power is legitimate only if it has, and can demonstrate in reasoned opinions that is has, a valid theory, derived from the Constitution, of the respective sphere of majority and minority freedom. If it does not have such a theory but actually follows its own predilections, the Court violates the postulates of the Madisonian model that alone justifies its power. It then necessarily abets the tyranny either of the majority or of the minority.[7]

Claims of the illegitimacy of courts straying beyond the constitutional text or framers' intent are premised on the assumption that a fundamental difference exists between law and politics. As Bork argues:

[Judges] must not make or apply any policy not fairly to be found in the Constitution or a statute. It is of course true that judges to some extent must make law every time they decide a case, but it is minor, interstitial lawmaking. The ratifiers of the Constitution put in place the walls, roofs, and beams; judges preserve the major architectural features, adding only filigree.[8]

Those who advocate an interpretivist argument, which accords binding authority to the text of the constitution or the intentions of its adopters, have been subject to a number of criticisms. It is argued that there may not be a singular intent in any provision, it is difficult to determine intent, the values espoused by the eighteenth-century drafters of the constitution may not be suitable or comprehensive enough to deal with contemporary moral dilemmas, and the open-ended wording of much of the constitutional text does not provide adequate guidance for determining what values and circumstances should be protected. While interpretivists are critical of all attempts to interpret the clause as a mandate to assess the substantive merits of legislation or executive decisions, they have difficulty explaining how a textual approach will provide apparent or coherent standards to review legislation, given the vague manner in which many rights are specified in the Bill of Rights. As John Hart Ely argues, constitutional provisions exist on a spectrum "ranging from the relatively specific to the extremely open-textured." The due process clause, which provides that no state shall "deprive any person of life, liberty, or property, without due process of law" is an example of the latter. Ely argues that the inability of this clause to provide determinate principles has resulted in its use to justify a diverse range of judicial interpretations from the economic due process interpretations in the *Lochner* v. *New York* era of the early part of this century to the declaration of a right to abortion in *Roe* v. *Wade* in the 1970s.[9]

Democracy as an Institutional Arrangement for Accountable Representative Government

Other constitutional scholars have sought alternative approaches to judicial review that recognize a strict reading of the constitution itself cannot provide the necessary answers to all constitutional disputes. But while disagreement exists with the methodology of interpretivism, many share the interpretivists' democratic objection to unelected courts making decisions that are not derived from explicit constitutional requirements. Thus, some have sought ways to interpret the constitution in a non-textual manner while at the same time trying to lessen the subjectivity of judge-made laws.

This second group of scholars reflect a vision of democracy that is largely process-oriented. Influenced by the judicial invalidation of a range of progressive policies seeking to prohibit the extension of slavery in the United States territory, restricting the use of child labour and New Deal policies attempting to deal with the effects of the depression, many judicial analysts have premised their democratic critique of judicial review on its "counter-majoritarian" aspects.[10] Democracy is seen primarily as a means of ordering and managing representative government in which the core principle is rule of the people, often equated with rule of the majority. The democratic tension posed by judicial review, which is generally assumed to be its counter-majoritarian tendencies, is tempered by the recognition that the values derived from the constitution must be protected and insulated from hostile political decisions.

The task of courts is to ensure that legislative and executive decisions respect these fundamental values that are derived from the themes of the constitution, although not always rooted in the specific words themselves. The constitution, in other words, is authoritative in that it is the paramount source of law, although the precise application of constitutional principles may require a certain degree of judicial elucidation. Courts must flesh out the open-ended and dated provisions to make them relevant to circumstances not anticipated by the drafters. But they must be careful to avoid the usurpation of legislative responsibilities by taking it upon themselves to read into the text their own normative or substantive conceptions of liberty or equality. To do so would be to assume legislative and executive responsibility for choosing between competing policy choices and, consequently, to frustrate a fundamental premise of representative government – that these kinds of decisions should be made by those who are elected and accountable to the people.

Those who base their democratic concerns of judicial review on its counter-majoritarian aspects but still believe that the constitution is incapable of providing clear answers to rights-based disputes have difficulty explaining the rationale for judicial review. If the constitution itself is of limited guidance in determining the contemporary meaning of values, then those who see democracy principally as an institutional arrangement for representative government have to grapple with several questions. Why should courts, rather than some legislatively accountable body, scrutinize the constitutionality of legislative and executive decisions? What principles should guide constitutional scrutiny or judicial review? Can constitutional values be protected from legislative excesses without undermining the principle that the people via their elected representatives, not judges, should rule?

Herbert Wechsler, writing in the early 1960s, tried to respond to this difficulty in a widely read defence of judicial review based on the assumption that courts should develop and adhere to neutral principles when interpreting the constitution. Wechsler disagreed with the interpretivists' desire to base all judicial review on the text or framers' intents. To read the text as "statements of a finite rule of law, its limits fixed by the consensus of a century long past," is to fail to leave room to adapt to competing and changing values that have a constitutional dimension. Despite his rejection of interpretivism, however, Wechsler did not intend courts to make value choices based on their own substantive views.[11] For Wechsler, judicial decisions must be controlled by principle. He defined a principled decision as "one that rests on reasons with respect to all the issues in a case, reasons that in their generality and their neutrality transcend any immediate result that is involved." When no sufficient reasons can be assigned for overturning the choices of government, courts ought not to substitute their vision or opinion of what is right.[12]

Wechsler's theory generated criticism from a different generation of constitutional scholars, who advanced theories of rights that required and presumed the kind of judicial intervention his theory precluded. One critic was Alexander Bickel who questioned which values, among adequately neutral and general ones, qualify as sufficiently important to be vindicated by the Court against other values affirmed by legislative acts? For Bickel the more important task was to determine how fundamental values are found and applied and what weights should be assigned to them when they come into conflict with other values or interests. These are questions that he thought a theory of neutral principles could not address.[13]

Ely offers a more contemporary approach. In his view, neither a strict interpretivist approach, which assumes that constitutional provisions are self-contained units, nor a search for an external source of values to guide interpretation of the constitution, provide a sufficient basis for judicial review. Instead courts should seek to improve the quality of the democratic process or, in his words, engage in a "participation-oriented, representation-reinforcing" exercise. What Ely means by this is that courts should be guided by the dominant theme of the constitution which he interprets as "the achievement of a political process open to all on an equal basis and a consequent enforcement of the representative's duty of equal concern and respect to minorities and majorities alike."[14]

Ely argues that the proper scope of judicial review should be confined to questions of participation and that judicial inquiries into the substantive merits of impugned political decisions should be avoided.[15] This approach is consistent with the constitution, which, he argues, is concerned more with procedural than substantive values. It is also more democratic because courts are not required to impose their normative or prescriptive views on citizens. The substantive choices that are made, therefore, are by elected and accountable officials and not by appointed and non-accountable judges.[16] While Ely is not willing to tolerate prejudicial considerations in law-making that disadvantage a discrete or insular minority or deny access to the political process, he can see no justification for courts to impose substantive requirements on legislatures, in the name of the constitution, beyond ensuring that the process for legislative decision-making is fair. To allow courts to base judicial review on substantive values denies the majority principle and is flagrantly undemocratic.[17]

Ely's process theory has generated considerable controversy. One of the difficulties Ely has is explaining the substantive character of so many of the constitutional values. It has been argued that much of American constitutional history can be written around three enduring themes – religious freedom, anti-slavery, and private property – which are ostensibly concerned with substantive values. An even greater conceptual difficulty for Ely is his lack of justification for a process-bound understanding of democracy. Laurence Tribe argues that Ely's advocacy of protecting procedural openness cannot be adequately understood, much less applied, without a developed theory of fundamental rights protecting individuals from the state.[18] Similarly, Ronald Dworkin argues that Ely's view that the proper role of the Supreme Court to police the process of democracy rather than review the substantive decisions made might be persuasive if democracy were "a precise political concept" with no room for disagreement as to whether some procedure was democratic. But since none of this is true, Ely's argument can only be read as putting forth his own conception of democracy and prescribing that courts identify and promote this vision.[19]

Democracy as Embodying Fundamental Rights Beyond Those Derived from the Text

A leading player in the American debate about the democratic implications of judicial review in the 1950s and 1960s suggested that the question of whether judicial review is compatible with democracy is one that must be examined anew by each generation.[20] At the time of his observation, the American debate focused on whether courts should exercise "judicial restraint" or "judicial activism," prompted in large part by the decisions of the Warren Court. These decisions, in particular the landmark school segregation case *Brown* v. *Board of Education*,[21] generated controversy by interpretivists and non-interpretivists alike. Both sides considered the decision neither authorized or required by the constitution, nor an interpretation or application of any value judgment of the interpreters.[22]

The dichotomous nature of the interpretivist/non-interpretivist debate has been rejected by some for masking the more meaningful question of whether courts should seek to enlarge the policy realm of judicial review and, if so, on what basis. Many commentators have advanced theories of fundamental rights as a model for judicial review. What sets this approach apart from others that consider democracy principally in process terms is the extent to which its advocates do not premise their approach on the claim that judges should be bound by the logic of the text when asserting the primacy of particular values over legislative decisions. Whereas the process-oriented critics tend to consider judicial review as anti-democratic or counter-majoritarian whenever courts invalidate legislative decisions for reasons other than enforcing what can be logically derived from the constitution, the fundamental rights' theorists envisage a far more expansive scope for judicial review to protect values, such as autonomy and privacy, which are not enumerated and cannot easily be inferred from the text. However, substantial differences of opinion exist as to which non-enumerated values are sufficiently fundamental to warrant limiting legislative decisions. For example, those who agree that enduring principles can be found in social consensus or derived from moral reasoning disagree about how these values should be applied and interpreted by courts.[23] But fundamental values are not determinate and their application is based on subjective and discretionary judicial opinions. Thus fundamental rights theorists are challenged to distinguish enduring values from the policy preferences of certain sectors of society and, if unsuccessful, to explain what theoretical understanding of democracy justifies an elitist and unaccountable institution, such as the judiciary, asserting the primacy of its views over the preferences of others.

Nowhere is this conflict clearer than in the work of Alexander Bickel. Bickel believed that government has a responsibility to serve society's enduring values and while he did not elaborate on what these are, he was of the opinion that courts are better suited than legislatures to engage in "the creative establishment and renewal of a coherent body of principled rules."[24] However, in later works Bickel expressed doubts about whether there is any consensus on how to define enduring values or whether courts have the capacity to develop "durable principles."[25]

Bickel's earlier confidence in the superiority of judicial over legislative decisions about the substance of fundamental values did not mean that he was comfortable about the possibility that courts would impose their own values. To do so would undermine confidence in the judiciary and bring into question the legitimacy of judicial review in a democracy. While Bickel recognized that no democracy operates by taking continuous head counts on the broad range of daily governmental activities, judicial review nevertheless conflicts with democratic principles because judicial decisions are not accountable, as are legislative ones, in the form of regular elections. When the Supreme Court declares unconstitutional a legislative act or the action of an elected executive, it exercises control not on behalf of the prevailing majority but against it. In this sense, judicial review is a "deviant institution" in American democracy.[26]

Other fundamental rights scholars have been less reticent in articulating enduring values and advocating a judicial role to promote them. Some argue that the constitution protects the rights of privacy and personhood while others argue that the constitution protects freedom of intimate association and freedom of lifestyle choices.[27] Proponents of the view that courts should read into the open provisions of the constitution substantive interpretations of privacy or personhood share considerable faith in the capacity of the courts to promote a higher morality than Congress or state legislatures. They also tend to view morality in evolutionary terms. Judicial review is not only a preferable way of deciding moral issues but may change (for the better) public moral awareness.

Michael Perry is a leading advocate of the view that through judicial review of difficult moral dilemmas courts will help facilitate a higher moral political culture. He believes that few contemporary human rights issues can be resolved through reference to the constitutional text or drafters' intent.[28] Like other non-interpretivists who believe that judicial review need not be bound by the logic or text of the constitution, Perry is challenged to explain which values courts should protect and how they can be discovered. He rules out tradition, consensus, and social ideals on his way to developing a theory of non-interpretive judicial review based on the search for "rights answers" to political and moral problems. Perry justifies this role for courts on the basis of comparative institutional competence. Courts are better equipped than legislatures to discover rights answers. Legislatures, he argues, do not have the capacity either to keep up with the moral evolution taking place in the United States or to redress issues such as distribute justice, freedom of political dissent, racism and sexism, the death penalty, or human sexuality. Legislative institutions, when they finally confront such moral issues, rely on established moral conventions and thereby ignore the occasion for moral re-evaluation because few values outrank re-election.[29]

Perry avoids explicit reference to democracy as the context for justifying a non-interpretive theory of judicial review. He is reluctant to use the word because it is "so freighted and misused" and instead prefers to talk about electorally accountable policy-making.[30] And while he does not accept that the objection to judicial review is its counter-majoritarian aspects (he accepts that few legislative decisions actually represent majority will) his concern that legislative decisions be electorally accountable is similar to the concern underlying Bickel's reference to judicial review as a "deviant institution" in American democracy:

Whether the function served by noninterpretive review in human rights cases constitutes a persuasive justification for such review – depends ultimately on whether noninterpretive review enables us to keep faith (or try to) with our commitment to moral growth – or, if you prefer, with the possibility that there are right answers – but in a manner that tolerably accommodates our other basic, constitutive commitment – our commitment to the principle of electorally accountable policymaking.[31]

Although reluctant to assess judicial review directly from a democratic perspective, Perry nevertheless seems compelled to explain why non-interpretive review can be thought of as consistent with the principle of electorally accountable policy-making. Perry's justification is based on the power of Congress under article 3 which provides that the Supreme Court "shall have appellate jurisdiction, both as to law and fact, with such exceptions, and under such regulations, as the Congress shall make." This power, Perry argues, could be used to allow Congress to confine the effects of those judicial decisions that are decided on the basis of non-interpretive review of the Constitution, to the immediate parties to the initial dispute.[32] Perry does not find much support for his argument that Congress's potential for limiting the jurisdiction of the Supreme Court is an effective political control over non-interpretive review. Congress has not used this power to deal with an unpopular Supreme Court decision in more than a hundred years, leading to conclusions that this power is both ineffective and "fraught with constitutional doubt."[33]

Not all fundamental rights' theorists feel the need to justify judicial review in democratic terms. Laurence Tribe, for example, recognizes that while the legitimacy of judicial power is subject to debate, he is sceptical of the limitations of all theories that attempt to render the enterprise legitimate and considers the search for legitimacy a pastime to be resisted:

In declining to join the recently renewed rush toward theories that purport to answer [questions about the democratic character of judicial review] and to provide foundational criteria that will render judicial review legitimate within – and only within – determinate boundaries, I by no means suggest that the legitimacy of judicial review (or, for that matter, of majority rule without judicial review) is ever unproblematic. On the contrary, it is largely because I believe that all exercises of power by some over others – even with what passes for the latter's consent – are and must remain deeply problematic that I find all legitimating theories not simply amusing in their pretensions but, in the end, as dangerous as they are unconvincing.[34]

Rather than worry about whether judicial review is consistent with democratic precepts, Tribe argues that courts instead should evaluate the validity of legislative choices that restrict personal autonomy on the basis of such questions as: Who is being hurt? Who benefits? By what process is the rule imposed? For what reasons? And with what likely effects? Tribe acknowledges few doubts about judges' capacities to address and find answers to these questions. The judiciary, he argues, has a unique capacity and commitment to engage in constitutional discourse – to explain and justify its conclusions about government authority in a common dialogue of rights: "This is a commitment that only a dialogue-engaging institution, insulated from day-to-day political accountability but correspondingly burdened with oversight by professional peers and vigilant lay critics, can be expected to maintain."[35]

Ronald Dworkin similarly justifies his theory of rights on the basis of judges' special capacity to engage in legal reasoning. Dworkin's moral theory of law and the constitution is predicated on the egalitarian ideal that government must treat all its citizens as equals in the following sense: political decisions and arrangements must display equal concern for the fate of all. Dworkin argues that a distinction must be made between the strategies a government uses to secure the general interest, as a matter of policy, and individual rights which, as a matter of principle, have primacy over these collective strategies.[36] Rights, according to his theory, should "function as trump cards held by individuals" against policies that would impose some particular vision of the good on society as a whole.[37]

Dworkin believes that the task before courts is fundamentally different from that of legislatures. What is required of judges is no less than "a fusion of constitutional law and moral theory."[38] Judges do and should rest their judgments in controversial cases on arguments of political principle even in hard cases where no explicit rule firmly decides the case either way.[39] He exudes great confidence in the ability of judges to invoke entirely legal and principled decisions which, even in hard cases, are not based on their personal preferences but reflect their best judgment of what the law requires. Even when judges are wrong, he believes it is preferable for society to have asked judges to "reason intuitively or introspectively" about different conceptions of equality or other contested concepts than to subject decisions of individual rights to legislative responsibility. To do so would be to suppose that the ordinary voter has better capacity to engage in moral argument than judges.[40]

Arguments that courts should seek recourse to moral philosophy or read into the constitution substantive rights such as personal autonomy have attracted criticisms that this approach is an invitation for judges to impose their own normative views on the substantive requirements of liberty or freedom.[41] One of its harshest critics is Ely. He believes that judicial review based on the discovery and enforcement of fundamental values is anti-democratic, and he disagrees with the premise that a "method of moral philosophy" exists that can guide judges.

The invitation to judges seems clear: seek constitutional values in – that is, overrule political officials on the basis of – the writing of good contemporary moral philosophers, in particular the writings of Rawls. Rawls's book is fine. But how are judges to react to Dworkin's invitation when almost all the commentators on Rawls's work have expressed reservations about his conclusions? ... One might be tempted to suppose that there will be no systematic bias in the judges' rendition of "correct moral reasoning" aside from whatever derives from the philosophical axioms from which they begin. ("We like Rawls, you like Nozick. We win, 6–3. Statute invalidated.")[42]

A different variation of the fundamental rights approach comes from feminist and minority scholars who look to equality rights as an important source of empowerment.[43] For many, a normative requirement of democracy is the fair and equitable treatment of all citizens. Thus, a different perspective on the democratic implications of judicial review looks to the potential of rights-based claims to broaden avenues of participation and to enhance membership of those individuals or groups who traditionally have lacked power or influence over decision-making.

Many of those advocating the use of equality rights as an instrument for social reform are responding and reacting to a body of North American legal theory known as "critical legal studies" (CLS). CLS scholars, including both legal academics and social scientists, offer a critique of liberal legal and political philosophy, an integral part of which is the rejection of liberalism's ideology of rights as a valuable social and political contribution.[44] The liberal distinction between law and politics, or public and private, is denied by CLS scholars who view law as "simply politics dressed in different garb; it neither operates in a historical vacuum nor does it exist independently of ideological struggles in society."[45] Further, CLS views the reference to rights as not only failing to resolve societal conflicts, because rights are indeterminate, but as being harmful because rights-talk "impedes advances by progressive social forces."[46]

While some minority and feminist scholars share some of the critical claims of CLS, they reject, and in some cases resent, the CLS' dismissal of rights and rights theory as a vehicle for social reform.

The attack by the Critical Legal Studies movement on rights and entitlement theory discourse can be seen as a counter crusade to the hard campaigns and long marches of minority peoples in [the United States]. Minority people committed themselves to these struggles, not to attain some hegemonically functioning reification leading to false consciousness, but a seat in the front of the bus, repatriation of treaty-guaranteed sacred lands, or a union card to carry into the grape vineyards.[47]

Although many minority and feminist scholars reject the use of rights as a strategy for social reform, others believe rights are important not only for use in litigation to redress specific injustices but also in their rhetorical power to mobilize forces for change. Critics argue that CLS scholars' dismissal of liberal rights and rights theory fails to recognize a benefit arising from the force of rights talk and does not offer a theoretical alternative to overcome injustice and inequality:

The frequent attacks by CLS on both rights and entitlement discourse represent direct frontal assaults on the sole proven vehicle of the European-derived legal tradition capable of mobilizing peoples of color as well as their allies in the majority society.

... Among the perils of CLS for peoples of color is its tendency to abandon and marginalize reliance upon what it regards as a false vision ... It is far too easy for someone on a law professor's salary to offer open-ended reconstructive projects which may bring immense benefits to a future generation. Minority law professors, however, who enjoy the sinecurial comforts of an academic life, cannot afford the luxury enjoyed by our CLS colleagues of not speaking to the real and immediate needs of our respective peoples. The trust placed in us demands the highest fiduciary standards.[48]

Minority and feminist scholars do not generally feel compelled to discuss their advocacy of rights in terms of the democratic legitimacy debate engaged in the law/politics literature. Given the overriding importance they assign to substantive equality, it is not too surprising that they do not see a conflict between judicial review and democracy. If democracy requires the fair and equitable treatment of all citizens, an expansive interpretation of equality by the courts, even if not textually driven from the constitution, promotes rather than undermines democracy.

CANADIAN JUDICIAL REVIEW AND DEMOCRACY DEBATE

Democracy and Fundamental Rights

Since the idea of entrenching rights assumed a prominent position on the constitutional agenda in the late 1960s, Charter supporters have greatly outnumbered critics both in popular and academic quarters. For these enthusiasts, the Charter will ensure that individual or minority rights are respected in the course of policy-making. Courts, in applying principles to assess the justification of rights, are expected to offer better protection for fundamental rights by insulating these from majority preferences, administrative expedience, and other "utilitarian" considerations. In short, the Charter introduces "a positive and energizing influence on decision-making by forcing policy-makers to heed to fundamental human rights and by giving a voice to minorities and the disadvantaged."[49]

Unlike many American commentators who feel compelled to justify judicial review in democratic terms, many of those who are most enthusiastic about the Charter's potential do not address the democratic question, at least as traditionally defined in the literature on judicial review. This disinterest may be due to the different vintages of the Bill of Rights and the Charter. The dated text of the Bill of Rights is recognized by all but the most strict interpretivists as incapable of providing a sufficient framework to address contemporary constitutional conflicts. Thus many American commentators have addressed the following concerns. In light of the indeterminacy of the text, on what basis should courts define values that are constitutionally worthy of invalidating legislative choices? And if judicial review rests on anything less than applying apparent and non-contested values in the constitution, should courts be involved at all? Would it not be more appropriate in a democratic polity for these decisions to be made by elected officials who are accountable to the people?

The relative newness of the Charter, as well as its explicit authorization for judicial review, may for some provide sufficient reason for not having to expound on the relationship between judicial review and democracy. Yet the recent vintage of the Charter does not resolve the democratic issue in light of the vague manner in which protected rights are stated as well as the wide-open concept of a free and democratic society as the context for evaluating the reasonableness of impugned legislation under section 1. The reluctance of Canadian fundamental rights advocates to confront the question of whether judicial review conflicts with democratic precepts is also explained by their aversion to confront the subjective nature of defining rights or applying reasonable limits. As David Beatty, one of the keenest supporters of the Charter, describes judicial review: "The Court [has] put in place a model of constitutional review which it [has] derived objectively from the most basic principles and values which underlie the Charter and which [has] the potential of enhancing both the quality of social justice and political participation in the country."[50]

An even more emphatic pronouncement by Beatty on the objectivity of protected rights is his criticism that because certain members of the Court have failed to apply these "objective" principles correctly they "have themselves acted unconstitutionally."[51] Lorraine Weinrib is similarly reluctant to acknowledge the subjective nature of judicial responsibilities under the Charter. She does not anticipate that interpretations of a "free and democratic society" will involve contested assumptions or differing philosophical opinions.

The second stage of the Charter adjudication [the application of reasonable limits] does not invite the state to rehearse in the judicial forum the entire range of considerations upon which the executive or the legislature acts. On the contrary, when the state argues the justifiability of its impugned policy, it urges the court to find consistency with a stable body of constitutional values and not an ad hoc equilibrium between the right and the policy in issue.[52]

Democracy: The Counter-Majoritarian Objection to Judicial Review

Although Charter enthusiasts have greatly outnumbered critics, a number of legal and political scholars have been critical of entrenchment because they believe it undermines democracy. One of the harshest critics of the Charter is Michael Mandel. A democratic polity, in Mandel's view, is one in which the people, through associations with like-minded or sympathetic groups or their elected representatives, make policy decisions. The problem with the Charter is that it transfers power not to the people but to judges. Mandel sees most of the Charter provisions as "vague incantations of lofty but entirely abstract ideals, incapable of either restraining or guiding the judges in their application to everyday life."[53] Mandel rejects claims that judges, when interpreting the Charter, base their decisions on principles qualitatively different from those undertaken in the legislative process.[54] Mandel believes that once it is realized that judicial review is not a principled, policy-neutral exercise, it is extremely difficult to reconcile the Charter with democracy.[55]

At the core of his democratic objection to the Charter is his normative preference for the primacy of legislative decisions. While Mandel does not assume that representative government is without its problems, he prefers this form of government for reasons which essentially boil down to a preference for majority rule.

What does it mean for one person to succeed at everyone else's expense? Majority rule can sound authoritarian, but it is merely the political expression of the profoundly egalitarian idea of "one-person-one-vote." To treat as irrelevant the unrepresentativeness of a claim is to allow some claimants to be more equal than others ... The Charter is admittedly a revolt against majoritarianism. But it does not substitute a new kind of democracy for it. In allowing individuals to shortcircuit representative institutions and groups, and to advance claims which "trump" more representative claims on the basis of consistency with abstract rights embedded in the status quo, it is a perversion of democracy.[56]

While Mandel recognizes that the Charter does contain some abstract formulations of rights that should interest socialists like himself[57] he does not advocate any theory of rights that would legitimize judicial review. Thus, he has difficulty in explaining his enthusiasm for the *Morgentaler* decision, the "only unqualified good result" to come out of the Supreme Court. The reason for his praise is that the decision "has removed a law whose only concrete effect was to make life more difficult for women in the already excruciating difficulty of an unwanted pregnancy."[58] The difficulty for Mandel, however, is to justify why the Court should have set aside an abortion law that was duly enacted by Parliament, in light of the vagueness of section 7 that could just as easily support a pro-life decision as a pro-health or pro-choice one. In the absence of a theory of rights – for example, a right to terminate an unwanted pregnancy or, as Justice Bertha Wilson characterized it, the right to have autonomy over personal decision-making – Mandel cannot explain his praise for this decision other than in terms of his personal policy preference.

Democracy and Community Values

Patrick Monahan offers an alternative critique of judicial review which relies on his interpretation of the Charter as being based on two foundations: democracy and communitarianism. Democracy, as he understands it, "is the forum and the means" for debate about the "idea that there is a difference between the way things are and the way they might be."[59] As such, democracy requires citizen participation, valued not only for its role in producing better informed and tolerant citizens, but also as a means of ensuring greater responsiveness on the part of the state to the needs and desires of the public. Monahan's version of democracy consists of three requirements: political institutions should facilitate ongoing political participation, or at the very least, should not discourage it; important political and moral decisions, such as those affecting justice and fairness, should remain at the political level, not determined by judicial elites; and finally, political and judicial decisions should embrace and reflect the community and collective identity that is part of Canada's heritage and culture.[60]

Monahan's theory of judicial review is influenced by the work of Ely. Monahan adopts Ely's normative position that democracy requires that the choice of substantive political values be made by elected representatives rather than by unelected judges. His rejection of an approach to judicial review in search of "right answers" is rooted in the belief that the text of the Charter is so vague and indeterminate, particularly section 1, that it invites the Court to "devise its own theory of freedom

and of democracy."[61] At the heart of Monahan's theory is the claim
that judicial review should be confined to the purpose underlying the
Charter which, he argues, is to improve and perfect the democratic
process and to protect community values.[62]

Ely's process theory, upon which Monahan relies, has been criticized
for advocating moral relativism and for relying on a faulty distinction
between process and substance.[63] Monahan admits that this proce-
dural/substantive distinction is "a weak link in Ely's argument."[64] But
Monahan believes his approach can be saved because the Charter does
not resemble those aspects of the Bill of Rights that are premised on
ideals of "limited government." Because the Charter is not bound up
by attempts to secure the private realm of property from the public
realm of state action, the kinds of substantive provisions that challenge
Ely's theory do not appear in the Charter.[65]

My claim is that a democratic conception of judicial review, although originally
formulated in the American context, actually offers a far more convincing account of the purposes underlying the Canadian *Charter*. My claim is that the
drafters of the Canadian *Charter* embraced those elements of the American
constitution designed to protect the democratic process, while largely excluding provisions aimed at guaranteeing particular substantive goods or values
deemed fundamental.[66]

Monahan's explanation has left many unconvinced. A frequent criticism is that reliance on a process-perfecting model of democracy does
not provide the framework to resolve many of the substantive conflicts
that will arise under the Charter.[67] Monahan fails to explain how a
democratic process theory can resolve minority language disputes or
conflicts pertaining to mobility claims. Also, he does not address the
more serious conceptual challenge that a process-bound theory itself is
rooted in a normative and substantive theory of democracy.

Monahan does not elaborate on the linkage between democracy
and communitarianism although it is implied. A healthier civic polity,
encouraged by open democratic processes and robust participation,
will produce a responsible democratic polity more likely to embrace
community values and enrich the lives of individuals residing in these
communities. Monahan's assumption of the intrinsic value of community can be criticized for failing to acknowledge conflicts between community and individual values. While he rejects the idea that conflict
necessarily exists between community and individual values, he does
not delve into what kinds of community values can justifiably be promoted or consider what effects these values might have on individuals
who are adversely affected.[68] As the case of the language and culture

debate in Quebec illustrates, communities are not hermetically sealed and their values and choices affect other individual members who reside geographically within the constituency if not culturally or philosophically in the community. With one important exception, his communitarianism does not address whether certain individual rights exist independent of community values. That exception is democratic values. As Monahan acknowledges,

No genuine democracy could function without basic guarantees regarding free expression, a free press and freedom of association. The same can be said of the democratic rights in ss. 3 to 5 [the right of citizens to vote and run as a candidate, and the requirement that the House of Commons and Legislative Assembly sit at least once every year and not for longer than five years after an election].[69]

According to Monahan's theory of judicial review, courts are justified in setting aside legislative decisions that impose barriers to participation in democratic debate and argument. But he does not define what constitutes a barrier to participation in political argument: specifically, does being a minority within a community constitute a barrier, if minority status ensures that one's rights or interests are adversely affected by the pursuit of collective values? And are democratic rights in sections 3–5 of the Charter the only values that should be protected and insulated from community values?

CLS Charter Critique

Some of the most serious democratic objections to the Charter come from Canadian legal scholars who wish to see greater state intervention in social and economic spheres and are concerned that the Charter embodies a conception of negative liberty that will frustrate affirmative state action. These critics contest many of the assumptions upon which a system of entrenched rights is often defended. These include the idea that codified rights will provide a sufficient framework for courts to review legislation; that judicial review will be based on reasoning that is qualitatively different from the kind of reasoning that takes place in the legislative sphere; that a public/private distinction adequately demarcates the Charter's sphere of protection; and that the law is neutral in that it is not predisposed to give preferential treatment to certain kinds of claims over others.

Alan Hutchinson and Andrew Petter are concerned that a public/private dichotomy, as a prescription for judicial review, will insulate a considerable source of inequality from affirmative state action and, when combined with the liberal emphasis that private interests should be free from regulatory interferences, will allow powerful interests to use rights as a way to resist government regulation that would seek to improve conditions for the disadvantaged.[70] As Petter argues, the Charter is,

a 19th century liberal document set loose on a 20th century welfare state. The rights in the Charter are founded upon the belief that the main enemies of freedom are not disparities in wealth nor concentrations of private power, but the state ...

This "systematic bias" is reinforced by a highly selective view of what constitutes the state. The presumption underlying the Charter is that existing distributions of wealth and power are products of private initiative as opposed to state action. Never mind that these distributions depend for their existence and legitimacy upon a panoply of state sponsored laws and institutions. They are nevertheless viewed as outside politics and beyond the scope of Charter scrutiny. Thus far from being subject to Charter challenge, such distributions comprise the "natural" foundation upon which Charter rights are conferred and against which the constitutionality of "state action" is to be judged.[71]

It is not just that particular judicial decisions may be regressive if based on a negative conception of liberty; the problem is deeper and is entrenched in the very liberal philosophical tenets that underlie both the law and the Charter. This philosophy is premised on the liberal understanding that the market demarcates the public from private spheres and that the Charter's application is limited to the former. Hutchinson and Petter argue that this distinction has grown out of the assumption in liberal theory that individuals possess an autonomous sphere that does not depend upon the state. The major task of the state in liberal theory is to police the boundary to protect individual liberty from state interference. Classical liberal theory assumed that the state crossed the line when it interfered with or failed to protect common law entitlements. The authors' criticism of this belief is the assumption that the market is somehow a product of natural order, that it does not implicate the state. They argue that since the market depends upon the state, the public/private distinction is a myth which, if allowed to "police the boundary between the two spheres," will continue to perpetuate substantive injustice.[72]

While Hutchinson and Petter's criticism of the liberal assumptions of the Charter is not framed explicitly in democratic terms, a democratic objection is implicit in their argument. In their view, adherence to this public/private distinction serves a political purpose that allows the judiciary to influence policy decisions: it enables courts to decide whether certain values should be subject to Charter review on the basis of an ostensibly neutral determination as to whether they are "public" or "private" in nature. The difficulty Hutchinson and Petter have with this justification is that an unelected and unaccountable judiciary can influence the priorities that are given to particular values by insulating a considerable source of inequality from affirmative state intervention.

> The effect of limiting Charter application to actions of the legislative and executive branches of government is to exclude from Charter scrutiny the major source of inequality in our society: the maldistribution of property entitlements among individuals ...
>
> The decision that an entity is "private" not only permits it to act without fear of breaching the moral imperatives contained in the Charter; it also makes it more likely that the entity will be permitted to mobilize the Charter as a weapon to resist government regulation and to insulate itself from popular scrutiny and control.[73]

Hutchinson and Petter do not offer any alternative theory of judicial review. They suggest only that a challenge exists to envisage a "substantive vision of social justice that is capable of responding to the vast inequalities of economic and political power that liberalism ... condone[s]."[74] They make it clear that they would prefer a non-Charter political regime to the current one, but they do not discuss any normative theory of politics that would be capable of pursuing the substantive vision they discuss. For example, are there certain fundamental values that should be protected independent of whatever vision of social justice is implemented, and if so, why is Parliament better able to protect these values than courts?

Democratic Objections to Judicial Activism

An alternative school of criticism focuses not on the limitations of negative liberty but on the implications of judicial attempts to broaden the scope of Charter entitlements. F.L. Morton and Rainer Knopff are concerned that liberal judges may interpret the Charter to promote a particular substantive vision of liberty or equality that is not derived from the Charter's obvious or textual meaning and yet imposes obligations on the state. They are particularly critical of the Charter's use by feminists and other equality-seeking groups to "wrest power from the 'unenlightened' majority"[75] in order to advance a social and political agenda of reform in the undemocratic branch of government – the courts. Their concern is not that the Charter is predicated on a negative conception of liberty, as was the case of Petter and Hutchinson, but rather that interest groups will successfully engage the Charter in a positive manner to expand state activities and obligations.

Morton and Knopff attribute the popularity of the Charter to the politics of post-materialism. They argue that the Charter undermines rather than enhances the democratic character of Canadian politics. While it has encouraged individuals and interest groups to become more involved in policy-making, this is not a mass movement but a politics of elite participation (well-educated and affluent feminists, bureaucrats, intellectuals, and the media). Their criticism of the use of the Charter by these groups (referred to pejoratively as "the Court Party") is that such organizations pursue their interests and agendas in the judicial arena of legalized politics "that intentionally bypasses the traditional democratic processes of collective self-government through popular elections and responsible parliamentary government."[76]

Morton and Knopff argue that the Supreme Court has encouraged this change by transforming itself from a traditional, British-style adjudicatory court to one that seeks to solve social problems "by issuing broad declarations of constitutional policy." The Supreme Court has facilitated the use of interest group litigation by adopting new and more open rules for intervenor status and by relaxing the doctrine of standing to make it easier for interests groups to pursue their causes before courts. The consequence of these changes is that judicial review is no longer characterized by its traditional role as a conservative check on democratic change but rather is engaged in the wholesale scrutiny of governmental policy initiatives.

Morton and Knopff imply that judicial activism is undemocratic. Courts ought not to act as agents of policy reform by assuming for themselves "a free hand to 'discover' new meaning in broadly worded constitutional principles." Thus their difficulty with the Supreme Court for having "liberated itself from the interpretive confines of fidelity to the framers' intent" is its insistence on interpreting the Charter in a manner that reflects a substantive vision of liberty or equality that goes well beyond the legitimate basis of judicial review, which in their view is to ensure limited government.[77]

Knopff and Morton raise another democratic objection to judicial review, one which is based on their reading of the appropriate division of institutional labour. They argue that for judicial review to be democratic it must comport with the principle of the separation of powers. While they acknowledge that this doctrine is a more accurate description of American political institutions because the Westminster cabinet system in Canada blurs the distinction between executive and legislative responsibilities, they nevertheless argue that the institutional separation between the judiciary and other branches of government is just as strong in the Canadian parliamentary system as it is in the American system.[78]

Knopff and Morton argue that competing, although not mutually exclusive, judicial interpretive approaches have different conse-quences for the integrity of the separation of powers.[79] Of these two approaches, adjudicative and oracular, they view the former as being consistent with the separation of powers doctrine while the latter trans-gresses it. The differences between the two approaches is the extent to which they emphasize adjudicating concrete disputes as opposed to in-terpreting the law in a manner that is not derived from the text or cir-cumstances before the court. Differences also embrace the relative impact of the decision on the other branches of government. An adju-dicative approach is said to give greater recognition to the role of other branches of government in interpreting those parts of the con-stitution for which they have responsibility.[80] This contrasts with the oracular approach which assumes, first, that while the correct legal meaning may not always be obvious, judges are better equipped to determine this and, secondly, that even when not required for the im-mediate dispute or derived specifically from the text at hand, judicial decisions are binding on the other branches of government. What concerns Knopff and Morton is that the traditional adjudicative view is steadily losing ground to the oracular perspective. In the process, they see it as undermining the appropriate separation of powers and raising democratic concerns.[81]

No one will challenge the legitimacy of appointed and politically independent judges settling concrete disputes, and the lawmaking incident to that function is likely to be accepted as long as it is seen as the unavoidable corollary of the primary adjudicative function, and is closely circumscribed by the adjudicative context. When the relationship between the two judicial functions is reversed, however, with the concrete case becoming a mere pretext for the authoritative declaration of what the law requires in circumstances extending well beyond the confines of the case, the problem of democratic legitimacy looms much larger.[82]

Knopff's and Morton's failure to expand on how they view democracy makes it difficult to assess their conclusion that the oracular as opposed to the adjudicative approach to judicial review is more susceptible to democratic objections. What is required is an explanation for why judi-cial review that goes beyond interpreting the obvious or implied logic of the constitutional text should be considered undemocratic.

This criticism is not intended to challenge the validity of the con-cerns Knopff and Morton raise. They share assumptions common to

Thayer's early discussions of judicial review, which remains one of the most authoritative discussions of the tension between judicial review and democracy. These assumptions include that society should not be misled into thinking there is only one constitutional answer to contemporary problems; that courts should address only those circumstances where the constitution clearly implicates governmental action; that other branches of government should not be unduly paralysed by judicial decisions; and that the citizenry should not abdicate responsibility for making difficult and contentious moral and political decisions. The concerns raised by Knopff and Morton warrant empirical analysis of the Charter's institutional and societal effects.

Rights as a Source of Empowerment

As serious as the interest in maintaining an appropriate division of institutional labour, however, are concerns about meaningful participation in political decision-making and in the just and fair distribution of societal benefits and burdens. Concerns exist within Canadian feminist scholars as to the merits of rights-based litigation strategies. They cite the possibility that definitions of formal equality may be imposed by courts, resulting in sameness of treatment that denies the biological and social differences that exist between women and men. Further, the legal mode of reasoning could make it difficult to place in context the experiences and circumstances of those who are not similarly situated to men. Despite these limitations, many Canadian feminists believe that, given the entrenchment of rights in the Charter, it is essential that feminists embrace rights-based claims of equality. Not only has the language of rights been privileged by the Charter (sexual equality is specifically protected in the Charter unlike the American Bill of Rights) but the indeterminacy of equality – whether it protects sameness between sexes or protects substantive results – ensures that its constitutional meaning and scope have yet to be determined. Thus many feminists believe that they should try to influence how the Court interprets equality to ensure that it does not adopt alternative interpretations that may be harmful in addressing the substantive inequalities facing women. As Diane Majury argues, "Pragmatically, at least in Canada, women have no choice but to address equality-based arguments; at the very least, we have to be ready to respond to arguments framed in terms of equality. Equality is, at present, too much a part of the dominant discourse in Canada to be ignored."[83]

As is the case in the United States, those who see rights as a source of empowerment and as a vehicle for social reform have objectives other than to engage in a discussion of the democratic implications of judicial review. In response to the argument by Knopff and Morton that it is inappropriate and illegitimate for courts to fashion social reform out of vague constitutional rights, two responses can be inferred from feminist scholarship. The first is that democracy presumes the fair and equitable treatment of all citizens and therefore requires progressive social reform to address systemic inequalities. Courts, no less than other political institutions, share in the responsibility to achieve this. A second, and different, response is that if liberal democracy precludes substantive equality, then some other version of democracy needs to be promoted.

While equality-seeking scholars are not generally engaged in the debate about whether judicial review is consistent with democracy, their prescriptive approaches nevertheless have democratic implications. Equality is among the most contested concepts in liberal democracies, particularly around fundamental issues such as whether equality should be interpreted in a formal manner or in terms of generating equal outcomes. Feminists themselves disagree about whether equality should result in women being treated the same as men, with or without consideration for biological differences, or should instead ensure that the differences between men and women, whether social or biological, real or perceived, do not result in substantive differences in women's quality of life or experiences. Even among those who agree with an outcome approach to equality, disagreements inevitably occur over questions such as which measures are appropriate to ensure that gender differences are costless. Given the range of equality-based reforms and disagreement about which measures can best attain the equality ideal, those who would prescribe that courts deliver a particular substantive outcome may wish to give more thought to the democratic justification of judicial elites giving authoritative standing to one, among many, interpretations of equality.

Enhancing Democratic Participation

For some, the question of whether the Charter facilitates or undermines democracy should be assessed on the basis of its effects on political participation. Many view this part of the Charter as having a salutary effect on political participation by "giving individuals direct access to some public decisions affecting their lives."[84] Clearly, this is part of Monahan's theory of judicial review – that one of foundations for the Charter is to improve political representation by removing barriers to political discussion. Beatty also identifies one of the benefits of the Charter as providing a new way in which "individuals and groups, who traditionally have not had much influence in the process of politics, can now make their voices heard."[85]

Peter Russell similarly emphasizes political participation when evaluating the democratic implications of judicial review. But rather than viewing the Charter as a necessarily positive contribution, Russell expresses concern that it may in fact discourage political participation. He does not have much sympathy for the simplistic proposition that it is anti-democratic for courts to resolve fundamental policy issues because this does not represent majority rule.[86] But he does believe that any society that aspires to be democratic should resolve the most important of its social priorities through its elected legislatures rather than in courts. Among the most difficult tasks of any democratic polity, Russell argues, is not protecting rights but determining the appropriate limits that can be imposed upon them. As we move away from those values that reflect ideals of common to all contemporary liberal democracies (political freedom, religious toleration, due process of law, and social equality) we incur considerable dilemmas in determining what limits are appropriate for less universal and more contested values.

As we move out from the central core of these values, we encounter restrictions and limits on each, and considerable controversy about the right limits … It is in the way we deal with [questions about the appropriate limits on protected values] that the Charter will have its main effect. A constitutional charter guarantees not that there will be no limits to rights and freedoms but that a change will be made in the way our society makes decisions about these limits.[87]

Russell believes that the legislative, rather than judicial, process is more likely to facilitate the kind of discussion and reflection desirable in making these difficult decisions. The virtue of having the legislature rather than courts engage in the balancing of social priorities is that the former is the branch of government whose deliberations are most exposed to public purview and are more likely to encourage political debate and discussion. Russell believes that the Charter, by establishing the judicial branch as the most important forum for the systematic application of Charter standards, may have a democratizing effect through opening the law reform process. Yet he is concerned that an over-reliance on the judicial process for resolving contentious policy disputes will weaken rather than strengthen the democratic character of a polity.

The danger here is not so much that non-elected judges will impose their will on a democratic majority, but that questions of social and political justice will be transformed into technical legal questions and the great bulk of the citizenry who are not judges and lawyers will abdicate their responsibility for working out reasonable and mutually acceptable resolutions of the issues which divide them.[88]

OVERVIEW OF CANADIAN AND AMERICAN DEMOCRACY DEBATES

Much of the discussion of the democratic character of their judicial review in the United States and Canada shares the following assumptions: unelected courts cannot help but interpret and make the law when reviewing the vague and indeterminate constitutional provisions; when doing so, they make decisions that have the effect of giving priority to some values over others; these decisions impose financial and policy obligations on governments; in a democracy, elected legislators, accountable through periodic elections, should make these kinds of policy decisions; when an unaccountable political institution such as the judiciary invalidates the choices of a legislature, this is inconsistent with democratic principles.

There is broad acceptance of the function of judicial review; in the United States it is seen as a necessary institutional device to preserve the separation of powers and to enforce the standards in the constitution, and in Canada as an explicit constitutional responsibility. Therefore those scholars whose evaluation of the democratic character of judicial review is influenced by its counter-majoritarian aspects have addressed their critiques to several questions. If the values in the text are insufficient to provide the answers, how should the court determine the values worthy of invalidating legislative choices? And if the exercise rests on anything less than applying apparent and non-contested values in the constitution, why should courts be involved at all? Would it not be more appropriate in a democratic polity for these decisions to be made by elected officials who are accountable to the people?

The difficulty in responding to these questions is aggravated by the treatment of democracy in much of the law and politics literature. Democracy is discussed not as an ideal – for example, a social and economic environment that best enables citizens to express their diverse views and pursue different courses of action in their private and public lives – but as a descriptive statement of the actual practices and institutions of those polities that are assumed to be liberal democracies. Rather than pursuing questions of whether democracy has a normative component, democracy is often assumed to be the sum of current practices of representative government.

An additional constraint encountered by those who base their objection to judicial review on its counter-majoritarian character is how to justify arguments about the primacy of elected institutions in light of the fact that neither the American nor Canadian political systems are designed to express majority will. Those who argue that judicial review is inconsistent with democracy do not explain why one should presume that there is any obvious linkage between the decisions of a legislature and a majority of people it is supposed to represent. Not only is there little account of the significant role of the bureaucracy in the age of the large and complex state, this perspective does not confront the composition or dynamics of elected institutions. For instance, if political institutions like the US Senate cannot be characterized as giving an equal voice to all citizens (in the sense that all citizens have an equitable influence on who will govern) because representation is based on equality of the states rather than population, how can it be suggested that legislative decisions are an expression of majority will? This objection to characterizing legislative decisions as reflecting majority will is equally relevant for Canada where the single-member plurality electoral system combines with a constituency system that deviates significantly from the principle of one-person/one vote. Further, it is misleading to suggest that political representatives represent the wishes of a majority of their constituents. In Canada the convention of cabinet government and the practice of strict party discipline represent substantial constraints on the capacity of elected representatives to assume the role of delegate for their constituents.

Fundamental rights' scholars consider that such rights should have primacy over all other legislative or societal initiatives. Yet their treatment of democracy is also underdeveloped. What needs to be explained more fully is how those values that are to be protected against legislative decisions should be defined, given the vagueness of constitutional provisions. Also, in light of substantial disagreement about how to identify or interpret these enduring values, why should the views of a handful of appointed judges veto the collective judgment of elected legislatures? The recent vintage of the Charter does not eliminate this imperative for those who believe that rights should be interpreted as paramount to all other societal values. The vagueness in how rights are expressed and the contested nature of section 1 obliges fundamental rights' scholars to explain how these values should be interpreted, how conflicts between important values should be reconciled, and what is the theoretical justification for courts to assume the primary responsibility for these tasks.

Those who view the democratic issues in terms of participation also have a normative understanding of democracy that emphasizes the importance of participation in decision-making that affects citizens' lives. Does the Charter improve participation, by providing a new process and opportunity for those who lack influence on policy development, or does it encourage citizens and their elected representatives to renege on their responsibilities to engage in the discussion and reflection necessary to make difficult social and political decisions? These arguments need to be assessed empirically as experience with the Charter accumulates.

In thinking through my own assumptions of democracy as it relates to judicial review, democratic arguments that emphasize the Court's influence on participation seem to offer the most persuasive grounds for critical evaluation.

DEMOCRACY DEBATE RECAST

The limitation clause of section 1 is integral to understanding whether and how judicial review of the Charter conflicts with democratic principles. The Charter's unique structure – of both guaranteeing rights and allowing limits on them – establishes the opportunity for debate on how the Charter should effect governing, the obligations of legislatures when promoting policies, and the values that should be promoted in a responsible and caring society.

The question of which values justify limiting protected rights and how these should be evaluated are critically linked to questions of how democracy should be conceived. Because it is intended to be a normative standard, the word "democratic" in section 1 can only be understood as referring to an ideal, rather than to a descriptive account of existing political practices. As an ideal, democracy is both about protecting rights and about facilitating the public discussion and reflection necessary to assess the relative weight and priority that should be attached to conflicting rights and values. One of the aims of a democratic political system is to enhance the role and involvement of citizens in contributing to decisions that affect their public and private lives. This does not necessarily imply direct citizen participation, but stresses the contributing role of discussion and debate in assessing and influencing the decisions taken by elected representatives and public officials.

But public debate is not the only goal of a democratic polity. Policy choices should respect fundamental rights, those contained explicitly in the Charter and others related to its core values. Among the most important of these are the individual autonomy in decision-making essential to one's dignity and sense of person; equality; the right of a citizen to vote in elections and to be a candidate for public office; the right to be free from persecution and discrimination based on personal characteristics such as religion, gender, age, physical or mental capacity, sexual orientation, race, or ethnicity; the right to express opinions freely on political and social practices and developments; the right to communicate with others about issues and ideas; and the rights to physical security of one's person, protection against unreasonable search or seizure, and to a fair trial. Policy choices that undermine the essential purpose of these fundamental rights should be extremely difficult to justify – considerably more so than policies that impose limits on more peripheral rights-based claims.

The Charter's single most important contribution from a democratic perspective is the obligation it imposes on all branches of government to give effect to its values and to evaluate the implications of policy choices for protected rights. This requirement is due, in a formal sense, to changes in Canada's constitutional principles: courts are now charged with the responsibility of interpreting and defining rights and granting the appropriate remedy where rights have been infringed or denied. As important as the formal responsibility to respect judicial interpretations of protected rights under the constitution, however, is the obligation of representative institutions to give life to the Charter in day-to-day policy development. This obligation, I argue, arises both from the democratic ideals of governing through discussion and debate and from the difficulties inherent in judicial review of the reasonableness of impugned policies.

These democratic ideals oblige representative institutions to not only abide by judicial decisions but to justify policy choices in terms of their implications for protected rights. Rigorous legislative debate about the merits of policy choices and the rationale of alternative measures should be an essential part of justifying policies. If the governing party is expected to defend its policy choices in the legislature in terms of how they affect protected rights, it will become more difficult to pursue policies that deny core rights or impose too great an infringement on other protected rights.

The importance of debate is not that it will produce "right answers." While there is no reason to assume that the dominant opinion emerging from parliamentary debate will always represent the best way of resolving the conflict in a manner that gives due respect to those whose rights are adversely affected, it will generate a better, and more principled, answer to complex and contested issues than a policy process where rights-based assessments are absent. The importance of debate is to contribute to, reflect on, and evaluate critically legislative obligations under the Charter and to assess whether policies which impose limits on protected rights are justified, given the nature of the affected right and in the face of claims of compelling societal values and interests. Debates where those defending policy choices must justify the effects of these on protected rights would better expose the discriminating effects of policies or possible unintended consequences that impair or undermine protected rights.

If governments and opposition parties discuss openly the justification for policies and their effects on protected rights, media coverage and scrutiny by interested individuals and groups of legislative records should stimulate a broader public debate on the merits of policies that conflict, prima facie, with protected rights. While promoting public debate is by no means a new role for representative institutions the Charter should sharpen the quality of debate about legislative obligations and the priorities that should be attached to conflicting values. Instead of debating policies in the context of reconciling competing interests, the terms of the debate will embrace rights and democratic values more directly. The significance is not simply a change in semantics. It is more difficult to justify the reasons for pursuing policies that require limiting protected rights than it is to pursue competing interests. Not only is the rhetorical impact of "rights" stronger than "interests," the Charter has privileged rights as it has not interests.

The purpose of emphasizing the potentially salutary effects that arise from discussion about the merits of conflicting values is not to imply that legislative priorities should be equated with the preferences of a legislative majority or determined on the basis of public opinion. Answers to rights-based conflicts are not necessarily those for which substantial agreement exists. The presence of robust parliamentary debate would not justify policies that exact an unnecessary rights-burden on some. Nor would a robust debate validate a majority's or community's preference that results in a serious deprivation of a core right and which would not represent a compelling democratic value. In short, the mere fact of debate cannot justify "bad" policies that are incongruent with the fundamental values of a free and democratic society. Even if representative government were an effective way of translating majority will into policy preferences, democracy is not simply the sum of its processes and practices. While democracy is very much a contested concept, the interpretation offered here emphasizes the ideal of enhanced citizen participation which must coincide with respect for fundamental rights and values.

A second reason legislatures have an obligation to give life to the Charter, I argue, is due to the difficulties inherent in judicial review of the reasonableness of impugned policies. What makes debate and reflection so important is the indeterminacy of the Charter. The vague manner in which rights are expressed in the Charter, when combined with the broad purposive interpretation given to them by the Supreme Court, implicates a wide range of legislative activity.

Although courts are given the responsibility for reviewing the reasonableness of impugned policies, this responsibility is one that requires discretionary evaluations as to whether less restrictive legislative means are practically available. Only infrequently does the court declare that the legislative objective itself is not worthy of limiting a protected right. Most often when legislation is rejected as a reasonable limit it is because the Court deems that the legislation has not been designed carefully enough. An important component of a reasonableness test is whether better legislative means, which impose a less severe restriction on a protected right, should have been undertaken.

But despite courts' responsibility to review the reasonableness of impugned policies, judges are poorly situated to evaluate whether better or less restrictive legislative means are available. Judicial principles or precedents are of little relevance when assessing the reasonableness of legislation. In some cases courts may not have serious difficulties assessing whether a policy is poorly designed – where, for instance, the objective is attained by means that impose an obviously severe restriction on a protected right that far exceeds what is warranted. But in general, the complexity of policy development makes it difficult for those external to the process to make an informed judgment as to whether the policy scheme represents the best arrangement possible in terms of reconciling conflicting rights and values.

In light of the inherent difficulties a court faces when trying to assess the reasonableness of legislative objectives that conflict with protected rights, it is imperative that courts have more to rely on than arguments for judicial deference, rhetorical assurances that the policy is justified, or attempts at "reading the tea leaves of Parliament."[89] What they require are sound arguments and evidence, where possible, about why a policy objective is being pursued and the reasons for the manner in which it is has been designed. In short, courts need an indication that Parliament or provincial legislatures have sincerely reflected on the choices before them, that they have been sensitive to the affected right, and have tried to accommodate that right as much as is reasonably or practically possible in the pursuit of the desired objective.

Most Charter commentators think of section 1 solely as the principal judicial standard for evaluating the constitutionality of legislation. The limitation clause, as interpreted by the Supreme Court, also represents a useful framework for legislatures to assess the justification of their proposed policies. The very questions the Court asks when scrutinizing legislation should be asked by representative institutions. If the claim I made earlier is compelling – that the virtue of the Charter from a democratic perspective is that it imposes a requirement and obligation on representative institutions to consider the effects of policy choices on protected rights – then the extent to which the Charter shapes and influences policy debate is important.

Governments that promote policy values which impose limits on protected rights should be prepared to explain the justification for the policy, its potential effects on protected rights, whether these rights are core and fundamental or marginal and peripheral, and why the policy is being designed in a particular manner. A government can facilitate debate about the merits of competing values by circulating policy analysis undertaken by public officials and departmental and justice lawyers that explains the rationale of the legislation in light of the Charter and its likely effects on protected rights. Alternatively, the ministers for departments of Justice and Attorney General could be required to sign a declaration that explains the policy rationale, merits, and effects of a particular proposal.[90] Either approach would sharpen the level of rights-based scrutiny in legislative proceedings. Not only would this encourage a policy process more sensitive to the Charter, but the public attention derived from media scrutiny of policy statements, ministerial declarations, and legislative proceedings would stimulate a larger public debate about the importance of contested moral and political values. This in turn would facilitate the democratic ideal that citizens take a more active role in assessing decisions that affect their social and private lives.

In arguing that legislatures have an obligation to give life to the Charter by scrutinizing policy initiatives in terms of their effects on rights and their consistency with a free and democratic society, my intent is to argue neither that legislatures should be preoccupied with second guessing and anticipating how courts will assess their policies nor that governments should avoid making difficult decisions that may result in a Charter challenge.

The purpose of legislative debate is not to anticipate what may or may not pass judicial scrutiny but rather to express a collective judgment on what policies are necessary and responsible in light of the Charter. It is important to distinguish between the role of parliamentary Charter debate discussed here and the kind of Charter analysis undertaken when policies are initially being developed by government lawyers in the departments of Justice and Attorney General. Patrick Monahan and Marie Finkelstein suggest that while governments have responded to the Charter in different ways, they share the intent to consider rights issues early in the policy process. This objective has increased the role and status of attorneys generals and their legal advisers who, in many governments, now constitute a new central agency.[91] Government lawyers evaluate the likelihood that a proposed policy will attract Charter problems and can give some indication, based on accumulated Supreme Court jurisprudence, on the difficulty of defending the policy in court. This kind of Charter scrutiny is both expected and welcome. To those charged with policy responsibility, both public officials in departments and agencies and ministers who bear ultimate accountability, it signals some of the specific legal difficulties that can be anticipated. With this information, public and political officials are able to revisit the policy objective, assess alternative means and objectives, and ultimately make a decision about whether to recommend that the policy be enacted.

But it should not be presumed that this process of behind-the-scenes "Charter-proofing" exhausts political and legislative obligations to give life to the Charter or that government lawyers alone have the answers to Charter-related questions. To defer all judgment on Charter issues to government lawyers is to argue that the constitution involves exclusively legal issues, that it provides clear and authoritative answers to constitutional questions (to the extent that Supreme Court decisions can be forecast with precision), and that legislatures do not have political responsibility to challenge and contest legal assumptions about the scope of their responsibilities and of democratic values. It is one thing for governments to take heed of criticisms when pursuing policies that may unduly or unjustifiably limit a protected right. It is quite another for them to renege on the political responsibility to make difficult decisions in the public interest simply because these decisions attract rights-based objections. This is particularly true where the rights' dispute is based not on a core value but on a more peripheral claim. It is important that the Charter not undermine the political will and resolve to promote contentious values that promote a compelling societal interest.

Political scientists have not studied the effects of entrenched rights on policy development in Canada in a systematic manner. What work has been done is largely impressionistic and focuses primarily on the constitutional arena, where the Charter is said to have helped bring about a transformation in citizen identities from passive spectators to assertive rights-bearers.[92] Students of the policy process suggest that the Charter has the potential to alter policy agendas and to "build the foundations of a higher purpose of value to which state officials themselves can adhere."[93] But in the absence of empirical research these assessments can be treated as little more than informed speculations. My own reading of parliamentary debates that have raised rights-based issues suggests that while the language of rights has increasing prominence, governments have not generally been willing to explain why policies justify imposing limits on protected rights or how they promote values essential to democracy.[94] Thus there is little legislative record to explain why a policy that conflicts with protected rights has been endorsed or why it has been designed in the manner it has.[95] This is not surprising since parliamentary debate in Canada has traditionally been a relatively ineffective way of influencing policy. The principle of responsible government encourages party loyalty and discourages members of Parliament from assessing and criticizing policy an in independent manner. The weakness of the legislative committee system reinforces Parliament's ineffectiveness to assess and influence government initiatives.

CONCLUSIONS

The ability of legislatures to exert considerable influence in determining which values warrant limiting protected rights and also whether impugned policies have been carefully enough designed to impose a reasonable limit should be seen as imposing an obligation on representative institutions to ensure that the policies they promote, which conflict with protected rights, are really justified. Representative institutions should engage in and promote robust legislative debate about the justification of policy objectives, in terms of their effects on rights, and the merits of alternative measures. Not only would this debate subject policies to critical assessments of legislative obligations under the Charter, but debate would better expose the discriminating effects of policies or possible unintended consequences that impair or undermine protected rights.

Debate on when policies must be justified in terms of the Charter would also be a prudent way of responding to the democratic concerns that arise from judicial uncertainty about whether legislation represents a reasonable limit. If the Court were to require clear evidence that the impugned policy is the product of meaningful and deliberative debate about the worthiness of a policy objective and the reasonableness of its means, judges could be more confident about their decision about whether to uphold or set aside legislation under section 1.

The decision to uphold the legislative response to a complex policy problem, which does not compromise a core right and which has been the product of rigorous and sincere debate about its justification and the merits of alternative means, would be consistent with the democratic ideal of governing through discussion and debate. To nullify legislation, under these circumstances, would generate justifiable criticisms that the Supreme Court was simply second-guessing the choices of those who are better situated to evaluate policy and who are ultimately accountable to public scrutiny.

Where legislation compromises a core right, the Court may not be satisfied that the legislative decision is the proper one, even where the policy has been subject to rigorous legislative debate. The ideals of governing through discussion and debate co-exist, with some tension, with the ideal of respecting the normative rights and values of the Charter. The constraints on legislatures imposed on the Charter are welcome and justified where legislation imposes an unreasonable limit on a core right or where legislation discriminates against or imposes an unfair burden on a particular individual or group, whether or not intended.

Where legislation that imposes limits on protected rights has not been the product of rigorous debate about alternative options, or where the policy has not been scrutinized by other organizations such as royal commissions or inquiries, judicial deference may be neither warranted nor appropriate. Where the Supreme Court has no basis to verify a government's claim that the effects of the policy are reasonable, the Court cannot be assured that its decision to uphold the policy will result in a reasonable limit being imposed on a protected right. Under these circumstances, a judicial decision to set aside legislation because of a lack of sensitivity in pursuing legislative objectives may itself generate the desired public and political deliberation on the merits of legislative choices that adversely affect protected rights.

6 Rights and Federalism

Much has been said of the Charter of Rights and Freedoms's nation-building effects for Canada, particularly in transforming citizens from passive spectators to assertive rights-bearers in constitutional debates.[1] What has not received the same attention, however, is the institutional side of the nation-building thesis. When entrenched rights were first included in the constitution many predicted that the Charter would undermine the territorial-based pluralism contemplated by Canadian federalism.[2] Yet little has been done to test the thesis in light of more than a decade of Charter jurisprudence.[3] In this chapter the question of whether and how the Charter frustrates the territorial pluralism of Canadian federalism will be revisited. It will analyse Supreme Court federalism/rights jurisprudence and will consider whether the structure of the Charter, with its inclusion of explicit limitation and legislative override clauses, will allow for provincial diversity in the Charter's interpretation and application. The chapter will begin by examining American developments relating to the application of the Bill of Rights to the states. It will consider the extent to which judicial review of entrenched rights undermines the autonomy of the constituent parts of a federal system by encouraging the homogenization of public policies.

Debates in Canada and the United States about the effects of entrenched rights on provincial or state policies reflect differences in how the relationship between entrenched rights and federalism have evolved. While both countries chose federalism to allow sub-national units to exercise autonomy, the subsequent reasons for curtailing this autonomy by subjecting provincial and state decisions to judicially interpreted national rights diverge in significant ways. Unlike Canada's experience, in which the decision to apply the Charter to the provinces was a political one, recognized at the time as imposing the most radical break ever made with the Canadian constitutional and legal order "hitherto characterized by continuity and incremental development,"[4] the decision to apply the Bill of Rights to the states was made gradually and at the discretion of courts.

RELATIONSHIP BETWEEN THE US BILL OF RIGHTS AND STATE AUTONOMY

Distrust of government was an enduring theme both before and after the American Revolution. One way this distrust was expressed was in the enumeration in state constitutions of rights guaranteed to the people. So secure did the protection of state rights seem that a federal bill of rights was not seriously considered at the Philadelphia Convention of 1787.[5] The decision to confine the Bill of Rights to the federal government is consistent with "American tradition, almost Jeffersonian in its nobility and localism, of hostility to federal equity."[6] An 1833 Supreme Court decision confirmed that states were not subject to federal constitutional rights.[7]

The passage of the fourteenth amendment after the Civil War resulted in a fundamental change in federal-state relations. The amendment prohibits states from making or enforcing any law "which shall abridge the privileges or immunities of citizens of the United States; nor shall any State deprive any person of life, liberty, or property, without due process of law; nor deny to any person within its jurisdiction the equal protection of the laws." The significance of this amendment for federalism was not immediately evident. Between 1868 and 1897 the Supreme Court rejected repeatedly the idea of applying these amendments to the states.[8] The Court held that the primary purpose of the Civil War amendments was to guarantee freedom for blacks and that privileges and immunities were to be protected by the states, not the national government. However, by the end of the century the Supreme Court had decided that certain portions of the Bill of Rights should be applied to the states.

The Court's turnaround began in 1897 when it held that protection against taking private property for public use without just compensation was embodied in the fourteenth amendment's proscription "nor shall any state deprive any person of ... property, without due process of law." This coincided with the Court's laissez faire interpretation of the fourteenth amendment as conferring a substantive entitlement to freedom of contract and property.[9]

The extension of other amendments to the states was gradual. In 1925 the Court applied the first amendment's protection of freedom of speech and of the press to the state level and in 1949 extended the fourth amendment's prohibition against unreasonable searches and seizures to the states. It was not until the 1960s, however, that the Court engaged in the wholesale incorporation into the fourteenth amendment of many of the detailed provisions of the Bill of Rights. In 1961 the Court applied the exclusionary rule to state proceedings and from 1962 to 1969 extended to the states many of the specific clauses in the Bill of Rights:

- the eighth amendment's prohibition of cruel and unusual punishment;
- the sixth amendment's requirement that the accused in all prosecutions shall have the assistance of counsel, which was interpreted as a requirement that counsel must be provided for in every court in all states;
- the fifth amendment right against compulsory self-incrimination was extended to the states which was incorporated as a requirement that police give warnings to a suspect before custodial interrogation;
- extensions of the sixth amendment of the right of an accused to be confronted by the witnesses against him or her, the right to a speedy and public trial, the right to a trial by an impartial jury, and the right to have compulsory process for obtaining witnesses;
- the right against double jeopardy in the fifth amendment.

The Court's willingness to subject state activities to federally interpreted national rights was not confined to criminal legal rights. The Court interpreted the fourteenth amendment to include the non-enumerated right to privacy and struck down a state law banning the dispensing of contraceptive devices. The first amendment was interpreted as the basis to set aside state policies which reflected community religious and cultural preferences: the guarantee of separation of church and state was used to prohibit state-required prayers in public schools while freedom of speech and the press was interpreted to prevent public officials from recovering damages for defamatory statements relating to their official conduct unless actual malice could be proven. In addition, the Supreme Court confronted and challenged a distinction in American constitutional jurisprudence between rights of entitlement and privilege. Traditional constitutional wisdom has held that while rights are subject to constitutionally protected safeguards, privileges could be terminated without the constitutional requirement of a hearing or other procedural safeguard. This distinction was repudiated by the Court in

1970, by ruling that the fourteenth amendment prevents a state from terminating welfare payments without granting a quasi-judicial hearing to ensure that those who are entitled to benefits receive them.[10]

The application of the Bill of Rights to the states, described in the American law and politics literature as the incorporation doctrine, has had the effect of establishing a new floor of protection for citizens – a minimum of federally protected rights that the states are now constitutionally obligated to respect. Unlike Canada, which has a hierarchical and integrated judicial system in which decisions of the Supreme Court are binding on all other courts, the United States has two major court systems – the national and state courts. At the apex of each state system is its final court of appeal which usually has the last word in the state on all constitutional questions. Its decisions are final as to state and local law. However, on rare occasions, where a substantial federal question has been validly raised in the proper state court below and all remedies at the state level have been duly exhausted, the Supreme Court may exercise its discretion to review the case.[11]

What is particularly noteworthy of the Supreme Court in the 1960s under Chief Justice Earl Warren was its willingness to exercise this discretion to ease access to federal courts for litigants who claimed a violation of their rights at the state level. The Warren Court, which played the largest role in applying many of the specific rights in the Bill of Rights to the states, has ___ ___   ·   __ __ having been "carried along by the centralizing currents" in American life and by "its own sense of judicial responsibility for reforms which would better protect the individual and the oppressed."

The impetus came from the broad trend toward nationalization, from distrust of state tribunals in matters arising out of the civil rights revolution, from enthusiasm for enlarging the constitutional protection for individuals and minorities, and from awareness that state courts were slow to respond to the reforming trend of constitutional decisions.[12]

In contrast, the subsequent Burger Court limited access and indicated that federal courts should interfere with pending state prosecutions only under extraordinary circumstances.[13] This has lessened the extent to which state autonomy has been undermined by federally interpreted national rights. Commentators observe that the states continue to enjoy discretion to diverge from national standards where, for example, they wish to accommodate community standards by regulating obscenity or to give local effect to the federal right to a jury trial by establishing juries with less than twelve members and by accepting non-unanimous verdicts.[14]

The Burger retreat has encouraged a renewed interest in state constitutions. Under the Warren Court, public and political officials saw
state constitutions and bills of rights as adding little to their federal
counterpart. However, as it became more difficult to seek federal relief
from the 1970s on, a renewed interest arose in state bills of rights. This
debate has been fuelled by the Burger Court's decision not to review
state court decisions which, while raising federal questions, nevertheless rest on independent and adequate state law grounds. As a consequence, considerable discretion has been conferred on state court
judges to formulate their arguments on grounds other than interpretations of the constitution or Supreme Court precedents. While some
observers see this as a welcome development in the revitalization of
federalism by allowing for inter-state diversity and the opportunity to
experiment, others contend that the renewed emphasis on state constitutional law creates a confusing multiplicity of rules, subverts the
idea of America as one nation, and undermines the public's confidence in the Supreme Court and the rule of law.[15]

An additional wrinkle in the debate about the appropriate interpretation of state bill of rights has been decisions by the Burger Court to
reverse state court decisions where these exceed the requirements of
the national Bill of Rights. Instead of reversing state judgments because they fall below minimum federal requirements, the Court "now
regularly upsets state court decisions because too much protection has
been afforded individuals in the name of the Bill of Rights," which
means that the Bill of Rights is now being used by the Supreme Court
"to police the 'outer limits' of state court civil liberties decisionmak-
ing." This practice has been criticized for undermining the state's role
in promoting social reform. Critics argue that state courts may be reticent about expanding protection for individual rights if they are subject to oversight by federal courts.[16]

THE CHARTER'S EFFECTS ON
FEDERALISM IN CANADA

Unlike developments in American federalism, in which the decision to
apply the Bill of Rights to the states was made at the discretion of the
Supreme Court, the decision in Canada to graft an entrenched Charter on to a parliamentary federal system was made by political leaders.

The Charter has been characterized as a centralizing force in Canada not because it confers additional powers on the federal Parliament but because it imposes constraints on the extent to which the
provinces can promote community values based on a set of priorities
different from other jurisdictions. In this sense the Charter strength-

ens "Canadian as against provincial identities."[17] The Charter clearly has implications for federalism, attributable in large part to Canada's hierarchical judicial system in which the Supreme Court's jurisprudence is binding on all other courts. By establishing an authoritative role for courts in evaluating the constitutionality of legislative and executive decisions, the Charter is expected to encourage national standards on the parameters of protected rights and the justification of governmental initiatives that impose limits on these rights. While the articulation of rights is expected to constrain the policy choices of both provincial legislatures and the federal Parliament, its impact is expected to be greater at the provincial level. This is because provinces, which are less heterogenous than the broader Canadian society, are more apt to promote policies that promote particularities that diverge from national norms and conflict with protected rights.[18] In a more specific way, the Charter affects federalism in that it has transformed what traditionally has been a matter of provincial jurisdiction – minority education language policy – to an entrenched right that is national in scope.

Tension between federalism and the Charter has been particularly acute among political leaders in Quebec. Quebec was the only province that refused to agree to the constitutional reforms in 1981 which included an entrenched Charter of Rights. Given the importance to Quebec of provincial autonomy, it is hardly surprising that the Charter, which will be interpreted by a national court and whose members are appointed at the discretion of the prime minister and federal justice minister, has been viewed in that province with scepticism and criticism.

A time bomb for Quebec stems from the Charter of Rights and Freedoms, which will inevitably leave wide powers to the Supreme Court. With the often vague wording of the Charter, the judges will be called upon to play a substantial legislative role in addition to a judicial one, which does not augur well for the future of democracy in Canada. In addition, the Charter, which will be interpreted by federally-appointed judges, is likely to have a profound impact on many Quebec laws, particularly in the areas of language and economic policy.[19]

Concerns in Quebec about the Charter arise largely from its influence on the province's ability to determine its own cultural and language policies. Language policy has been a vital part of Quebec's political agenda since the Quiet Revolution, not in a narrow linguistic sense but in its connection to Quebec nationalism and culture. It is not difficult to see why the entrenchment of minority education language rights in section 23 raised concerns in Quebec. Its technical precision, which reads more like a statutory instrument than a constitutional provision, suggests that this clause was intended to challenge directly Quebec's Bill 101.

This inclusion of minority education language rights in the Charter has been interpreted by some in Quebec as a direct intervention into exclusive provincial autonomy over education as well as an assault on the ability of the Quebec government to promote cultural values through the primacy of the French language. Indeed, section 23 was intended to allow no legislative redress for Quebec.[20] The Supreme Court, in one of its earliest Charter cases, ruled that the provisions in Quebec's Bill 101 restricting access to English schools violated the right in section 23 to minority education language rights and constitutionally were not justified.[21] Conflicts between the Charter and policies intended to promote Quebec's cultural objectives have not been confined to school language instruction. In one of the most anxiously awaited Supreme Court decisions, *Ford v. Quebec (Attorney General)* the Court, in an unsigned judgment, ruled that Quebec legislation which required public signs, commercial advertising, and firms' names be in French only was an unjustified restriction on the constitutional guarantee of freedom of expression.[22]

Based on these decisions in which rights-based claims have provided the justification for setting aside aspects of Quebec's cultural policy, it is understandable why the Charter is seen by many in Quebec as frustrating the ability of the Quebec state to promote cultural policies. Since policies affecting education and commercial practices are within provincial jurisdiction, the Charter is undermining the federalism principle of provincial autonomy over local matters. However, while there is no denying that the Charter has constrained Quebec's ability to control its language policy, it may be premature to assume that on other matters the Charter will undermine substantially the federalism principle.

Much of the rationale for federalism in a culturally diverse nation such as Canada has been to allow provinces to promote community or local preferences rather than national perspectives. The Charter has neither superseded federalism nor altered its logic. To conclude that provincial-based diversities historically authorized by federalism are now precluded by the Charter dismisses the potential for a federalist interpretation of the Charter – which recognizes legitimate provincial differences both in the priorities that are attached to conflicting values and in the configuration of how legislative objectives are reconciled with protected rights.

SUPREME COURT AND CHARTER/ FEDERALISM JURISPRUDENCE

Federal laws have been struck down more often than provincial ones.[23] The Supreme Court has indicated a greater sensitivity to the concerns of the provinces to address their problems in different ways than may have been anticipated. This has occurred both in the interpretation of substantive rights and also in the assessment of whether legislative objectives impose reasonable limits on protected rights. At both stages the Supreme Court has been receptive to arguments that the Charter should not be interpreted in a manner that disregards federalism.

The first indication that members of the Court were sympathetic to federalism concerns arose in *R.* v. *Edwards Books.* A majority of the Court held that when attempting to reconcile the legislation with protected rights, there is no constitutional obligation on a province to adopt the same legislative arrangement used elsewhere. This is because these choices require an in-depth knowledge of all circumstances and are choices that must be made by the particular legislature in question: "The simple fact is that what may work effectively in one province (or in a part of it) may simply not work in another without unduly interfering with the legislative scheme."[24]

The Court has rejected arguments that province-based differences constitute an abridgement of equality rights in three cases. In two the issue was whether provinces can administer federal laws in diverse ways, while the third involved the question of whether differences between provincial and federal legislation on a similar issue infringes equality.

The first of these equality-based challenges was *R.* v. *Turpin* in which an accused, charged with murder, argued that different interpretations by provinces of the federal Criminal Code violate the Charter. The code provides that for certain indictable offences an accused in all provinces but Alberta shall be tried by a court composed of a judge and jury. In this case Turpin, who preferred to be tried by a judge alone but who lived in Ontario and therefore was not eligible, argued that this distinction violated equality. The unanimous decision held that this difference in treatment did not constitute a violation of equality.

The Court has interpreted equality in two stages: the first is to determine whether an individual has been denied equality before the law, and the second is to assess whether this denial results in discrimination. Discrimination arises, in the Court's view, when distinctions are made for reasons based on the enumerated grounds in section 15 –

race, national or ethnic origin, colour, religion, sex, age, or mental or
physical disability, or analogous categories. The distinction in this case,
the Court held, could not be considered discrimination.[25]

A second challenge based on the different applications of federal
legislation, *R. v. S.(S.)*, involved the Young Offenders Act which allows
provinces to designate "alternative measures" to deal with a young person alleged to have committed an offence instead of judicial proceedings under the act. At issue was Ontario's decision not to designate
alternatives. In rejecting the argument that equality was denied because of the different treatments between provinces the Court, in an
unanimous judgment, offered its most explicit statement on the need
to recognize and protect province-based diversities in a federal system.
In arguing that differential applications of federal law in provinces can
be a legitimate means of promoting and advancing the values of a federal system, the Court warned that to assume that interprovincial
distinctions constitute discrimination for equality purposes would undermine seriously the federal system.[26] It would "potentially open to
Charter scrutiny every jurisdictionally permissible exercise of power by
a province, solely on the basis that it creates a distinction in how individuals are treated in different provinces."[27] The Court elaborated on
the tension between federalism and the Charter and indicated it would
be reticent to interpret the Charter in a manner that is not cognizant
of the diversities authorized by federalism:

Obviously, the federal system of government itself demands that the values underlying s. 15(1) cannot be given unlimited scope. The division of powers not
only permits differential treatment based upon province of residence, it man-
dates and encourages geographical distinction. There can be no question,
then, that unequal treatment which stems solely from the exercise, by provincial legislatures, of their legitimate jurisdictional powers cannot be the subject
of a s. 15(1) challenge on the basis only that it creates distinctions based upon
province of residence ... To find otherwise would be to completely undermine
the value of diversity which is at the foundation of the division of powers.[28]

The most recent defence of federalism in Charter review is the *Haig*
case which questioned whether the absence in federal referendum
legislation of provisions to respond to the different residency requirements for the Quebec referendum, which had the effect of disenfran-
chising newcomers to Quebec from elsewhere in Canada, violated
freedom of expression, the right to vote and equality. Both the federal
and Quebec referendums were held 26 October 1992 and put to the
electorate identical questions about approval of the Charlottetown Accord. On enumeration day for the federal referendum Mr Haig was no

longer a resident in Ontario, but having lived in Quebec for less than six months did not meet Quebec's eligibility requirements. As a result he was not enumerated and could not vote.

At issue was whether the Charter extends an entitlement to vote even if one does not meet the enumeration requirements of either the federal or Quebec referendum.[29] The claim before the Court was that the Charter litigant should not have lost his residence status for the purpose of voting in the federal referendum until he had qualified as an elector in Quebec. The Court rejected this claim on two grounds: the right to vote in section 3 is limited to the elections of provincial and federal representatives and does not extend to a referendum[30]; and this interpretation would undermine provincial autonomy and the federalism principle.

The appellants are asking the Court to conclude that ordinary residence under the *Referendum Act* (Canada) cannot be lost until one is entitled to vote under the *Referendum Act* (Quebec) ... Such a conclusion would strike a blow at the autonomy and independence of legislative bodies in a federal system. It is clear that, carried in different settings, such an interpretative approach would have incredible and untenable consequences.[31]

The Court not only rejected the claim that a federal referendum should contain provisions to enumerate individuals in provinces where they do not meet a province's eligibility criteria but also held that a federal referendum should be national in scope and apply to all provinces. The Court argued that, unlike national elections, a referendum is a consultative process that does not have to be held in all jurisdictions.[32] In coming to this conclusion, the majority opinion disagreed with the suggestion, implicit in the claim of a national referendum, that the federal government "allowed" Quebec to administer part of what really was a "national" referendum. Haig had claimed that "the differential application of federal law to the provinces can only be tolerated if it is 'legitimate' and advances the values of a federal system." In his view, the decision to hold a referendum in only nine provinces did not advance these values. To this claim the Court replied:

Though the federal government may well have taken note of the results of the Quebec referendum, it would be unfounded in law to suggest that the federal government "allowed" Quebec to administer part of what was really a "national" referendum. Quebec did not need the authorization of the federal government to hold its referendum, and the Quebec referendum legislation was not within federal control or authority. Had the federal government wished to hold a "national" referendum, it could have included Quebec in the proclamation. Though it had every right to do so, it chose not to, as it also had the right to do.[33]

While the previous federalism cases considered provincial differences in administering federal law, the Court implied in *Haig* that this principle is also applicable to differences between federal and provincial laws. It indicated that the mere fact of such differences does not constitute a violation of equality. To presume otherwise would undermine the division of powers in the federal system: "Section 15(1) of the Charter, while prohibiting discrimination, does not alter the division of powers between governments."[34]

One exception to the Court's willingness to allow for provincial diversity is the *Morgentaler* decision.[35] The Court ruled that the federal abortion law, section 251 of the Criminal Code, which prohibited the procurement or performance of an abortion without prior approval from a therapeutic abortion committee at an accredited hospital, violated the principles of fundamental justice in section 7. The majority opinion was that the procedure required to obtain approval for a legal abortion imposed undue burdens on women that resulted in a danger to health. The decision touched on the issue of provincial diversity. The then Chief Justice, Brian Dickson, who wrote one of the three separate judgments on the majority side, referred to an earlier decision in which Justice La Forest had urged the Court to ensure that provinces are given sufficient opportunity to make choices regarding the type of administrative structure that will suit their needs unless the provincial structure itself is "so manifestly unfair, having regard to the decisions it is called upon to make, as to violate the principles of *fundamental* justice."[36] The abortion policy, in the opinion of Dickson, is precisely the kind of arrangement that contradicts the principles of fundamental justice. His difficulty in allowing for provincial diversity is that the differences within and between provinces in providing for therapeutic abortions ensures that many women may not be able to have access to the medical procedures necessary for their health.

The structure [of the abortion law] – the system regulating access to therapeutic abortions – is manifestly unfair. It contains so many potential barriers to its own operating that the defence [to criminal prosecution] it creates will in many circumstances be practically unavailable to women who would prima facie qualify for the defence, or at least would force such women to travel great distances in order to benefit from a defence that is held out to be generally available.[37]

The majority's rejection of varying levels of access to therapeutic abortions is seen as contradictory to the intent of the 1969 law which, as Christopher Manfredi argues, responded to a complex legislative objective, to liberalize access to abortion in a manner that would allow local authorities to control access to ensure that the policy accords with a community's moral views.[38] Local autonomy was implicitly recognized in the law's failure to define health or require that all hospitals establish therapeutic abortion committees, and by leaving enforcement of section 251 to the provinces. While these aspects of the legislation "virtually guaranteed unequal access to abortions both among and within provinces"[39] Manfredi argues that the Court's decision to nullify the procedural scheme of section 251 was tantamount to the Court rejecting local diversity as a legitimate policy objective in the application of a national abortion policy.[40]

Four of the five preceding cases provide compelling reasons to question assumptions that Charter jurisprudence will necessarily result in uniform interpretations of rights that are insensitive to regional differences. While this chapter is not arguing that the Charter imposes no constraint on the provinces' capacity to promote values rooted in community values, customs, or culture, the jurisprudence provides strong indication that the Court is sympathetic to concerns that provinces be given some latitude to enact different policies or to administer federal policies in different ways. In *Morgentaler*, where the Court disallowed provincial diversity in the administration of federal policy, it merely expressed a qualification on provinces' abilities to differ in how they administer a federal law: in other words, that local, community, or provincial standards do not impose a threat to the principles of fundamental justice.

The Charter poses the greatest constraint on provincial autonomy when legislation is in direct conflict with a protected right that is specific in its definition. This was the case in the conflict between Quebec's Bill 101 and the minority education language rights of section 23 of the Charter. However, the majority of protected rights are stated in vague and abstract terms. Therefore the constraint on Quebec's capacity to determine school language instruction policy should not serve as the basis for a general proposition that the pursuit of cultural objectives or community values by provinces will inevitably be vetoed by the Charter.

The remainder of this chapter will argue that the structure of the Charter should signal caution to those who claim, in the absence of more jurisprudence, that the Charter will inevitably undermine federalism by promoting the homogenization of Canadian public policy.

LIMITATION CLAUSE OF SECTION 1

For reasons discussed earlier, many find it difficult to reconcile conceptually the ideas of protecting rights but of allowing for limits on them, or entrenching rights but interpreting them in a federalism context. This difficulty has been attributed, in part, to the tendency to think of the Charter as ushering in a completely new political regime, one characterized by the primacy of rights over limits and principles over policies.[41] The view that rights should be paramount to all other policy values has obvious implications for federalism. It denies the legitimacy of provinces promoting community or cultural objectives if these affect adversely protected individual rights.

But the Charter should and need not be interpreted from the perspective that individual rights are the only values that are important in Canada. An expansive interpretation of section 1 would allow Parliament and the provincial legislatures to promote, where justified, values other than those specifically enumerated in the Charter. This would enrich the Charter by embracing collective values that, like individual rights, are relevant to Canadian conceptions of a just and democratic society yet are not adequately captured by the Charter's highly individualist language.

This interpretation of section 1 would not only help expand the scope and depth of the Charter but would help reconcile protected rights with a federal system. The Charter should be seen not as an exhaustive statement of protected rights but as the framework for fundamental values in Canada that can be amplified where legislatures are able to convince courts that the non-enumerated values they wish to promote are consistent with a free and democratic society and do not unduly impair protected rights. Thus, depending on the justification of these objectives, the constitution could embrace and protect non-enumerated values that reflect a collective, cultural, or community orientation. An interpretation of section 1 that recognizes the legitimacy of provincial differences, where these are not manifestly unfair, would also allow provinces to experiment with how policies are designed and administered to better reflect the needs and wishes of provincial populations. This idea of giving to the provinces local control over local affairs is a vital part of the justification for federalism in a nation as large and diverse as Canada.

LEGISLATIVE OVERRIDE OF SECTION 33

Like the limitation clause of section 1, the legislative override has generated divergent responses as to the appropriate relationship between individual rights and community values. It has raised questions of whether enumerated rights should at all times be given priority over non-enumerated values. From a federalism perspective, the debate is clear. Can provinces promote policies that have a differential effect on protected rights than other provinces? And can provinces promote collective values that may adversely affect protected rights?

Outside of Quebec, the override has been used only once.[42] In protest of the constitutional changes of 1982 that brought Canadians the Charter and were ratified despite Quebec's lack of assent, the Parti Québécois introduced legislation to systematically enact the legislative override of section 33 in all provincial legislation. This practice ended under the Liberal regime of Robert Bourassa. Although the blanket use of the override in Quebec did result in the practice being challenged,[43] the systematic use of the override did not evoke widespread public condemnation. The use of the override by the Bourassa government in 1988 to protect its signs law policy, however did stir up public response. More than any other issue, the question of whether the promotion of collective cultural goals in Quebec can be given primacy over specified rights has polarized opinions.

Although some analysts remain critical of the limitation clause, their concerns have been placated to some extent by changes to its earlier versions to ensure that the government bears the burden for demonstrating the justification of a limit. However, critics have not similarly warmed to section 33. The legislative override continues to be characterized as being incompatible with entrenched rights. While many predicted that the popularity of the Charter and public sentiment would ensure that it would be difficult for legislatures to use the override, the language of rights has so captivated our public discourse that section 33 has now, except for the francophone majority in Quebec, generally assumed the mantle of being constitutionally illegitimate. This became particularly clear following Quebec's decision to enact the legislative override, in response to the Supreme Court's decision that its signs law policy violates the Charter, in order to exempt new legislation from potential judicial review.

This decision, particularly at a time when the proposed Meech Lake amendments dominated the national constitutional agenda, reinforced criticisms of the distinct society clause in the failed Meech Lake constitutional reforms. While rarely analysed in conjunction with each other,[44] the distinct society clause and legislative override were intricately related, particularly in the context of how the Quebec government views its political responsibilities for promoting French culture in light of the Charter.

Critics of the distinct society clause argued that the clause prescribed a shift away from the pan-Canadian model and represented a turning away from our newly enacted Charter regime. By failing to provide explicitly for the Charter's exemption from the distinct society clause, they feared that the clause would undermine equality and minority language rights and would remodify the political system to the extent that some decisions about limiting rights, particularly in Quebec, would effectively remain in the hands of politicians.[45]

The distinct society clause became even more controversial when it became clear that Premier Bourassa regarded it in a similar light as he did section 33 – as a way of accommodating and promoting Quebec culture despite the protected rights in the Charter. Bourassa suggested that had the distinct society clause and the Meech Lake Accord been ratified, the use of the override would not have been necessary.[46] Bourassa's statement suggests one of two things: that the Court might have decided the signs language case differently in light of the distinct society provision; or that he would have been justified in enacting the override to redress what his government considered an inappropriate interpretation of the relationship between Quebec's signs laws and the distinct society clause. Either suggestion is incompatible with many Canadians' views, particularly outside Quebec. Bourassa's explanation and his subsequent statement about the need for collective values to prevail in this instance gave ammunition to those who had argued that the distinct society clause, like the override, is inconsistent with a Charter because it could be used to subordinate protected rights.

When two fundamental values clash, someone has to make a choice, and find a balance between both. An unavoidable arbitration has to take place. Anywhere else in North America, the arbitration would have been made in favour of individual rights ...

At the end, when a choice had to be made between individual rights and collective rights, I arbitrated in favour of collective rights, by agreeing to invoke the notwithstanding clause.

... I am the only head of government in North America who had the moral right to follow this course, because I am, in North America, the only political leader of a community which is a small minority.

Who can better, and who has more of a duty to protect and promote the French culture if not the Premier of Quebec? ... I chose to do what seemed to me to be vital for the survival of our community.[47]

The reaction of many of the political proponents of Meech Lake was immediate and pronounced. The federal Progressive Conservative government cautiously condemned Quebec's decision to use the override, suggesting that the legislation subverts fundamental rights,[48] while the Liberal opposition demanded an immediate first ministers conference.[49] The most significant reaction in terms of the future of the Meech Lake amendments came from then Manitoba premier, Gary Filmon, who abruptly withdrew his minority government's support for the accord in response to Bourassa's signs law.[50] Labelling Bourassa's use of the override a national tragedy, Filmon suspended debate on the constitutional amendment to protest Quebec's new signs legislation. Filmon had introduced a resolution supporting the accord days before Bourassa's decision and had voiced support for the Meech Lake proposal.[51]

The use of the override also provoked public reaction outside Quebec. Tension between French-speaking Quebec and English-speaking Canada goes a long way towards explaining the overwhelming critical public response levied at Bourassa's use of the override. With the Charter, critics could express their dislike for Quebec's language policies in the powerful rhetoric of rights. They could, as Roger Gibbins suggests, "wrap themselves in the flag of the Charter and come charging forward in defence of universal human rights."[52] But there is more to the explanation than longstanding grievances based on ethnic, language, and regional factors. The answer also lies in how the relationship between entrenched rights and limits is viewed by the academics, the media, politicians, and the public at large.

The public debate after Bourassa's use of the override renewed suggestions that the Charter is insufficient as long as it contains the override.[53] [Underlying these concerns is the belief that protected rights are too important to be subject to the discretionary decisions of political leaders who may wish to promote the values of a community or legislative majority that undermine individual rights.]The debate has also signalled fundamental disagreement about the importance of the right to expression in the signs law issue. One view is that the ability to advertise in one's preferred language is a vital aspect of free speech. It relates to one's identity and autonomy and is an essential condition of mobility so that an individual can be free to live and establish a business anywhere in the country. Therefore, this right should not be circumscribed for any reason. A second perspective is that the right to advertise is not a core aspect of speech in that it does not relate to the ability to express opinions on political and social issues. Given the importance of protecting and promoting Quebec's culture, the right to advertise can justifiably be limited. Further, the Charter is not generally concerned with economic issues; organized labour has not been granted economic rights and therefore business interests should not be protected under the Charter.

The public and political debates have emphasized the first view with little regard for the second. Quebec's decision to use the override was portrayed in the rest of Canada as a threat to fundamental rights. It was seen as an unwelcome and residual element of parliamentary supremacy and was deemed illegitimate because it contradicts the belief that the virtue of entrenched rights lies in the fact that decisions about limiting rights are removed from the political process. Peter Russell has stated:

In the hue and cry which then arose outside Quebec we could hear how the rhetoric of constitutional rights invests political discourse with a deep sense of moral rectitude ... There was no need to give any heed to French Quebecers' beliefs about what was necessary for the survival of their culture. Clifford Lincoln's words, "Rights are rights and will always be rights," brought tears to his own and to English Canada's eyes. Freedom to advertise in the language of one's choice was now elevated to the status of a fundamental human right that must override any other human right or social interest. The Meech Lake Accord must die because its recognition of Quebec's distinct culture posed too severe a threat to fundamental rights.[54]

What is interesting about differences in opinion in the legitimacy of sections 1 and 33 is that conceptually the two clauses serve similar purposes. This might seem a strange statement; rather than being viewed as inconsistent with entrenched rights, the override should be viewed as a similar, although more extreme, form of limiting protected rights. Just as limitations on protected rights may be justified to pursue important democratic objectives, the override can similarly be considered as a way of conferring constitutional protection on collective or non-enumerated values. The difference between the two clauses falls primarily in how justification of these policies is assessed. While courts evaluate the justification of policies that pursue collective or non-enumerated values under section 1, the public scrutinizes the merits of objectives enacted through the use of section 33. The override requires renewal in five years to ensure an opportunity for public scrutiny in an election. Some who defend the override have argued persuasively that, although the concept is itself consistent with entrenched rights, it should be more difficult to use. The threshold for legislative approval should be higher, the override should not be used pre-emptively before the Court has ruled on the issue of whether the impugned legislation is a reasonable limit on a protected right, and public consultation should occur whenever it is used.[55]

Just as care must be taken when reviewing legislative decisions under section 1 to ensure that community or general welfare values do not unduly transgress important fundamental rights and freedoms, so the same concern exists for the override. The justification of the override should not be to allow legislative majority preferences to veto protected rights but rather to preserve the capacity of the public, through debate within and beyond its representative institutions, to make difficult decisions about the priorities that should be attached to conflicting values. Occasionally the justification may be to reverse a judicial decision, but this should happen only after the Supreme Court has ruled on the dispute under section 1. Only when a policy has been pursued in the course of meaningful and rigorous debate about its justification and effects on protected rights should there be such a reversal. The importance of debate is not to validate the demands and preferences of a legislative majority or community but to contribute to, reflect on, and evaluate critically legislative obligations under the Charter and to assess whether decisions that impose limits on protected rights are justified.

The lack of public debate prior to the use of the override by Bourassa may have contributed to the overwhelmingly critical response this action received. Bourassa chose to invoke the override as a pre-emptive measure rather than encourage debate in the National Assembly on whether the legislation represented a reasonable limit under section 1. In the context of Bill 178 and the role it played in the Meech Lake debate, it is ironic that the constitutional validity of the signs policy may not have required the override.

The Supreme Court's ruling in the *Ford* case, which found the policy an unreasonable limit on freedom of expression, was based on the province's earlier unilingual policy and not on Bill 178. Far from being an unqualified victory for the primacy of the Charter over federalism, the Court's decision was receptive to federalism concerns. In making its decision, the Court did not find that the objective itself was unreasonable. In fact, it went a long way towards reading a distinct society interpretation into the limitation clause. The Court agreed with the Quebec government's claim that a rational and justifiable legislative response to the survival of the French culture was the protection of the French language to assure the "reality of Quebec society is communicated through the 'visage linguistique'." This approach extended section 1 protection to the collective and cultural values promoted by the Quebec government even though these values are not readily identifiable in the specific enumerated sections of the Charter.

What troubled the Court, however, was the means by which the policy objective was sought. In the Court's view, while the Quebec government's objective was a serious and legitimate one, the requirement of French only was unjustified. It held that the Quebec attorney general did not demonstrate why the policy requires the exclusive use of the French language. The Court speculated about alternative forms of the legislation that would impose a less severe restriction on the freedom to advertise in other language and indicated that two alternative means would be to require the predominant display of the French language or the requirement that French be in addition to any other language.[56]

One could argue that Quebec's policy under Bill 178, which required that public signs be in French only on the outside of stores while allowing for the use of other languages inside stores, might be interpreted by the Court as a reasonable attempt to ensure that the promotion of the policy objective did not impose an overly severe restriction on freedom of expression. Given the Court's indication in *Ford* that the problem with the legislation was not its objective but its failure to accommodate any use of advertising other than French, there is reason to speculate that the Court might have ruled that the signs policy of Bill 178 imposed a reasonable limit on freedom of expression. Arguably, the inside/outside distinction in Quebec's policy is consistent with the Court's own suggestion that an acceptable approach would require the predominant display of the French language.

Quebec, however, chose to use the override pre-emptively rather than to argue the merits of the legislation under section 1. In doing so it encouraged claims that the province was disregarding the protected rights in the Charter. The context of the constitutional debate at the time, in which Bourassa was under pressure within his own province to demonstrate that the proposed constitutional reforms went far enough, helps to explain why the premier chose to use the override. It served to bolster his claim that the distinct society clause, when combined with the override, would allow Quebec to promote its cultural policies despite the emphasis in the Charter on individual rights. Further, given pressures from nationalists, Bourassa would understandably have been reluctant to give the appearance of being uncertain about the province's legal capacity to promote its signs law policy by waiting for a renewed Charter challenge and the opportunity to argue that the policy imposed a reasonable limit on speech.

OVERVIEW: ENTRENCHED RIGHTS
AND FEDERALISM

It is difficult to discern just from reading the Canadian Charter of Rights and Freedoms and the American Bill of Rights the extent to which protected rights will undermine provincial and state autonomy by encouraging the homogenization of public policies. What is significant of the American experience is that judicial discretion, rather than the structure of the constitution, has been the most important factor in determining to what extent entrenched rights at the national level will undermine the autonomy of sub-national units. While the Bill of Rights was intended to apply only to the federal government, judicial discretion has resulted in the widespread application of many of its detailed provisions to the states. One implication of judicial discretion is that attitudes and principles about the relationship between federalism and rights can vary with changes in the composition of the Supreme Court, particularly with changes in who is the Chief Justice. Many of the important judicial decisions of the Warren Court which expanded upon the incorporation doctrine were close decisions, and wholesale changes in the people appointed to the Supreme Court are not necessary to produce substantially different outcomes. This was evident in decisions of the Burger Court to reject a more centralizing role for the Court to scrutinize the constitutionality of state policies. It did this by tightening access to federal courts for litigants wanting relief for alleged violations of the Bill of Rights at the state level.

While many of the rights in the Charter can be distinguished from those in the United States, particularly in the inclusion in the Charter of association and group rights, the most important differences are the explicit recognition of limits on protected rights. The Bill of Rights has no institutional or theoretical equivalent for the limitation clause of section 1 and the override of section 33. Questions that arise in light of the American experience are: Will the limitation and override clauses make a difference in terms of accommodating community or province-based values and priorities? Or is judicial discretion the most significant factor in determining the extent to which provincial autonomy is insulated from the homogenizing effects of entrenched rights?

It is difficult at this early stage to provide an authoritative answer to this question. Only a small Charter-federalism jurisprudence exists, and judicial and political attitudes on sections 1 and 33 are still evolving. So a speculative response will have to suffice. It is difficult to discount the potential of these two clauses in accommodating interprovincial differences. The legislative override of section 33 clearly allows for the most direct way of promoting the community or collective values of federalism under the Charter. However, the perceived lack of legitimacy for the clause, particularly outside Quebec, has meant that political leaders are reticent to invoke it. One consequence of the differences of opinion on its appropriateness might be that Canada will follow two paths in reconciling community values with protected rights: one in Quebec, with a greater willingness to use the override to protect values distinctive to it, and a different one in the rest of Canada, where the override will either not be used or will be invoked only on rare occasions after careful consideration of whether the benefits exceed the political costs.

In light of the legitimacy problems associated with section 33, the more systematic way that provincial legislatures will likely promote community or collective preferences that conflict with protected rights is to argue that the policy is justified under section 1. To understand the potential of section 1 in accommodating federalism values it is important to consider both the uniqueness of the clause and also the American lessons about the significance of judicial discretion. Such discretion in the United States was evident both in decisions to apply the Bill of Rights to govern state policies and in judgments about access to federal tribunals to review alleged state breaches, and the significance of judicial discretion for federalism in Canada lies, principally, in how the Court interprets section 1.

The Supreme Court of Canada has indicated that section 1 provides a unique context for the evaluation of the justification of legislative policies that conflict with protected rights. This context, it has held, differentiates assessments of what might be reasonable in Canada from other jurisdictions. As then Chief Justice Brian Dickson held:

Section 1 has no equivalent in the United States ... Of course, American experience should never be rejected simply because the *Charter* contains a balancing provision, for it is well known that American courts have fashioned compromises between conflicting interests despite what appears to be the absolute guarantee of constitutional rights. Where s. 1 operates to accentuate a uniquely Canadian vision of a free and democratic society, however, we must not hesitate to depart from the path taken in the United States. Far from requiring a less solicitous protection of *Charter* rights and freedoms, such independence of vision protects these rights and freedoms in a different way.[57]

Justice Wilson similarly argued that section 1 differentiates Canada from the United States because it invites assessments of reasonableness unique to Canadian social, cultural, and political values:

The uniqueness of the Canadian Charter of Rights and Freedoms flows not only from the distinctive structure of the Charter as compared to the American Bill of Rights but also from the special features of the Canadian cultural, historical, social and political tradition. Thus ... the pre-eminent role of s. 1 of our Charter which differentiates our constitution from that of our American neighbours.[58]

These statements suggest a domestic element to the reasonableness assessment that is inherent in judicial review of entrenched rights. The question for the Court is not necessarily what have other countries accepted as reasonable legislative policies, in light of protected rights. Rather, it is what is a reasonable limit in Canada? The values integral to a free and democratic society are not necessarily universal in their dimension; as Brian Dickson suggested in his statement quoted above, they underlie a uniquely Canadian perspective.

Neither of these judicial statements refer explicitly to federalism in their discussion of section 1; nevertheless, a connection can be inferred. Federalism is an institutional response to the cultural, ethnic, and geographical diversities in Canada. It allows provinces to promote policies that reflect the priorities and values of their regional communities. Thus one can infer from these judicial pronouncements that part of the rationale for section 1's role in reflecting Canada's distinctive "cultural, historical, social and political tradition[s]" is the accommodation of province-based differences in how the Charter is interpreted.

While the uniqueness of the limitation clause could make a difference in terms of which values are constitutionally upheld because of its role in domesticating the issue of reasonable limits, the American lesson about the importance of judicial discretion cannot be ignored. The limitation clause establishes that a free and democratic society is the context for evaluating the reasonableness of impugned legislation. But it does not give courts further instruction on how to recognize which policies further these values or assess whether they have been carefully enough drafted. Further, the limitation clause is silent on the issue of whether the Charter commands a negative liberty interpretation or whether positive or affirmative state actions are justifiable limits on protected rights. Hence, section 1 gives judges extraordinary discretion to shape the Charter according to judicial views of what fundamentally contested values such as freedom and democracy should mean in Canada and what threshold representative institutions must meet to pursue policies that conflict with protected rights.

The importance of judicial discretion in determining what role section 1 will play in accommodating federalism values is underscored by the Supreme Court's reluctance to reject directly governmental claims that an impugned policy represents an objective sufficiently pressing to warrant limiting a protected right. This approach gives the provinces greater opportunities to pursue collective or community values than if the Court were to confine section 1 justification to those rights that are specifically enumerated in the Charter. The Court's decision in the signs law case of *Ford* is an important example of this flexibility. Although the outcome of *Ford* was that Quebec's signs law was an unreasonable limit on freedom of expression, the decision nevertheless reveals both the importance of judicial discretion and the relevance and legitimacy of federalism in resolving Charter conflicts. The decision in *Ford* confirms the potential importance of section 1 as a means of allowing provinces some latitude to pursue values that reflect their own particular priorities, provided that these policies are carefully drafted so as not to impair protected rights more than necessary and are not fundamentally incongruent with democratic values.

CONCLUSIONS

There is no disputing that the Charter conflicts with the territorial diversity authorized by federalism by imposing constraints on the capacity of provinces to promote community values based on their own set of priorities. However, it is premature to assume that the Charter will result in the homogenization of Canadian policies. The structure of the Charter provides strong incentives for the provinces to argue against a uniform or universal interpretation of how to reconcile individual with community values. The legislative override provides the most direct way for provinces to ensure the primacy of values that conflict with protected rights. But widespread hostility towards the legislative override clause, particularly outside Quebec, suggests that section 1 will be the more likely context for arguments that the Charter should accommodate territorial-based diversities.

While the Court has not encountered many cases where federalism questions arise directly, the small body of jurisprudence that addresses the relationship between the Charter and federalism should be viewed with cautious optimism by those who would argue against the assumption that the Charter presumes a singular interpretation of the Charter – one that transcends provincial differences. This does not mean that provinces should escape the requirement that they respect protected rights. Provinces have an obligation to justify why the values they pursue warrant constitutional protection and why alternative and less restrictive means have not been adopted.

It is too soon to predict how much latitude the Supreme Court will confer on provinces to pursue divergent priorities. This jurisprudence does suggest that provinces retain a measure of discretion to pursue policies that represent values not specifically enumerated, provided that they can justify these in democratic and reasonableness terms. It also suggests that provinces that choose to enact policies in a manner different from other jurisdictions or apply federal provisions differently do not risk, solely on the basis of difference, implicating equality rights.

Many are concerned that collective or community values, particularly in Quebec, are simply a way of promoting the preferences of legislative majorities over the rights of minorities that the Charter is intended to protect. Nevertheless, it is wrong to assume that Quebec, as the one province most willing to promote collective values, lacks respect for individual rights. Charles Taylor's reflections on our shared values, in which minimal divergences exist between French and non-French segments of Canada on what constitutes fundamental values,[59] is demonstrated by extensive survey research which found both in English and French Canada a high level of support for the fundamental values of political freedom, due process of law, and social equality.[60] As Peter Russell argues, "so far as civil liberties are concerned, Quebec is not a distinct society."[61]

There is one other reason for questioning the view that the Charter has fundamentally compromised federalism: this view implies that without a Charter provinces would be free of all rights-based constraints. Increased public sensitivity to equity issues and the plight of vulnerable groups in society suggest that it is a mistake to presume that the Charter represents the only constraint on provinces' capacity to pursue community values. Moreover, one cannot presume that without a Charter provinces would be free of all judicially imposed constraints in their pursuit of collective or community values. The Supreme Court's record in the 1950s reveals how, despite the constraints of parliamentary supremacy, many of the Supreme Court justices were willing to engage in creative means to set aside provincial legislation that seriously transgressed fundamental or core rights, even in the absence of a constitutional Charter.[62]

7 Conclusions

Although the Charter of Rights and Freedoms purports to *guarantee* rights, the symbolism implied in this word is unfortunate. Common sense dictates that rights cannot possibly be absolute. In a civilized society we can no more embrace the idea that liberty allows people to act in any manner they wish than we can give sanction to murder as a protected form of expression. Courts not only have to define and give scope to the Charter's vague provisions but must determine under section 1 when, under what circumstances, and for what reasons, rights can be limited.

The significance of section 1 goes well beyond the symbolic recognition that rights are not absolute. There is an element of danger to the limitation clause because of the possibility that it will be used to uphold policy objectives that do not warrant constitutional protection and that impose unnecessary or undue burdens on those whose rights are adversely affected. Nevertheless, the virtue of section 1 is its breadth and potential to expand the reach of the Charter to embrace fundamental values that were not anticipated by its drafters or that change over time.

The Charter establishes that a free and democratic society is the context for evaluating the reasonableness of impugned policies, but it provides no further guidelines on how reasonable limits are to be determined. In an attempt to give some structure to the task of resolving competing social values – a task the Supreme Court itself characterized shortly before the Charter was enacted as "arbitrary" and best left to elected representatives – the Court has decided that the section 1 standard for justifying limits on protected rights is not universal in its dimension but may accentuate a uniquely Canadian vision of a free and democratic society. But even with the domestication of reasonableness, questions about which values are integral to Canadian conceptions of freedom and democracy do not elicit obvious or uncontested answers from the Charter but require normative and philosophical inquiries.

The contested nature of a free and democratic society has encouraged the Court to give substantial weight to how representative institutions define these values. Since the Court developed its framework for evaluating the reasonableness of impugned policies, it has only once rejected a government claim that the policy it promotes represents a sufficiently important objective that warrants limiting protected rights. The section 1 task has focused almost exclusively on the question of whether these policies have been carefully enough designed to constitute a reasonable limit on protected rights.

However, reasonableness assessments pose even greater difficulties for courts. They presume an evaluation of the merits of impugned legislation in terms of how the policy was conceptualized and drafted, a task courts are ill-equipped to perform. Although the Court has established a number of guidelines from which to assess the reasonableness of impugned policies, these guidelines have not provided the basis for a coherent and consistent body of section 1 jurisprudence. Instead they have encouraged discretionary and ad hoc evaluations of the merits of policy which reflect normative views of liberty or institutional assumptions about the proper role of courts in a representative democracy. The problem is not that the Court has selected the wrong guidelines or has made mistakes in applying these. The difficulty is inherent in the requirement that courts assess the reasonableness of legislation and whether alternative or better legislative means were available. The complexity of policy development ensures that courts will often be uncertain about the question that underlies reasonableness inquiries: were better and less restrictive legislative means available?

This uncertainty has presented the Court with a fundamental dilemma. Given the discretionary nature of reasonableness inquiries, once the Supreme Court has accepted that the legislative objective is sufficiently important to impose limits on protected rights, should judges scrutinize the internal dynamics of a policy at the risk of second-guessing complex legislative decisions and potentially invalidating compelling objectives? Or should judges defer to governmental claims about the reasonableness of the impugned policy, at the risk of discouraging Parliament and the provincial legislatures from taking the responsibility of respecting protected rights as seriously as they should?

This dilemma and the Court's response to it raise serious democratic concerns. If the Court is uncertain about whether less restrictive legislative means are available and yet it nevertheless sets aside a compelling policy objective for not having been carefully enough drafted, its decision may unjustifiably frustrate the promotion of important public policies intended to help vulnerable individuals or groups or to promote the general welfare. If judges are unsure about how to evaluate the criteria they apply, the substitution of the collective judgment of elected representatives for their own discretionary judicial opinions compromises the democratic ideal of governing through discussion and debate.

On the other hand, if the Court upholds impugned legislation yet is uncertain about whether the limit imposed is reasonable, judicial deference could undermine the democratic ideal that rights be duly respected in the course of policy decisions. This concern may not necessarily be confined to the specific case in question but could become systemic if, because there is little risk that legislation will be nullified, legislatures do not routinely and rigorously evaluate the effects of policy choices on fundamental human rights.

In responding to this dilemma the Court has assumed a deferential posture in the realm of social policy. It has changed how it evaluates reasonableness. The requirement that legislatures place limits on protected rights only when these constitute minimal impairment to an affected right has devolved to the substantially lesser requirement that governments have a "reasonable basis" for making policy choices that conflict with protected rights. The Court is no longer inclined to ask whether less restrictive means are available, but instead whether the legislative choice is "reasonable" under the circumstances. This devolution in the reasonableness standard has greatly reduced the extent to which the Charter constrains the decisions of Parliament and the provincial legislatures, particularly in the realm of social policy.

The significance of the Court's relaxation of the reasonableness standard, when combined with its reluctance to disallow particular policy objectives themselves, is difficult to overstate. Parliament and the provincial legislatures have been able to exert considerable influence in determining not only which values warrant limiting protected rights but also whether impugned policies have been carefully enough designed to impose a reasonable limit. Contrary to prevailing opinion about the purpose of a Charter, they have helped define the very constraints that the Charter was intended to impose on them.

This development raises serious concerns about whether the Charter is effective in requiring that governments respect fundamental rights when making policy choices, a concern that the breadth of the limitation clause intensifies. What is particularly troubling about how Charter jurisprudence is evolving is that judicial deference does not seem to correspond with evidence, from legislative proceedings, that policy decisions are being discussed and assessed in terms of how they affect protected rights. The relative failure of representative institutions to require that governments justify their policy choices in rights-based terms shields from public and judicial purview evidence of what assumptions have influenced these policies, how rigorous they have been scrutinized, and whether less restrictive measures have been contemplated.

Although these concerns are serious, it may be premature to conclude that the limitation clause irreparably undermines the salutary benefits that arise when representative institutions are required to heed fundamental rights in their policy decisions. The entrenchment of fundamental rights and freedoms in the Charter underscores the difficult task of distinguishing between the legitimate sphere of state action and the protected sphere of human activity. Section 1 makes visible, but is not responsible for, this tension between rights and limits. Although the reference in the limitation clause to a free and democratic has expanded the range of values that can be upheld as justifiable limits on protected rights, courts would have to reconcile conflicting values regardless of whether the Charter included a different version of section 1 or contained no limitation clause.

The seriousness of the judicial dilemma of how to reconcile conflicting values and its implications for democracy leads me to conclude that contrary to conventional wisdom, the requirement of ensuring that legislative decisions are reasonable is not primarily the responsibility of the Supreme Court. Rather, Parliament and the provincial legislatures share this responsibility. Although interpreting the limitation clause has been a source of frustration for the Court, the very questions section 1 contemplates are precisely those that representative institutions should be asking themselves when scrutinizing policy proposals. The limitation clause, rather than being a blight on the Charter, has the potential to improve the quality of political decisions that impose limits on protected rights and to enrich the Charter by protecting compelling values that are not specifically enumerated.

The benefit of section 1 is that by framing debate specifically in terms of the tension between rights and limits, it has the potential to structure a positive and useful discourse about justifying policy choices under the Charter. Its dual purpose of both recognizing fundamental rights and yet allowing limits has encouraged an approach that asks both whether a right has been infringed and if so whether the limit is reasonable. This "yes ... but" approach reinforces the idea that what is required of a polity, particularly one that has entrenched rights, is to take the issue of limits on rights seriously: to scrutinize and evaluate, within and beyond representative institutions, the justification of policies that implicate protected rights and the merits of alternative measures.

The inclusion of an explicit limitation clause is more conducive to a rigorous and open debate about the merits and justification of policy choices than if the Charter was silent on the question of limitations. In the absence of an explicit limitation clause, the emphasis in debate would likely turn on the primacy or lack of rights. Without a limitation clause a rights claimant would be encouraged to frame his or her argument in terms of the primacy of rights. This language, which implies that rights act as trumps, would arrest rather than encourage further debate about whether the disputed policy was justified. Conversely, those resisting these claims who argue that no such right exists – a posture that assumes the justification of the policy where no right has been infringed. The difficulty with arguments based on the primacy or absence of rights is that the absolute nature of their assumptions deflects attention from the more pressing task of assessing and rebutting claims of whether the impugned policy is justified.

By establishing a free and democratic society as the framework for evaluating the justification of limits, section 1 provides the opportunity for representative institutions to debate the merits of non-enumerated values and their justification in light of their effects on protected individual rights. Although both individual and collective values are integral to Canadian conceptions of democracy, the latter are not adequately captured by the highly individualist language of the Charter. Section 1 can be interpreted in a manner that infuses the Charter with collective or community values where these are justified and yet cannot be easily captured by the specific language of the Charter. By recognizing the justification of collective or community values that do not compromise core rights or exact undue burdens on protected rights, section 1 enhances the Charter by expanding the range of fundamental values that can and should be subsumed under the Charter's protection.

Discussion within and beyond representative institutions to evaluate critically legislative proposals is a vital part of the democratic ideal of governing. Questions in legislative debates about why a policy is justified and whether alternative legislative means are available would put pressure on governments to justify their policy choices, invite contrary perspectives, and, where possible, incorporate alternative means that impose less severe restrictions on protected rights. Unlike courts, representative institutions have the necessary resources to assess the multiple dimensions of a complex social issue and the capacity to elicit expert opinion from those who have the policy expertise and analytical skills necessary to evaluate conflicting social science data and alternative policy options. The Court's contribution is not to scrutinize the merits of the particular legislative scheme but to evaluate the quality of how the legislative decision was made and to ensure that core rights have not been unduly compromised.

Although political debates where governments must justify the effects of policy proposals on protected rights would better expose their discriminating effects or possible unintended consequences, no political institution is infallible. Even where policy issues have been subject to rigorous debate, core rights may at times be compromised in the face of contradictory pressures and partisan disagreements. Courts are insulated from the pressures of electoral politics, federal-provincial conflicts, and national unity debates. They may therefore be better positioned than Parliament or the provincial legislatures to ensure that core rights are not neglected amidst pressures from other interests and claims which, in the heat of the legislative moment, may command more attention. The ideals of an active citizenry and governing through discussion and debate coexist, with some tension, with the ideal of respecting the normative values of the Charter. The constraints on legislatures imposed by the Charter are welcome and justified where legislation imposes an unreasonable limit on a core right or where legislation discriminates against or imposes an unfair burden on a particular individual or group.

However, where legislative records reveal that a policy has been the product of meaningful and deliberative debate about the worthiness of its objective and has been sensitively drafted, a judicial decision to nullify legislation may undermine the democratic ideal of governing through discussion and debate. Under these circumstances, unless the Court is relatively certain that shortcomings identified in debate had not been adequately rectified, or that the legislation restricts a core right or imposes a limit that is obviously excessive or unreasonable, little justification exists for judges to nullify these decisions.

By the same token, where legislative decisions have not been the product of careful deliberation about why the policy is justified, judicial deference may be neither appropriate nor consistent with democratic ideals. By refusing to accept the justification of impugned policies where rights' concerns have not been fully considered, the Court will provide an important incentive for representative institutions to pay more attention to the effects of policy choices on protected rights.

Notes

1 Keith Banting and Richard Simeon, "Federalism, Democracy and the Constitution," in Banting and Simeon, eds., *And No One Cheered: Federalism, Democracy and the Constitution Act* (Toronto: Methuen 1983), 21.

2 Donald Smiley, "A Dangerous Deed: The Constitution Act, 1982," in ibid., 89.

3 In addition to the limitation clause of s. 1, the Charter contemplates two other ways in which limits can be imposed on protected rights. First, the legislative override of s. 33 enables governments to impose temporary exemptions to the applicability of the Charter to legislation, with the exception of voting rights and guarantees of general elections, mobility rights, and minority language rights. Second, many of the specified rights in the Charter are accompanied by explicit qualifications which allow governments to pursue competing values. S. 15 proclaiming equality rights, for example, both specifies categories of prohibited discrimination and yet provides for exemptions if the law is intended to ameliorate the conditions of disadvantaged individuals or groups.

4 The term "protected rights" is used here intentionally instead of "Charter rights" to convey the idea that the circumstances protected by the Charter might be broader than the specific enumerated rights.

5 For a good discussion on limitations on rights in the American jurisprudence, see C. Edwin Baker, "Limitations on Basic Human Rights – A View from the United States," in Armand de Mestral, ed., *The Limitation of Human Rights in Comparative Constitutional Law,* (Cowansville, Quebec: Les Éditions Yvon Blais 1986), 76–102.

6 The override cannot be invoked for violations of rights under ss. 3–5 (democratic rights of citizens and requirements that legislatures sit regularly and not longer than five years), s. 6 (mobility rights), s. 23 (minority education language rights), and s. 28 (gender equality).

7 Berend Hovius and Robert Martin, "The Canadian Charter of Rights and Freedoms in the Supreme Court of Canada," *Canadian Bar Review* 61 (1983): 369.

8 Paul Bender, "Justifications for Limiting Constitutionally Guaranteed Rights and Freedoms: Some Remarks about the Proper Role of Section One of the Canadian Charter," *Manitoba Law Journal* 13 (1983): 666.

9 Peter H. Russell, "Political Purposes of the Canadian Charter," *Canadian Bar Review* 61 (1983): 30–54.

CHAPTER TWO

1 Pierre Elliott Trudeau, *A Canadian Charter of Human Rights* (Ottawa: Queen's Printer 1968).

2 Pierre Elliott Trudeau, *The Constitution and the People of Canada: An Approach to the Objectives of Confederation, the Rights of People and the Institutions of Government* (Ottawa: Queen's Printer 1969).

3 Pierre Elliott Trudeau, Constitutional Conference, first meeting, verbatim record (Ottawa: February 1968), 268–9.

4 Trudeau, *Canadian Charter of Human Rights*, 18.

5 Ibid., 16–17.

6 The desire to limit rights in an emergency situation followed the earlier precedent in which the War Measures Act was amended to provide that upon a proclamation of war duly approved by Parliament, nothing done under the act would be deemed to abridge the rights or freedoms in the Canadian Bill of Rights. Trudeau, *Constitution and the People of Canada*, 60.

7 The Bill of Rights was not a constitutional document but rather a federal statute that applied only to the federal government.

8 The interrelationship between constitutional renewal and the redistribution of powers was particularly evident in Quebec's proposition for a distribution of powers, which was intended to serve as a methodological framework for the entire process of constitutional revision. Canadian Intergovernmental Conference Secretariat, *The Constitutional Review 1968–1971: Secretary's Report, Canadian Intergovernmental Conference Secretariat* (Ottawa: Information Canada 1972), 68–72.

9 Ibid., 51–3, 483–4. The purpose of this sub-committee was to define the substance and scope of fundamental political rights, to explore the question of the guarantee or protection of rights through federal or provincial legislation, and to study the effects of clauses relative to due process. These constitutional sub-committees were characteristically staffed by fact-finding

technical groups which worked in specialized areas on behalf of either the continuing committee of officials or the committees of ministers. In the case of the Sub-committee on Fundamental Rights, it reported to a committee of ministers. Generally, the atmosphere at these meetings was considerably less political than meetings at other levels, particularly meetings of ministers.

10 Information obtained from author's interview with Mr Justice Barry Strayer, 7 December 1987, who was one of the senior federal officials involved in the process of constitutional renewal which began in 1968. Strayer, who was instrumental in drafting the limitation clause, served as an adviser to the Special Counsel on the Constitution when the 1968 Trudeau policy paper was developed. He was a director of the Constitutional Review section of the Privy Council from 1968 to 1974 and was assistant deputy minister of justice in public law from 1974 to 1983.

11 Canadian Intergovernmental Conference Secretariat, *Constitutional Review 1968–1971*, 126–7; interview with Barry Strayer, 7 December 1987.

12 The four western provinces commissioned a paper by Douglas Schmeiser, a legal academic, and relied frequently on his arguments that judicial review of entrenched rights is undemocratic, is prone to the personal values of judges, is ineffective, will lead to silly frivolous litigation and generate a "litigation syndrome," and will undermine the federal principle. Douglas Schmeiser, "Preliminary Study on Entrenchment of Fundamental rights and Judicial Review," paper commissioned by the provinces of British Columbia, Alberta, Saskatchewan, and Manitoba, 28 October 1969.

13 Harry Strom, Premier of Alberta, "Alberta's Position on Reports of Sub-Committees On Fundamental Rights and Judicial Review" (Federal-Provincial Conference of First Ministers on the Constitution, Ottawa, December 1968), 13.

14 Ibid., 13–14.

15 W.A.C. Bennett, Premier of British Columbia, "Opening Statement of the Province of British Columbia to the Constitutional Conference," Federal-Provincial Constitutional Conference of First Ministers on the Constitution, Ottawa, 10–12 February 1969, 7–8.

16 Canadian Intergovernmental Conference Secretariat, *The Constitutional Review 1968–1971*, 68.

17 In a briefing paper the Continuing Committee on the Constitution expressed concern that entrenched rights could conceivably conflict with collective concerns and urged that care must be taken to ensure that certain freedoms were not guaranteed to the extent that they could be used to violate other freedoms. For example, the committee suggested that free speech should not extend to the point that defamation of character cannot be prevented. The committee also expressed concern that criminal proceedings must not be unduly hampered by the entrenched rights;

otherwise citizens' rights to the protection of the law might be weakened. Continuing Committee of Officials on the Constitution, "A Briefing Paper on Discussions within the Continuing Committee of Officials," Ottawa, 12 December 1968, 41.

18 Ontario, "Propositions of the Government of Ontario," Brief submitted to the Continuing Committee of Officials on the Constitution, December 1968, 22.

19 A.A. Wishart, on behalf of the Ontario government, Constitutional Conference, Ottawa, 10–12 February 1969, verbatim transcript, 259–61.

20 Author's interview with Barry Strayer, 7 December 1987.

21 The agreement at Victoria provided that the proposed Charter would be reported to all eleven governments for consideration and that if its acceptance as a whole was communicated to the secretary of the constitutional conference by 28 June, eleven days after the conference concluded, each government would then take the further step of recommending the Charter to its respective legislative assemblies or Parliament. By 28 June all governments except Quebec and Saskatchewan had advised the secretary that the Charter was acceptable. Quebec had informed the secretary on 23 June that it could not recommend the Charter to its National Assembly because the clauses dealing with income security (articles 44–45) were not in keeping with the objectives of constitutional review. Moreover, Quebec would not guarantee that its answer would be different if the clauses were improved. In Saskatchewan there was a provincial election 23 June which produced a change of government. The deadline for agreement was extended so that premier-designate Allan Blakeney could select a cabinet and discuss the document. Saskatchewan never did report its position.

22 Canadian Intergovernmental Conference Secretariat, *Proposals on the Constitution 1971–1978* (Ottawa: Information Canada 1978), 68.

23 Author's interview with Barry Strayer, 7 December 1987.

24 The Special Joint Committee of the Senate and of the House of Commons on the Constitution of Canada, Final Report, 4th sess., 28th Parl., 1972, 21.

25 Roy Romanow, John Whyte, Howard Leeson, *Canada Notwithstanding: The Making of the Constitution 1976–1982* (Toronto: Carswell/Methuen 1984), 232–3.

26 Task Force on Canadian Unity, *A Future Together* (Ottawa: The Task Force 1979), 108. The task force's recommendation that protection of minority language rights be left to incremental provincial improvements did not satisfy federal officials who were intent on having language rights firmly entrenched in the constitution. Romanow et al., *Canada Notwithstanding*, 233–4.

27 Information obtained from author's interview with Fred Jordan, 19 November 1987. Jordan was one of the drafters of the 1981 charter. He was director of the Constitutional and International Law section in the Department

of Justice from 1972 to 1980 and senior counsel for the Constitutional Law section between 1980 and 1982.

28 Ibid.

29 Federal-Provincial Conference of First Ministers, *The Constitutional Amendment Bill: Text and Explanatory Notes* (Ottawa, 30 October – 1 November 1978).

30 Although some of the provincial regimes had changed in the past seven years, the three westernmost provinces, which had been among the most reluctant to support the limited entrenchment of rights in Victoria, had not changed their position. One of the provincial premiers, Peter Lougheed of Alberta, had been in office at the Victoria conference. Saskatchewan Premier Allan Blakeney, who was elected later, was one of the chief critics of entrenched rights during the late 1970s. In British Columbia, while the leadership of the Social Credit had changed since the Victoria conference, Premier Bill Bennett was no more supportive of entrenched rights in 1978 than his father's government had been. Moreover, provincial opposition to entrenched rights was strengthened by the 1977 Manitoba election of Sterling Lyon's Conservative government. Premier Lyon, as attorney general in the late 1960s, was a chief proponent of "legislative supremacy."

31 The federal government's strategy had been to enact Bill C-60 in two stages. The deadline for phase one was 1 July 1979. Aside from the charter, phase one had included the entrenchment of the Supreme Court of Canada and Senate Reform. See David Milne, *The New Canadian Constitution* (Toronto: James Lorimer & Company 1982), 44.

32 A Special Joint Committee of the Senate and of the House of Commons was established in June 1978, under co-chairs Maurice Lamontagne and Mark MacGuigan. The mandate of the committee was to report on government proposals related to the constitution. The principal matter before the committee was Bill C-60, *Constitutional Amendment Act*, 1978, 3rd Sess., 33rd Parl., 1977–78.

33 One of the strongest arguments against the limitation clause came from Professor Walter Tarnopolsky, who suggested that it would act as a substitute for s. 6 of the Bill of Rights. This section ensures that the rights can be limited by the invocation of the War Measures Act. The danger of this in Bill C-60, argued Tarnopolsky, was that while the War Measures Act requires a specific proclamation by government and is subject to the political constraints that accompany such a proclamation, the limitation clause in Bill C-60 would be operational at all times. Tarnopolsky suggested that the charter could be strengthened by narrowing the construction of the clause and specifying that limitations could only apply to the fundamental rights and freedoms and not to the individual legal rights. Special Joint Committee of the Senate and of the House of Commons on the Constitution, hearings, 12 September 1978 (Ottawa: Queen's Printer 1978), 12:17–18, 12:25.

See also the testimony of Professor Ed Ratushny who, in suggesting that the limitation clause be eliminated, argued that in its absence rights would not be interpreted in unqualified terms. Ibid., 20 September 1978, 16:13.

34 Special Joint Committee of the Senate and of the House of Commons on the Constitution of Canada, Second Report to Parliament (Ottawa: Queen's Printer 1978), 10 October 1978, 20:14.

35 The limitations on rights envisaged in Bill C-60 were discussed in a paper on constitutional reform by Justice Minister Otto Lang. The justifiable limits, he indicated, were those in the interests of public safety or health, the peace and security of the public, and the rights and freedoms of others. Lang suggested that these limits were generally recognized by courts "when properly circumscribing any individual right." The significance of the charter, however, is that these restrictions would be tested by the courts to determine if they were valid in each case in terms of being justified on one of the bases specified. Lang's position clearly assumed that governments would have to confine limitations to the grounds specified and that the courts would have the final say on whether the limits were reasonable. Otto Lang, "Constitutional Reform: Canadian Charter of Rights and Freedoms, Federal-Provincial Conference of First Ministers" (Ottawa, 30 October–1 November 1978), 16.

36 A second recommendation was that legal rights should not be subject to limitations, even in times of war. Joint Committee of the Senate and of the House of Commons on the Constitution, Second Report to Parliament, 10 October 1978, 20:14.

37 The Quebec government ordered a referendum, to be held on 20 May 1980, involving a quest for a mandate to negotiate "a new agreement with the rest of Canada, based on the equality of nations." There was a promise of a second referendum on the actual issue of sovereignty. In the referendum, 59.56 per cent of voters voted no, rejecting the proposal for negotiation, while 40.44 per cent registered yes. Quebec, Directeur général des élections du Québec, *Rapport des Résultats Officiels du Scrutin: Référendum du 20 Mai 1980* (Quebec: Directeur général des élections du Québec 1980).

38 See, for instance, Romanow et al., *Canada Notwithstanding*, 60–3 and 101–3.

39 In the early summer of 1980 the Continuing Committee of First Ministers on the Constitution met and considered a discussion draft of the charter which, once again, eliminated the general qualifying clause altogether. (See Meeting of the Continuing Committee Montreal, 8–11 July 1980, 830–81/27.) When the draft was published the proposal was roundly criticized because limitation clauses were placed in every section of the charter. Rights would no sooner be granted than they would be immediately qualified. The optimism of June had lapsed by the end of summer as constitutional negotiations collapsed. While there was mutual commitment from all provinces but Quebec that renewal was necessary, there was no consen-

sus on what reforms were necessary. Trudeau's view of a strong central government and constitutionally entrenched rights was not compatible with a number of the provinces' desire for greater autonomy, more limited federal intervention, and the retention of parliamentary supremacy. Moreover, the federalist victory in the Quebec referendum meant that the provinces could afford to feel complacent about the Quebec problem. The premiers increasingly came to view constitutional renewal as a means of achieving solutions to their own regional grievances. The agenda pursued turned into a potpourri of federal and provincial interests without any obvious common thread to link the competing visions of how Canada should be governed. See Milne, *New Canadian Constitution*, 48.

40 Author's interview with Barry Strayer, 7 December 1987.

41 "Revised Discussion Draft of September 3, 1980 – *The Canadian Charter of Rights and Freedoms*" (Federal-Provincial Conference of First Ministers on the Constitution, Ottawa, 8–12 September 1980).

42 Author's interview with Barry Strayer, 7 December 1987.

43 Alberta Premier Peter Lougheed had first proposed the inclusion of a legislative override in 1979.

44 Author's interview with Fred Jordan, 19 November 1987.

45 Roger Tassé, deputy minister of justice, Special Joint Committee of the Senate and of the House of Commons on the Constitution Hearings, 12 November 1980 (Ottawa: Queen's Printer 1980), 3:78.

46 In earlier charters the clause had assumed a less prominent placement. The limitation clause was placed in article 3 in the Victoria Charter and in section 25 in Bill C-60.

47 Author's interview with Fred Jordan, 19 November 1987.

48 Joint Parliamentary Committee Hearings, Tassé, 12 November 1980, 3:14–15.

49 Ibid., Philip Cooper, vice-president, Coalition for the Protection of Human Life, 9 December 1980, 22:32.

50 Ibid., Nick Schultz, associate general counsel, Public Interest Advocacy Centre, 18 December 1980, 29:20.

51 Ibid., Walter Tarnopolsky, 18 November 1980, 7:9. Tarnopolsky argued that historically there have been a number of incidents in which the denial of minorities' rights was accepted by the majority, such as the treatment of Japanese Canadians in the Second World War and the discrimination against Jehovah's Witnesses in Quebec in the 1940s and 1950s.

52 Ibid., 7:10.

53 Ibid., Jean Chrétien, minister of justice, 15 January 1981, 38:42–5.

54 A similar effect was gained in the 1980 clause by including the reference to a parliamentary system of government.

55 *Reference re Amendment of the Constitution of Canada (Nos. 1, 2, 3)* (1981), 1 SCR 153.

56 Joint Parliamentary Committee Hearings, Professor M. Cohen, 28 October 1980, 7:86.

57 Ibid., Allan Blakeney, 19 December 1980, 30:39.

58 The rights that can be overridden include the fundamental rights and free-doms in sections 2 and 7 through 15.

59 On the eve of the accord, the provinces, minus Quebec, proposed a settle-ment which, among other things, included the entrenchment of a Charter with a legislative override. The federal government conceded the override to apply to legal and equality rights on the basis that the entrenchment of these rights might raise special problems for the provinces. The provinces, however, wanted the override to extend to fundamental freedoms as well. In what has been described as a "classic example of raw bargaining," Trudeau was persuaded to accept the extension of the override to funda-mental freedoms, but in return, the override would be limited to a five-year period. Romanow et al., *Canada Notwithstanding*, 211.

60 Interview with Fred Jordan, 19 November 1987.

61 Joint Parliamentary Committee Hearings, Barry Strayer, assistant deputy minister, Department of Justice (Public Law), 25 January 1981, 38:45.

62 Ibid., Alan Borovoy, general counsel, Canadian Civil Liberties Association, 18 October 1980, 7: 25–6.

63 Canada, House of Commons, *Debates*, Yvon Pinard, 15 October 1980, 3704.

CHAPTER THREE

1 John Rawls, *A Theory of Justice* (Cambridge: The Belknap Press of Harvard University Press 1971).

2 Robert Nozick, *Anarchy, State, and Utopia* (New York: Basic Books, Inc. 1974); Friedrich M. Hayek, *The Constitution of Liberty* (Chicago: University of Chicago Press 1978).

3 William M. Sullivan, "Bringing the Good Back In," in R. Bruce Douglass, Gerald R. Mara, and Henry S. Richardson, eds., *Liberalism and the Good* (New York: Routledge 1990), 149.

4 Ronald Dworkin, "Liberalism," in Michael Sandel, ed., *Liberalism and its Critics* (New York: New York University Press 1984), 64.

5 Will Kymlicka, *Liberalism Community and Culture* (Oxford: Clarendon Press 1992), 78.

6 Hayek, *The Constitution of Liberty*, 153–61.

7 Ibid., 141.

8 Ibid., 232.

9 See, for example, Allan Hutchinson and Andrew Petter, "Private Rights/Public Wrongs: The Liberal Lie of the Charter," *University of Toronto Law Journal* 38 (1988).

10 Duncan Kennedy, "Form and Substance in Private Law Adjudication," *Harvard Law Review* 89 (1976): 1732.

11 "Tortious Interference with Contractual Relations in the Nineteenth Century: The Transformation of Property, Contract, and Tort," *Harvard Law Review* 93 (1980): 1539. For a criticism of contemporary theoretical inconsistencies with contract law, see Roberto Mangabeira Unger, "The Critical Legal Studies Movement," *Harvard Law Review* 96 (1983).

12 Grant Gilmore, *The Death of Contract* (Columbus: Ohio State University Press 1974), 9.

13 Rawls, *A Theory of Justice*, 3–4.

14 Ronald Dworkin, *Taking Rights Seriously* (Cambridge, Mass.: Harvard University Press 1977), 269.

15 Lorraine Weinrib, "The Supreme Court of Canada and Section One of the Charter," *Supreme Court Law Review* 19 (1988): 483.

16 Ibid., 505 (emphasis added).

17 Ibid., 494.

18 Ibid., 491–2.

19 Peter H. Russell, "Canada's Charter of Rights and Freedoms: A Political Report," *Public Law* (Autumn 1988): 394.

20 *Reference re ss. 193 and 195.1(1)(c) of the Criminal Code (Man.)* [1990] 1 SCR 1123; *Reference re Provincial Electoral Boundaries (Sask.)* [1991] 2 SCR 158.

21 Dworkin, *Taking Rights Seriously*, 194.

22 Janet Hiebert, "Rights and Conceptions of Government: Are We in a Period of Transition?" *International Journal of Canadian Studies* 7 (1993).

23 Janet Hiebert, "Representation and the Charter: Should Rights Be Paramount?", in David Smith and John Courtney, eds., *Drawing Boundaries: Legislatures, Courts and Electoral Values* (Saskatoon: Fifth House Publishers 1992).

24 Weinrib, "The Supreme Court of Canada and Section One of the Charter," 496.

25 G. Horowitz, "Conservatism, Liberalism and Socialism in Canada: An Interpretation," *Canadian Journal of Economics and Political Science* 32, no. 2 (1966).

26 See, for example, H.V. Nelles, *The Politics of Development: Forests, Mines and Hydro-Electric Power in Ontario, 1849–1941* (Toronto: Macmillan Company of Canada 1974).

27 Janet Hiebert, "Interest Groups and Canadian Federal Elections," in F.L. Seidle, ed., *Interest Groups and Elections in Canada* (Toronto: Dundurn Press 1991).

28 See Janet Hiebert, "Fair Elections and Freedom of Expression under the Charter," *Journal of Canadian Studies* 24 (Winter 1989–90).

29 *Somerville v. Canada (Attorney General)* (25 June 1993), Calgary, Queen's Bench.

30 See, for example, the testimony of Professor Edward Ratushny before the Special Joint Committee of the Senate and of the House of Commons on the Constitution (Ottawa: Queen's Printer 1978), 29 September 1978, 16:13.

31 Paul Bender, "Justification for Limiting Constitutionally Guaranteed Rights and Freedoms: Some Remarks about the Proper Role of Section One of the Canadian Charter," *Manitoba Law Journal* 13 (1983): 674–5.

32 Ibid., 672–4.

33 Ibid., 676.

34 *Bliss* v. *Attorney General of Canada* [1979] 1 SCR 183.

35 *Brooks* v. *Canada Safeway Ltd.* [1989] 1 SCR 1219.

36 The *Brooks* decision was based on a conflict with Human Rights legislation rather than the Charter.

37 Dale Gibson, *The Law of the Charter* (Toronto: Carswell Company Limited 1986), 137.

38 *Reference re Public Service Employee Relations Act (Alta.)* (1987) 1 SCR 313 at 398–9.

39 *Irwin Toy Ltd.* v. *A.G. Quebec* [1989] 1 SCR 927; *R.* v. *Edwards Books and Art Ltd.* [1986] 2 SCR 713; *R.* v. *Hufsky* [1988] 1 SCR 621; *R.* v. *Thomsen* [1988] 1 SCR 640; *R.* v. *Whyte* [1988] 2 SCR 3.

40 Janet Hiebert, "Debating Policy: The Effects of Rights Talk," in F.L. Seidle, ed., *Equity and Community: The Charter, Interest Advocacy and Representation* (Montreal: Institute for Research on Public Policy 1993).

CHAPTER FOUR

1 Peter Russell argues convincingly that the significance of the Charter is not in its "guarantee" of rights but how it changes the way decisions are made to impose limits on protected rights. Peter H. Russell, "The Political Purposes of the Canadian Charter of Rights and Freedoms," *Canadian Bar Review* 61 (1983): 44.

2 Peter H. Russell, *The Judiciary in Canada: The Third Branch of Government* (Toronto: McGraw-Hill Ryerson Limited 1987), 334.

3 Peter H. Russell, "The Paradox of Judicial Power," *Queen's Law Journal* 12 (1987): 422–3.

4 Berend Hovius and Robert Martin,"The Canadian Charter of Rights and Freedoms in the Supreme Court of Canada," *Canadian Bar Review* 61 (1983): 376.

5 In its earlier experiences with the Bill of Rights, the Supreme Court relied on the bill's lack of entrenchment to justify judicial restraint. The Court characterized it as a "quasi-constitutional instrument" representing a "halfway house between a purely common law regime and a constitutional one." See *Hogan* v. *The Queen* [1975] 2 SCR 574 at 597.

6 *Law Society of Upper Canada* v. *Skapinker* [1984] 1 SCR 357 at 366.
7 *Hunter et al.* v. *Southam Inc.* [1984] 2 SCR 145 at 155; *R.* v. *Therens* [1985] 1 SCR 613 at 638–9; *Singh* v. *Minister of Employment and Immigration* [1985] 1 SCR 177 at 209.
8 *Hunter et al.* v. *Southam.* at 154–5, 157.
9 The Court has not suggested that a purposive approach requires a narrow focus on the framers' intent for a particular Charter section or phrase. But it has indicated that it encompasses a broader consideration of the underlying historical and philosophical values that Charter provisions reflect. See, for example, Dickson's attempt to determine the purpose of freedom of conscience and religion, in which he argued that individual conscience and judgment lies at the heart of our democratic political system. Dickson held that the ability of citizens to make free and informed decisions is an absolute prerequisite for legitimate self government. It is the essential nature of this value that underlies our political tradition. *R.* v. *Big M Drug Mart Ltd.* [1985] 1 SCR 295 at 344–6.
10 Ibid. at 331–2.
11 The Court struck down two provincial and three federal laws. It declared invalid the portion of Bill 101 restricting assess to Quebec's English schools, a section of British Columbia's Motor Vehicle Act creating an absolute liability offence with a mandatory jail term for driving with a suspended licence, the search provisions of the Combines Investigation Act, the Lord's Day Act, and the section in the Narcotics Control Act which reversed the onus of proof. See *A.G. Quebec* v. *Quebec Association of Protestant School Boards* [1984] 2 SCR 66; *Re Motor Vehicle Act* [1985] 2 SCR 486; *R.* v. *Big M Drug Mart*; *Hunter et al.* v. *Southam*; and *Singh* v. *Minister of Employment and Immigration.*
12 *Operation Dismantle* v. *The Queen* [1985] 1 SCR 441 at 471–2.
13 The Court similarly attempted to distinguish between legal and policy inquiries in *Re Motor Vehicle Act.* At issue in this reference case was whether provisions of the act, which established minimum periods of imprisonment for driving without a valid driver's licence or while under suspension, even if the driver was unaware of his or her status, violated the principles of fundamental justice in s. 7. Justice Lamer, speaking for the majority, anticipated criticisms that the Court's decision to interpret the "principles of fundamental justice" to embrace substantive as well as procedural concerns would require that it make pronouncements on the wisdom of legislative decisions. Lamer, in addressing concerns that the judiciary was in danger of becoming a "super-legislature," tried to alleviate these fears by suggesting that the principles of fundamental justice do not lie in the realm of general public policy but in the basic tenets of the legal system which is "the inherent domain of the judiciary as guardian of the justice system." The assumption underlying this claim is that the development of the common law does not engage courts in a policy role. Thus, an interpretation of s. 7 which

goes beyond procedural safeguards will not require that courts make pronouncements on the merits or wisdom of legislative enactments because courts will simply be doing what they always have – protecting traditional legal norms. *Reference Re s. 94(2) of the Motor Vehicle Act (B.C.)* [1985] 2 SCR 486 at 497–503.

14 *Harrison v. Carswell* [1976] 2 SCR at 218.

15 The right of citizens of Canada to have their children receive publicly paid primary and secondary school instruction in the language of the English or French linguistic minority population of a province is subject to where numbers warrant.

16 *A.G. Quebec v. Quebec Association of Protestant School Boards* at 81–2 and 79.

17 Ibid. at 86–8.

18 *Singh v. Minister of Employment and Immigration.* Justices Beetz, Estey, and McIntyre also found that the procedures for determining Convention refugee status were unconstitutional but relied on the Canadian Bill of Rights.

19 Ibid. at 212–19.

20 Ibid. at 218.

21 *Hunter et al. v. Southam Inc.*

22 *Reference Re s. 94(2) of the Motor Vehicle Act (B.C.).*

23 *R. v. Oakes* [1986] 1 SCR 103 at 138–40.

24 Ibid. at 136–7.

25 The *Oakes* test did not receive unanimous support. Justices Estey and McIntyre offered no explanation for not signing the chief justice's judgment. In their curt opinion they simply stated that they were in agreement with both the result reached by Dickson and his analytical approach to s. 11(d) which distinguished the question of whether a right had been violated from the inquiry into the reasonableness of the legislation. But as far as deciding all other issues in the appeal, such as the standards for evaluating the reasonableness of legislation found to conflict with a protected right, Estey and McIntyre adopted the reasons of Judge Martin of the Court of Appeal. See ibid. at 143.

26 *R. v. Jones* [1986] 2 SCR 284 at 289.

27 La Forest did not take part in the *Oakes* judgment itself.

28 *R. v. Jones* at 299.

29 Ibid. at 304 (emphasis in original).

30 *R. v. Edwards Books and Art Ltd.* [1986] 2 SCR 713.

31 Ibid. at 778.

32 Ibid. at 768–9.

33 Ibid. at 779.

34 See McIntyre J. in *Andrews v. Law Society of British Columbia* [1989] 1 SCR 143 at 184; La Forest J. in *United States of America v. Cotroni; United States of*

America v. *El Zein* [1989] 1 SCR 1469 at 1489–90; and Dickson CJ. in *Slaight Communications Inc.* v. *Davidson* [1989] 1 SCR 1038 at 1051–2.

35 *R.* v. *Jones* at 318–19.

36 *R.* v. *Morgentaler* [1988] 1 SCR 30 at 74–5, 122, 181. While all three judgments agreed that Parliament's attempts to strike a balance between protecting the woman's life or health and fetal interests was a legitimate objective, they did not share the same opinion on what the primary objective of the legislation was. In Dickson's view the essential purpose of the legislation was to protect the pregnant woman's life or health, whereas for Beetz and Wilson the primary objective was the protection of the fetus.

37 Ibid. at 164.

38 Ibid.

39 Ibid. at 171–2. Wilson also found s. 251 to be in violation of a woman's right to security of the person under s. 7 because the legislation subjected women to considerable emotional stress and unnecessary physical risk.

40 Ibid. at 181.

41 F.L. Morton, Peter H. Russell, and Michael J. Withey, "The Supreme Court's First One Hundred Charter of Rights Decisions: A Statistical Analysis," *Osgoode Hall Law Journal* 30 (1992): 43.

42 Ibid., 42–3.

43 *Reference re Public Service Employee Relations Act (Alta.)* [1987] 1 SCR 313; *Government of Saskatchewan* v. *Retail Wholesale and Department Store Union, Locals 544, 496, 635 & 955* [1987] 1 SCR 460; *R.* v. *Public Service Alliance of Canada* [1987] 1 SCR 424. The majority approach to labour claims under freedom of expression and association was narrow and formalistic. Freedom of association was interpreted as primarily a formal right to create associations without protection for the activities of the association. The concurring reasons by McIntyre offered a more developed explanation for finding that freedom of association does not embrace the right of a trade union to strike. In contrast to the majority position which collapsed striking and collective bargaining and found that freedom of association does not afford constitutional protection to either, McIntyre ruled only on the constitutional validity of the right to strike. McIntyre's refusal to collapse the two claims might suggest that freedom of association, in the context of organized labour, is subject to constitutional protection. In *PSAC* he reinforced his position that the two activities could be distinguished for Charter purposes by asserting that just because there is not a constitutional guarantee of a right to strike, this does not preclude the possibility that other aspects of collective bargaining may receive Charter protection under s. 2(d). Given that an essential objective of the collective bargaining process is the ability to withdraw service in the form of striking as a fundamental process of

establishing working conditions, it is arguable that McIntyre might as well
have collapsed the two and found, as the majority judgment had, that there
is no constitutional protection for collective bargaining.

44 *Reference re Public Service Employee Relations Act* at 419–20.

45 Ibid. at 419–20.

46 *R. v. Morgentaler* at 141.

47 Ibid. at 140.

48 Russell, "Canada's Charter of Rights and Freedoms": 394.

49 *R. v. Thomsen* [1988] 1 SCR 640; *R. v. Hufsky* [1988] 1 SCR 621.

50 *R. v. Thomsen* at 649–53. This case differs from an earlier one involving
breathalyser tests. In *R. v. Therens* [1985] 1 SCR 613, the issue was whether
the requirement that an individual accompany the officer to a police sta-
tion and to submit to a breathalyser test resulted in detention under s. 10.
In *Thomsen* the issue focused on whether the requirement that an individual submit to a roadside breathalyser test results in detention. Justice Le
Dain who wrote the *Thomsen* decision held that the demand resulted in detention because it had legal consequences and criminal liability for refusal
to comply. Le Dain held that although the sample provided by the roadside
screening device could not be used as evidence, it could provide the basis
for a s.235(1) breathalyser demand. The appellant, therefore, had a right
to retain and instruct counsel without delay and to be informed of that
right, subject to limitation under s. 1. Having found that Thomsen was entitled to retain and instruct counsel, Le Dain had to determine whether the
limitation on Thomsen's right occurred as a result of the terms of
s. 234.(1) or its operating requirements, or arose out of the conduct of the
police. The former situation would be subject to s. 1 while the latter would
not. Le Dain held that a limit prescribed by law within the meaning of s. 1
may arise from the implication of the terms of a legislative provision or its
operating requirements. To qualify as a limit under s. 1, there need not be
an explicit limitation of a particular right or freedom. In Le Dain's view, the
failure to allow Thomsen to contact counsel prior to compliance with a
s. 234.(1) demand was an implication of the terms of the legislation. A
s. 234.1(1) screening device test is to be administered on the roadside, at
the time and place the motorist is stopped, and as quickly as possible. It
does not envisage an opportunity for those stopped to contact counsel. The
legislation, therefore, can be subject to limits under s. 1.

51 Ibid. at 653–5.

52 *R. v. Hufsky* at 636–7.

53 See, for example, Morton, Russell, and Withey, "The Supreme Court's First
One Hundred Charter of Rights Decisions": 35. One out of three governmental claims were accepted in 1986 as a reasonable limit, zero of two in
1987, five of nine in 1988, and three of five in 1989.

54 This characterization is made by Andrew Lokan, "The Rise and Fall of Doctrine under Section 1 of the Charter," *Ottawa Law Review* 24, no. 1 (1992): 184.

55 *R. v. Keegstra* [1990] 3 SCR 697 at 736–7.

56 *Stoffman v. Vancouver General Hospital* [1990] 3 SCR 483 at 550 (emphasis added).

57 Ibid.

58 *R. v. Chaulk* [1990] 3 SCR 1303 at 1375.

59 Ibid. at 1335, 1345, and 1372–5.

60 *R. v. Zundel* [1992] 2 SCR 731 at 761, 766.

61 Ibid. at 762.

62 *R. v. Keegstra* at 776.

63 *R. v. Butler* [1992] 1 SCR 452 at 491. A second objective was to promote the public interest in maintaining a "decent society."

64 Ibid. at 501–4.

65 *Irwin Toy Ltd. v. A.G. Quebec* [1989] 1 SCR 927.

66 Ibid. at 989–90.

67 *R. v. Chaulk* at 1343.

68 *Reference re ss. 193 and 195.1(1)(c) of the Criminal Code (Man.)* [1990] 1 SCR 1123 at 1138.

69 *R. v. Butler* [1992] 1 SCR 452 at 505.

70 *Lavigne v. Ontario Public Service Employees Union* [1991] 2 SCR 211 at 295.

71 *McKinney v. University of Guelph* [1990] 3 SCR 230 at 304–5.

72 *Irwin Toy* at 993–4.

73 *Reference re ss. 193 and 195.1(1)(c) of the Criminal Code (Man.)* [1990] 1 SCR 1123; *Ford v. Quebec (Attorney General)* [1988] 2 SCR at 778–9.

74 *Reference re ss. 193 and 195.1(1)(c) of the Criminal Code (Man.) Reference re Criminal Code (Man.)* at 1136.

75 *R. v. Keegstra* at 761–3.

76 See for example *Canada Human Rights Commission v. Taylor; Rocket.* See also the minority position in *Zundel.*

77 *R. v. Butler* at 500–1.

78 These cases are *A.G. Quebec v. Quebec Association of Protestant School Boards; R. v. Big M Drug Mart;* and *R. v. Zundel.*

79 Peter Hogg characterizes this aspect of the proportionality criterion as the "heart and sole of section 1 justification." Peter Hogg, "Section 1 Revisited," *National Journal of Constitutional Law* 1 (1991): 17.

80 *Dagenais v. Canadian Broadcasting Corporation* [1994] 3 SCR 927.

81 *Singh v. Minister of Employment and Immigration* at 218.

82 *R. v. Oakes* at 137.

83 *R. v. Keegstra* at 784–5.

84 *Chaulk,* at 1343 (emphasis in original).

85 *R*. v. *Butler* at 505.
86 *Sauvé* v. *Canada (Attorney General)* [1993] 2 SCR 438 at 440.
87 *Osborne* v. *Canada (Treasury Board)* [1991] 2 SCR 69 at 99.
88 Peter Hogg, "Section 1 Revisited,": 23–4.
89 *Dagenais* v. *Canadian Broadcasting Corporation* at 887–98 (emphasis in original).
90 Ibid. at 889 emphasis in original.
91 Ibid. at 889 and 892.
92 *R*. v. *Laba* [1994] 3 SCR 965 at 1010–11.
93 Hogg, "Section 1 Revisited," 23.
94 *R*. v. *Seaboyer* [1991] 2 SCR 577 at 612–16.
95 Ibid. at 634–6.
96 *R*. v. *Bain* [1992] 1 SCR 91. In this case the constitutional question was whether a disparity between the accused's and the Crown's right to challenge jurors violates ss. 7 and 11(d) of the Charter. A narrow four to three majority found that the legislation infringes s. 11(d) and is not justified under s. 1. The majority held that because no written or oral argument was made on the justification of the provision, the Crown did not discharge its burden of identifying a pressing concern which would justify a limitation (at 162). In *R*. v. *Morales* [1992] 3 SCR 711, the issue was whether ss. 515(6)(a) and 515(6)(d) of the Criminal Code, which require an accused to show cause why detention pending trial is not justified, violates s. 11(e) of the Charter. The majority held that the context for the show cause is the "public interest," a concept so vague and imprecise that it is incapable of framing the legal debate in any meaningful manner or structuring discretion in any way. The Court concluded that the violation of s. 11(e) was not justified under s. 1 because it failed all three of the proportionality criteria (at 734).
97 Robert Harvie and Hamar Foster, "Different Drummers, Different Drums: The Supreme Court of Canada, American Jurisprudence and the Continuing Revision of Criminal Law under the Charter," *Ottawa Law Review* 24, no. 1 (1992).

CHAPTER FIVE

1 Peter Russell has discussed the deceptive appearance of the concept of "protecting" rights. See "A Democratic Approach to Civil Liberties," *University of Toronto Law Journal* 19 (1969), and "The Political Purposes of the Canadian Charter of Rights and Freedoms," *Canadian Bar Review* 61 (1983).
2 Notable exceptions at the Supreme Court level are *R*. v. *Morgentaler* [1988] 1 SCR 30 (abortion), *R*. v. *Seaboyer* [1991] 2 SCR 577 (rape shield legislation), *Ford* v. *Quebec (Attorney General)* [1988] 2 SCR 712 (Quebec signs law), and *Rodriguez* v. *British Columbia (Attorney General)* [1993] 3 SCR 519 (medically assisted suicide for the disabled terminally ill).

3 James Bradley Thayer, *The Origin and Scope of the American Doctrine of Constitutional Law* (Boston: Little, Brown, and Company 1893), 3–4, 4–9, and 18.

4 Ibid 29–30.

5 For a good review of the different variations of originalism, understood as constitutional adjudication that accords authority to the text of the constitution or to the intentions of its adopters, see Paul Brest, "The Misconceived Question for the Original Understanding," *Boston University Law Review* 60 (1980).

6 Robert H. Bork, *The Tempting of America: The Political Seduction of the Law* (New York: Simon & Schuster 1990), 4–5.

7 Robert H. Bork, "Neutral Principles and Some First Amendment Problems," *Indiana Law Journal* 47 (1971): 8.

8 Bork, *The Tempting of America*, 5.

9 John Hart Ely, *Democracy and Distrust: A Theory of Judicial Review* (Cambridge, Mass.: Harvard University Press 1980), 14–15.

10 *Dred Scott* v. *Sandford*, 60 US (19 How.) 393 (1857); *Hammer* v. *Dagenhart*, 247 US 251 (1918); and *Schechter Corp.* v. *United States*, 295 US 495 (1935).

11 Herbert Wechsler, "Toward Neutral Principles of Constitutional Law," *Harvard Law Review* 73 (1959): 6–7, 19, and 27.

12 Herbert Wechsler, *Principles, Politics and Fundamental Law: Selected Essays* (Cambridge, Mass.: Harvard University Press 1961), 27.

13 Alexander Bickel, *The Least Dangerous Branch: The Supreme Court at the Bar of Politics*, 2nd ed. (New Haven: Yale University Press 1986), 55.

14 Ely, *Democracy and Distrust*, 99.

15 Ibid., 181.

16 Ibid., 87.

17 Ibid., 145–69, 59.

18 Laurence Tribe, *Constitutional Choices* (Cambridge, Mass.: Harvard University Press 1985), 11.

19 Ronald Dworkin, *A Matter of Principle* (Cambridge, Mass.: Harvard University Press 1985), 58–69.

20 Clifton McCleskey, "Judicial Review in a Democracy: A Dissenting Opinion," *Houston Law Review* 3 (1966): 354.

21 *Brown* v. *Board of Education*, 347 US 483 (1954).

22 Michael J. Perry, *The Constitution, the Courts, and Human Rights* (New Haven: Yale University Press 1982), 1.

23 See Paul Brest, "The Fundamental Rights Controversy: The Essential Contradictions of Normative Constitutional Scholarship," *Yale Law Journal* 90 (1981).

24 Bickel, *The Least Dangerous Branch*, 25

25 Alexander Bickel, *The Supreme Court and the Idea of Progress* (New Haven: Yale University Press 1978), 177, 99.

26 Bickel, *The Least Dangerous Branch*, 239, 18.

27 Laurence Tribe, *American Constitutional Law*, 2nd ed. (New York: The Foundation Press 1988), 1302–1435; Kenneth L. Karst, "The Freedom of Intimate Association," *Yale Law Journal* 89 (1980) 629; J. Harvie Wilkinson and G. Edward White, "Constitutional Protection for Personal Lifestyles," *Cornell Law Review* 62 (1977): 611–17.

28 Perry, *The Constitution, the Courts, and Human Rights*, 2.

29 Ibid. 93–96, 101–2.

30 Ibid., 4.

31 Ibid., 125–6.

32 Ibid., 130, 135–6. Interestingly, from a Canadian perspective given the inclusion in the Charter of the legislative override of s. 33, Perry acknowledges that while there may not be a substantial difference between the power to limit the effects and reach of judicial decisions and the power to overturn judicial decisions, he is not prepared to accept the legitimacy of the latter. In his view, the power to reverse or override judicial decisions would place the Court in a subordinate position, thereby undermining the appropriate inter-institutional tension between the judiciary and Congress.

33 Ely, *Democracy and Distrust*, 4.

34 Tribe, *Constitutional Choices*, 6.

35 Tribe, *American Constitutional Law*, 15.

36 Ronald Dworkin, *Law's Empire* (Cambridge, Mass.: Harvard University Press 1986), 381.

37 Ronald Dworkin, "Liberalism," in Stuart Hampshire, ed., *Public and Private Morality* (New York: Cambridge University Press 1978), 136.

38 Ronald Dworkin, *Taking Rights Seriously* (Cambridge, Mass.: Harvard University Press 1978), 149.

39 Dworkin, *A Matter of Principle*, 11, 13. Dworkin doubts that hard cases will arise frequently (pp. 144–5).

40 Ibid., 124–30.

41 Tribe, *American Constitutional Law*, 14. Tribe criticizes those who would argue that it is increasingly difficult to justify judicial review because fundamental values and beliefs cease to be widely shared. In his view, the difficulty with arguments about the political limits of constitutional law in an era of contested values is that it "undervalues the place of vigorously contested constitutional discourse and decision in political dialogue."

42 Ely, *Democracy and Distrust*, 57–8.

43 For a range of perspectives, see Richard Delgado, "The Ethereal Scholar: Does Critical Legal Studies Have What Minorities Want?"; Mari J. Matsuda, "Looking to the Bottom: Critical Legal Studies and Reparations"; Patricia J. Williams,"Alchemical Notes: Reconstructing Ideals from Deconstructed Rights"; and Harlon L. Dalton, "The Clouded Prism," all in *Harvard Civil Rights Civil Liberties Law Review* 22 (1987); Robert A. Williams, Jr, "Taking

Rights Aggressively: The Perils and Promise of Critical Legal Theory for Peoples of Color," *Law and Inequality* 5 (1987).

44 For a bibliography of critical legal studies, see *The Yale Law Journal* 94 (1984): 464–90. Two CLS critiques of rights are in Mark Tushnet, "An Essay on Rights," *Texas Law Review* 62 (1984), and Alan Freeman, "Antidiscrimination Law: A Critical Review," in David Kairys, ed., *The Politics of Law: A Progressive Critique* (New York: Pantheon Books 1982). For a stimulating critique of the critics, see Amy Bartholomew and Alan Hunt, "What's Wrong with Rights?" *Law and Inequality: A Journal of Theory and Practice* 9 (1990).

45 Allan C. Hutchinson and Patrick J. Monahan, "Law, Politics, and the Critical Legal Scholars: The Unfolding Drama of American Legal Thought," *Stanford Law Review* 36 (1984): 206.

46 Tushnet, "An Essay on Rights," 1364. Examples of the harmful effects of rights are said to include interpretation of the First Amendment which has prevented legislative efforts to address the effects of unequal wealth and resources in political advertising or to regulate the way in which advertising shapes public consciousness about societal problems and possible remedies (pp. 1387–8).

47 Williams, "Taking Rights Aggressively," 120.

48 Ibid., 121–3.

49 Robert Sharpe, "A Comment on David Beatty's 'A Conservative Court: The Politicization of Law'," *University of Toronto Law Journal* 41 (1991): 470.

50 David Beatty, *Talking Heads and the Supremes: The Canadian Production of Constitutional Review* (Toronto: Carswell 1990), 36.

51 David Beatty, "A Conservative's Court," 162.

52 Lorraine Weinrib, "The Supreme Court of Canada and Section One of the Charter," *The Supreme Court Law Review* 19: (1988): 506.

53 Michael Mandel, *The Charter of Rights and the Legalization of Politics in Canada* (Toronto: Wall & Thompson 1989), 39.

54 Dworkin, *Taking Rights Seriously*, 87. Dworkin has had considerable influence on a number of Charter proponents and some Supreme Court judges. Relying on the assumption that there is a fundamental distinction between arguments based on "principle" as opposed to "policy," Dworkin argues that courts must restrict their decisions to the former. Arguments of principle are intended to establish an individual right whereas arguments of policy are arguments intended to establish a collective goal. While legislatures are best equipped to decide on the collective welfare of the community, through representative institutions, rights-based conflicts are best decided by courts because they involve questions of principle. To leave these decisions to the political process would be to "make the majority judge in its own cause" which would be inconsistent with constitutionalism (the theory that the majority must be restrained to protect individual rights) and unjust.

55 Mandel, *The Charter of Rights*, 41–2.
56 Ibid., 60.
57 Harry J. Glasbeek and Michael Mandel, "The Legalisation of Politics in Advanced Capitalism: The Canadian Charter of Rights and Freedoms," *Socialist Studies* 2 (1984): 115.
58 Mandel, *The Charter of Rights*, 287.
59 Patrick Monahan, *Politics and the Constitution: The Charter, Federalism and the Supreme Court of Canada* (Toronto: Carswell 1987), 124.
60 Ibid., 97–138.
61 Patrick Monahan, "Judicial Review and Democracy: A Theory of Judicial Review, *UBC Law Review* 21 (1987): 89.
62 Monahan, *Politics and the Constitution*, 97–8.
63 Peter Russell, "The Paradox of Judicial Power," *Queen's Law Journal* 12 (1987): 432.
64 Monahan, *Politics and the Constitution*, 101.
65 Ibid., 109. Monahan argues that these classical liberal assumptions do not underlie the Charter. Nor does the Charter reflect a tension between the state and freedom. The overriding goal is to regulate and structure the way state power can be used, not to define the boundary between public and private spheres.
66 Ibid., 99.
67 Russell, "The Paradox of Judicial Power," 432.
68 Monahan, *Politics and the Constitution*. 98, 104–6, 111–20, 123–4.
69 Ibid., 110.
70 Allan Hutchinson and Andrew Petter, "Private Rights/Public Wrongs: The Liberal Lie of the Charter," *University of Toronto Law Journal* 38 (1988): 279.
71 Andrew Petter, "Immaculate Deception: The Charter's Hidden Agenda," *The Advocate* 45 (1987): 857–8.
72 Hutchinson and Petter, "Private Rights/Public Wrongs," 283–6.
73 Ibid., 294.
74 Ibid., 295–6.
75 F.L. Morton and Rainer Knopff, "The Supreme Court as the Vanguard of the Intelligentsia: The Charter Movement as Postmaterialist Politics," in Janet Ajzenstat, ed., *Canadian Constitutionalism: 1791–1991* (Ottawa: Canadian Study of Parliament Group 1992), 78.
76 Ibid., 58.
77 Ibid., 59–64.
78 Rainer Knopff and F.L. Morton, *Charter Politics* (Scarborough: Nelson Canada 1992), 138–9.
79 Ibid., 169–70. While these categories are not mutually exclusive (for example, courts often cannot adjudicate concrete disputes without pronouncing on the meaning of the relevant law), their particular characterization depends on which characteristic is primary.

80 Ibid., 195.

81 Ibid., 169–70, 176.

82 Ibid., 195–6.

83 Diana Majury, "Strategizing in Equality," in D. Kelly Weisberg, ed., *Feminist Legal Theory* (Philadelphia: Temple University Press 1993), 265–6.

84 Roy Romanow, John Whyte, and Howard Leeson, *Canada Notwithstanding: The Making of the Constitution 1976–1982* (Toronto: Carswell/Methuen 1984), 218.

85 Beatty, *Talking Heads and the Supremes*, 118.

86 Russell, "A Democratic Approach to Civil Liberties," 123.

87 Peter H. Russell, "The Political Purposes of the Canadian Charter of Rights and Freedoms," *Canadian Bar Review* 61 (1983): 43–4.

88 Ibid., 49.

89 This phrase is borrowed from a discussion between the author and Stephen Zaluski, Department of Justice Canada, 25 March 1994.

90 This suggestion is influenced by a conversation with Peter Russell, 3 June 1994.

91 Patrick J. Monahan and Marie Finkelstein, "The Charter of Rights and Public Policy in Canada," in Patrick Monahan and Marie Finkelstein, eds., *The Impact of the Charter on the Public Policy Process* (North York: York University Centre for Public Law and Public Policy 1993).

92 Alan C. Cairns, *Charter versus Federalism: The Dilemma of Constitutional Reform* (Montreal: McGill-Queen's University Press 1992).

93 Leslie A. Pal, *Public Policy Analysis: An Introduction* (Scarborough: Nelson Canada 1992), 108.

94 Research done by the author for the Ph.D dissertation and subsequent research, funded by a Queen's University Advisory Research Committee grant, examined a range of policies to identify whether and how the language of rights and awareness of the Charter were affecting the way issues were debated in Parliament and in legislative committees.

95 One notable exception is the debate on the rape shield legislation following the Supreme Court's decision in *R. v. Seaboyer.* See Janet Hiebert, "Debating Policy: The Effects of Rights Talk," in F. Leslie Seidle, ed., *Equity and Community: The Charter, Interest Advocacy and Representation* (Montreal: IRPP 1993).

CHAPTER SIX

1 Alan C. Cairns, *Disruptions: Constitutional Struggles, from the Charter to Meech Lake,* ed. Douglas E. Williams (Toronto: McClelland and Stewart 1991).

2 See, for example, Rainer Knopff and F.L. Morton, "Nation-Building and the Canadian Charter of Rights and Freedoms," in Alan Cairns and Cynthia Williams, eds., *Constitutionalism, Citizenship and Society in Canada*

(Toronto: University of Toronto Press 1985); Peter H. Russell, "Political Purposes of the Charter," *Canadian Bar Review* 61 (1983); Peter Hogg, "Federalism Fights the Charter of Rights," in David P. Shugarman and Reg Whitaker, eds., *Federalism and Political Community: Essays in Honour of Donald Smiley* (Peterborough: Broadview Press Ltd. 1989); Alan C. Cairns, *The Charter versus Federalism: The Dilemmas of Constitutional Reform* (Montreal: McGill-Queen's University Press 1992).

3 An exception is the work of F.L. Morton et al. which has examined the judicial nullification of statutes in the Supreme Court's first one hundred Charter cases. See F.L. Morton, G. Solomon, I. McNish, and D.W. Poulton, "Judicial Nullification of Statutes under the Charter of Rights and Freedoms, 1982–1988," *Alberta Law Review* 28 (1990). See also F.L. Morton, Peter H. Russell and Michael J. Whitey, "The Supreme Court's First One Hundred Charter of Rights Decisions: A Statistical Analysis," *Osgoode Hall Law Journal* 30 (1992). Alan Cairns also revisits the issue of the Charter's nation-building effects in Alan C. Cairns, "Reflections on the Political Purposes of the Charter," in Gerald A. Beaudoin, ed., *The Charter: Ten Years Later* (Cowansville, Quebec: Les Éditions Yvon Blais 1992).

4 Donald Smiley, "A Dangerous Deed: The Constitution Act, 1982," in Keith Banting and Richard Simeon, eds., *And No One Cheered: Federalism, Democracy and the Constitution Act* (Toronto: Methuen 1983), 89.

5 "Developments in the Law: The Interpretation of State Constitutional Rights," *Harvard Law Review* 95 (1982): 1326–7. Although James Madison, when supporting constitutional amendments to provide for a Bill of Rights, wanted to place restrictions on the states ability to violate the equal rights of conscience, freedom of the press or trial by jury in criminal cases, the Bill of Rights limited only the federal government. See Louis Fisher, *American Constitutional Law* (New York: McGraw-Hill 1990), 391.

6 Louise Weinberg, "The New Judicial Federalism," *Stanford Law Review* 29 (1977): 1196.

7 *Barron* v. *Baltimore* 7 Pet. (32 US) 243 (1833).

8 William J. Brennan, Jr, "State Constitutions and the Protection of Individual Rights," *Harvard Law Review* 90 (1977): 493.

9 *Missouri Pacific Railway Co.* v. *Nebraska*, 164 US 403 (1896); *Chicago, B & Q Railway Co.* v. *Chicago*, 166 US 226 (1897). *Allgeyer* v. *Louisiana*, 165 US 578 (1897); *Lochner* v. *New York*, 198 US 45 (1905).

10 *Goldburg* v. *Kelly*, 397 US 254 (1970).

11 Henry J. Abraham, *The Judicial Process*, 4th ed. (New York: Oxford University Press 1980), 146–52. Abraham argues that only in a handful of cases has the question been successfully brought to the discretionary attention of the Supreme Court.

12 Archibald Cox, "Federalism and Individual Rights," *Northwestern University Law Review* 73, no. 1 (1978): 2.

13 For a discussion of the new judicial federalism rules, see Louise Weinberg, "The New Judicial Federalism: Where We Are Now" and A.E. Dick Howard, "Garcia and the Values of Federalism: On the Need for a Recurrence to Fundamental Principles," both in *Georgia Law Review* 19 (1985); and Robert C. Welsh, "Whose Federalism? – The Burger Court's Treatment of State Civil Liberties Judgments," *Hastings Constitutional Law Quarterly* 10 (1983).

14 Fisher, *American Constitutional Law*, 393–5.

15 "Developments in the Law: The Interpretation of State Constitutional Rights," *Harvard Law Review* 95 (1982): 1328. See p. 1330 for a good discussion of the different schools of thought on the questions relating to how state bills of rights should be interpreted.

16 Welsh, "Whose Federalism?", 820–2.

17 Hogg, "Federalism Fights the Charter of Rights," 249.

18 Rainer Knopff and F.L. Morton, *Charter Politics* (Scarborough: Nelson Canada 1992), 148.

19 Pierre Fournier, "The Future of Quebec Nationalism," in Keith Banting and Richard Simeon, eds., *And No One Cheered: Federalism, Democracy and the Constitution Act* (Toronto: Methuen 1983), 159.

20 Minority education language rights of s. 23 are one of the few rights and freedoms in the Charter which cannot be subject to the legislative override of s. 33.

21 *A.G. Quebec* v. *Quebec Association of Protestant School Boards* [1984] 2 SCR 66.

22 *Ford* v. *Quebec (Attorney General)* [1988] 2 SCR 712.

23 In the first decade of Supreme Court jurisprudence, twenty-three federal statutes were nullified while eighteen provincial ones were declared invalid. F.L. Morton, Peter H. Russell, and Troy Ridell, "The First Decade of the Charter of Rights, 1982–1992: A Statistical Analysis of Supreme Court Decisions," paper presented at the annual meeting of the Canadian Political Science Association, University of Calgary, 12–14 June 1994.

24 *R.* v. *Edwards Books and Art Ltd.* [1986] 2 SCR 713 at 782, 802.

25 *R.* v. *Turpin* [1989] 1 SCR 1296 at 1329–33.

26 *R.* v. *S.(S.)* [1990] 2 SCR 254 at 289–92. The Court did not reject the possibility that some interprovincial differences in how federal laws are administered might constitute an infringement on equality. But these distinctions should be assessed on a case-by-case basis and in the context of a principled approach that recognizes explicitly the importance in Canada of federalism:

> It is necessary to bear in mind that differential application of federal law can be a legitimate means of forwarding the values of a federal system. In fact, in the context of the administration of the criminal law, differential applications is constitutionally fostered by ss. 91(27) and 92(14) of the *Constitution Act, 1867*. The area of criminal law and its application is one in which the balancing of national interests and local concerns has been

accomplished by a constitutional structure that both permits and encourages federal-provincial cooperation. A brief review of Canadian constitutional history clearly demonstrates that diversity in the criminal law, in terms of provincial application, has been recognized consistently as a means of furthering the values of federalism. Differential application arises from a recognition that different approaches to the administration of the criminal law are appropriate in different territorially based communities.

27 Ibid. at 285.

28 Ibid. at 287–8.

29 *Haig* v. *Canada (Chief Electoral Officer)* [1993] 2 scr 995 at 1028. An additional claim was that the federal chief electoral officer should have used the discretion of his office to extend the entitlement to vote for those persons who were not residents on the enumeration date in a province or territory where the federal referendum was held. The majority decision rejected this claim.

30 Ibid. at 1022, 1033.

31 Ibid. at 1024–5.

32 Ibid. at 1029–30. An argument made by the Charter claimant was that the Referendum Act (Canada) and the Canada Elections Act were inadequate because they did not make provision for all Canadians to vote in a national referendum. The Court also held that even if there was a right to vote in referendums, Mr Haig's claim that a "national" referendum confers the right to vote, even if an individual is not enumerated, was flawed because there was no "national" referendum but rather two referendums.

33 Ibid. at 1030.

34 Ibid. at 1046–7.

35 *R.* v. *Morgentaler* [1988] 1 scr 30.

36 *R.* v. *Jones* [1986] 2 scr 284 at 304, cited by Dickson in *Morgentaler* at 70 (emphasis in original).

37 *Morgentaler* at 73.

38 Christopher P. Manfredi, *Judicial Power and the Charter: Canada and the Paradox of Liberal Constitutionalism* (Toronto: McClelland and Stewart 1993), 163.

39 Ibid., 119.

40 Ibid., 163. Manfredi observes that, ironically, in the absence of a national abortion law, the Court's decision has resulted in even greater diversity as the provinces are regulating access to abortion under provincial health care laws.

41 See, in particular, Lorraine E. Weinrib, "The Supreme Court of Canada and Section One of the Charter," *Supreme Court Law Review* 19 (1988) and David Beatty, *Talking Heads and the Supremes: The Canadian Production of Constitutional Review* (Toronto: Carswell 1990).

42 The override was used by the Devine government of Saskatchewan in 1986 to override freedom of association and end a strike by the public service there.

43 The practice of a blanket override was challenged in *Ford* v. *Quebec (Attorney General)* in which the Supreme Court held that the omnibus nature of the declaration itself was not unconstitutional but the retrospective effect of the use was.

Similar issues were raised in *Alliance des professeurs de Montréal* v. *Procureur general du Québec* in which the Quebec Court of Appeal held that the standard override provision did not conform with s. 33 of the Charter. In that case s. 1 of An Act Respecting the Constitution Act, 1982, which added the standard override provision to all provincial legislation enacted up to 23 June 1982, was challenged. The objection to the act was that the provision did not sufficiently specify the guaranteed rights or freedoms which the legislation intended to override. The Court of Appeal held that the standard override provision did not conform with s. 33 of the Charter. It found that although more than one provision in s. 2 or ss. 7–15 could be validly overridden in a single enactment, it was not sufficient to refer solely to the number of the section containing the provision to be overridden.

The Supreme Court addressed the claim in *Ford* that the omnibus nature of Quebec's use of the override is unconstitutional. The Court rejected the key assumption in the Court of Appeal's decision in *Alliance des professeurs* that there are substantive conditions for reviewing the use of s. 33. In the Court's view s. 33 has only a procedural dimension and concerns for a fully informed democratic process are neither relevant nor helpful in reviewing s. 33. In finding that the standard override provision is a valid exercise of s. 33, the Court held that there is no requirement that a legislature make specific reference in words, rather than section numbers, to the right intended to be overridden. The Court also rejected claims that the "omnibus" character of the enactment is unconstitutional, again for the reason that there are no grounds for reviewing the substantive conditions of s. 33. The Court did find that the standard override provision has a retrogressive effect which is unconstitutional. See *Alliance des professeurs de Montréal* v. *Procureur general du Québec*, (1985) cs 1272, reviewed (1985) ca 376; *Ford* v. *Quebec (Attorney General)* (1988) 2 scr 712. See also Factum of the Intervenor the Attorney General of Ontario in the *Ford* case.

44 An exception is F.L. Morton, "Judicial Politics Canadian-Style: The Supreme Court's Contribution to the Constitutional Crisis of 1992," in Curtis Cook, ed., *Constitutional Predicament: Canada after the Referendum of 1992* (Montreal: McGill-Queen's University Press 1994), 138–46.

45 This view presumed that courts would have given a generous interpretation of the distinct society clause which would have granted the Quebec government significant latitude to enact limits on protected rights to promote cultural values.

46 "New Quebec policy to require French on outside signs," *Globe and Mail,* 19 December 1988, A1, A3.

47 "Bourassa's use of Charter clause shows his vision of distinct Quebec," *Globe and Mail,* 22 December 1988 A1, A5.

48 After numerous demands in the House of Commons by opposition members to comment on Bourassa's use of the override, Mulroney finally responded:

> The Quebec Bill, in my judgment, clearly does not meet the tests set out by the Supreme Court of Canada, and therefore, clearly, if it fails to do that, one of the tests being respect for the provisions of the Charter of Rights and Freedoms in the province of Quebec, surely in the absence of that, it offends against the Charter. Therefore, as I have indicated, anything that offends against the Charter is something that I find unsatisfactory both as a legislator and as a Canadian.

Mulroney's criticism of Bourassa's use of s. 33 is particularly mild in light of comments made a few months later when he suggested that because of the inclusion of the legislative override, the Charter was not worth the paper it was printed on. See Canada, House of Commons, *Debates,* 19–23 December 1988, 295–7, 424–5, 522–7, 615–21, 716–17.

49 "Mulroney condemns sign bill for subverting minority rights," *Globe and Mail,* 22 December 1988, A1, A4.

50 Manitoba agreed in principle to support the Meech Lake proposals under the then NDP government of Howard Pawley, who resigned as leader and whose party was defeated before the legislature had debated the amendment.

51 "Filmon being hailed as a hero for decision to withdraw accord," *Globe and Mail,* 21 December 1985, A5.

52 Roger Gibbins, "Constitutional Politics in the West and the Rest," in Robert Young, ed., *Confederation in Crisis* (Toronto: James Lorimer & Company 1991), 23.

53 The belief that rights are only meaningful if politicians cannot tamper with them has been fuelled, particularly at the popular level, by continued attacks on the override by public officials of the highest order. Prime Minister Mulroney, for instance, suggested that the constitutional accord proclaimed in 1982 is virtually worthless because, aside from dividing the nation, it fails to protect Canadians' rights. See *Ottawa Citizen,* 7 April 1989, A1–2. However, conflict arose within Mulroney's cabinet on the virtue of the override. Then Secretary of State Lucien Bouchard endorsed publicly the role of the override, claiming that it is "essential for the survival of certain fundamental Quebec values." These differences were downplayed by Mulroney, who implied that they amounted merely to nuances and were not a breach of cabinet solidarity. See Bouchard in House of Commons, *Debates,* 20 December 1988, 425. See also "Fight looms over opting-out clause: Bourassa disputes PM," *Globe and Mail,* 7 April 1989, A1-A2.

54 Peter H. Russell, "Political Purposes of the Charter," in Philip Bryden, Steven Davis, and John Russell, eds., *Protecting Rights and Freedoms: Essays on the Charter's Place in Canada's Political, Legal, and Intellectual Life* (Toronto: University of Toronto Press 1994), 36.

55 Christopher Manfredi argues that the threshold for using the legislative override should be three-fifths of Parliament. Manfredi, *Judicial Power and the Charter,* 209. Peter Russell argues that the legislative override should be subject to two separate enactments, both before and after an election. Peter H. Russell, "Standing Up for Notwithstanding," *Alberta Law Review* 29 (1991): 301–2.

56 *Ford* v. *Quebec (Attorney General)* at 778–80.

57 *R.* v. *Keegstra* [1990] 3 SCR 697 at 743.

58 *Lavigne* v. *Ontario Public Service Employees Union* [1991] 2 SCR 211 at 257.

59 Charles Taylor, "Shared and Divergent Values," in *Reconciling the Solitudes: Essays on Canadian Federalism and Nationalism* (Montreal: McGill-Queen's University Press 1993).

60 Paul M. Sniderman, Joseph F. Fletcher, Peter H. Russell, and Philip E. Tetlock, "Political Culture and the Problem of Double Standards: Mass and Elite Attitudes Toward Language Rights in the Canadian Charter of Rights and Freedoms," *Canadian Journal of Political Science* 22 (1989). See also by the same authors, "Liberty, Authority and Community: Civil Liberties and the Canadian political Community," paper presented at the annual meeting of the Canadian Political Science Association, Windsor, Ontario, 9 June 1988.

61 Russell, "Political Purposes of the Charter," 35.

62 These techniques included: a redefinition of sedition, one which was narrower than earlier common law interpretations, in a case in which the Quebec government had prohibited the distribution of religious pamphlets which were "expressive of a seditious intention" (*Boucher* v. *R.* [1951] SCR 265); an interpretation of the preamble of the Constitution Act which requires freedom of discussion and debate to set aside provincial legislation which required that newspaper presentation of the provincial policy satisfy the government's criteria of accuracy (*Reference re Alberta Statutes* [1938] 2 SCR 100); federalism grounds, to set aside Quebec legislation which sought to prohibit the propagation of communist ideology in the province (*Switzman* v. *Elbling and Attorney General of Quebec* [1957] SCR 285); and the interpretation of tort law which held Quebec Premier Maurice Duplessis personally liable for having caused the wrongful cancellation of a liquor permit in a personal vendetta against Jehovah Witnesses in the province (*Roncarelli* v. *Duplessis* [1959] SCR 122).

Index